After Midnight

After Midnight

THE LIFE AND DEATH OF
BRAD DAVIS

SUSAN BLUESTEIN DAVIS

with Hilary de Vries

POCKET BOOKS

New York   London   Toronto   Sydney   Tokyo   Singapore

POCKET BOOKS, a division of Simon & Schuster Inc.
1230 Avenue of the Americas, New York, NY 10020

ISBN: 0-671-79672-0

First Pocket Books hardcover printing April 1997

10 9 8 7 6 5 4 3 2 1

POCKET and colophon are registered trademarks of
Simon & Schuster Inc.

Printed in the U.S.A.

For Alexandra,
our light and our love

Acknowledgments

There are many without whose help this book would not have been possible:

I would like to thank: Larry Kramer, Rodger McFarlane, Mark Senak, Zane Lubin, Clifford Stevens, Joel Weisman, Mary Rocamora, Rick Rosenberg, Tim Thompson, Judith Weiner, Jeri Scott, Mark Rubin, Norbert Weisser, Tandy Parks, Neil Bell, David Eidenberg, John Erman, Lynda Gurasich, Alan Howard, Kathleen Letterie, Brad Wilson, Wynn Handman, Joy Harris, Michael Walker, Mignon McCarthy, Bill Grose, Tom Spain, Julie Rubenstein, Marcia and Tony Inch, Ellen Jacobs, Erica and Steve Itzkowitz, Marcia Ross, Howard Askenase, Shelley and Steve Goldman, Julie Garfield, Renee Rousselot, "My Group," and Marcie Jenner.

I give special thanks to Hilary de Vries, who captured my voice so well and gave me her unconditional support to complete this book.

I want to especially acknowledge with gratitude the people who make hard choices to protect those they love.

And to Patrick, my love and my thanks.

Susan Bluestein Davis

BRAD

In memory of Brad Davis

If there was ever a chance to go
    back,
Closer to my home,
Closer to what I had once loved
And still do
To see Susan again,
To hear her voice.
If I had not died,
Would I still be with her?
And my dear sweet child
Where is she?
My Alex had been so small,
So small.
Her hair so long and bright.
Has she grown?
Would she be taller than me?
Can AIDS be cured?
Or is it still a terror, a mystery?
If I could see them once again,
It would make me so happy,
Just once.
Could they hear me?
Could they see?
Would they understand
I would always be with them,
In the heart,
If they believed.

                    by Alexandra Davis, age 10

A man does not show his greatness by
being at one extremity, but rather
by touching both at once.
                              —Albert Camus

It has been more than five years since the death of my husband, Brad Davis, on September 8, 1991, time in which I have tried to put some distance between me and that event and our last bittersweet years together, years when we lived with lies and secrecy, the terrible silence we lived with during our—Brad's—years-long struggle with AIDS. It was the kind of silence known to many AIDS victims, famous or anonymous, on a daily basis. A silence that Brad and I hoped would end with this book.

This book, in fact, was conceived by Brad a few weeks before he died. During the six years we struggled with the disease, the war against AIDS was in its infancy. Information was hard to come by, and the little we had seemed to change almost daily. At the time, AZT was considered a possible cure, and for most of Brad's illness, we cherished the faint if naive hope he might actually recover.

But now, he'd come home from the hospital knowing he had not long to live and was determined to make good—no, better—use of the time he had left. I remember how he propped himself up in bed, legal pad and pen in hand, the pages piling up around him. Neither of us was prepared for how explosive his revelations would be— that Brad would be the first heterosexual Hollywood AIDS death, the first acknowledged IV-drug-user celebrity infectee—and that his death would make headlines across the country, in the *Los Angeles Times,* the *New York Times,* the network newscasts, even *Nightline.* Today, as AIDS has slipped from the front pages as, ironically, the number of victims continues to climb, including Magic Johnson and Greg Louganis, as well as any number of deaths, it is easy to forget how stunning Brad's news was in 1991.

But we were unprepared for the country's reaction after all our years of struggling with not one but two stigmatized illnesses in an industry where being labeled "victim" means all but certain ostracism. Brad had already fought one battle over his alcoholism and drug addiction. He had seen it almost kill his career, his fame that had begun virtually overnight in 1978 with the release of *Midnight Express.* Even after he got sober in 1981—and stayed sober for the next ten years—he never fully lived down his earlier reputation. Even when the entertainment industry went through its own recovery period, an era that began, symbolically at least, with John Belushi's death in 1982, Brad still bore the stigma. If *star* is a fickle label, Brad learned that *drug abuser* is not.

So in 1985, when we learned Brad was already one of the hidden victims of AIDS, he was not willing to add *HIV-positive* to those labels he already wore. Not in an industry when on any given day only 10 percent of the eighty-five thousand members of the Screen Actors Guild are working. Brad was enough of a survivor, and concerned enough about his family's welfare, to understand that his story would remain untold until his death. As he wrote in the proposal for this book, writing in his large, unkempt script:

> The purpose of this book is to reveal what it's like to be infected with HIV, to be receiving treatment, and having to remain anonymous at all costs—chronicling how I have done this for over six years. This may not be such a novel premise— nobody with this disease wants to walk down the street with a sign saying "AIDS" pinned to his or her shirt. The difference is that I am a recognizable celebrity. . . . I make my money in an industry that professes to care very much about the fight against AIDS—that gives umpteem benefits and charity affairs with proceeds going to research and care—but in actual fact, if an

actor is even rumored to have HIV, he gets no support on an individual basis. He does not work.

This book is also about a man and a woman who have been living together for twenty years—married for the last fifteen of those years. It is about a very deep love that has kept us together through good times and bad times. It is also about a very unhealthy codependent relationship. It is about having money, having no money, great success and recognition and celebrity, the insanity of alcoholism and drug addiction, great failure. . . . I would include in this book that I was a total drug addict—an alcoholic and IV drug user—a user of just about any kind of drug I could get. And I was sexually very promiscuous. I've never known any addicts who weren't. But it will only be there as it serves the story I want to tell, which is not a story about drugs and sex.

This is a story about great fear—starting in childhood and intensifying over the years—leading to a great addiction. It's a story of great ambition, of a man whose only dream since he was a boy of five years old was to be an actor. It's a story of love, anger, courage, of hiding in fear, of having to pretend, of being isolated. But it's ultimately a story of survival and of a man and a woman and the very long road they have shared.

Although he wrote those words, Brad didn't live long enough to write this book. That job fell to me, one that I undertook willingly but not without some trepidation. Part of that stems from what Brad touched on himself—the drugs and the sexual promiscuity. These were, without a doubt, the most painful parts of our life together. And to some extent they still are, especially when I consider our daughter, Alexandra. I know that rumors and stories about Brad still circulate in Hollywood. I know that many believe Brad was gay and that our marriage, in their eyes, was suspect. Brad had many gay friends, I have many gay friends, and I know that as a Hollywood star, he held a special place within the homosexual community. But Brad was not gay, that I also know. This book is not meant to be an apology for a complex and admittedly troubled man.

Rather it is in attempt to show the consequences of any deviation from Hollywood's norm.

As a casting director, I know only too well how intractable that rule remains: in Hollywood, appearances still count for everything. I saw it firsthand with Brad; I continue to see it in my work today, the countless ways, the extreme measures, that Hollywood actors—and not just stars—take to hide any illness or infirmity to preserve their careers. That has and continues to be an ironclad rule. Despite the success of such pioneering films as *Philadelphia* and HBO's *And the Band Played On,* artists and businesspeople alike still live in fear for their jobs, their careers, their images. Look at the impact on Burt Reynolds's career when rumors he had AIDS began to circulate, or look at Rod Steiger, who took enormous pains to hide his clinical depression out of fear for his career. In that light, Brad's story is more than one man's struggle with AIDS, being the quintessential Hollywood tale.

Whom then is this book for? Hollywood? Recovering addicts? AIDS victims? Of course, it is important that it reach all those now suffering with AIDS, especially those who feel as we did, that they must conceal their illness from even their closest friends and family members. I also hope that it speaks to those individuals whose spouses—both male and female—are HIV-positive and who live with the fear that by revealing the truth, they will be opening themselves and the most personal recesses of their marriages to public scrutiny and speculation. But mostly I hope that it reaches anyone who has ever been tempted to walk away from the challenges of his or her own life.

I know many of our friends often wondered about us when they saw how turbulent our relationship was. We were what Brad liked to call "a perfectly mismatched pair." I was Jewish, a lifelong New Yorker, while Brad was from one of the South's oldest families, whose lineage included Jefferson Davis. I was quiet and shy, while Brad was supremely confident in his ability to win anyone over. Brad was a sex symbol while I was a member of Overeaters Anonymous. We were, however, wildly attracted to each other, and our relationship, particularly at first, was highly charged.

But all this is part of the story, our early years in New York, the beginnings of Brad's drug and alcohol use, and later in Hollywood when he tested me with more drugs and alcohol and infidelity— behavior that I now know was part of Brad's deep fear of abandonment, but which led directly to his becoming HIV-positive. Yes, there was a lot about Brad's life I didn't now—and perhaps still don't know. And many of the more painful events in our life together I have blocked from memory. Brad was even more secretive than I was, the kind of person who, as our friend Rick Rosenberg said, "was a man of many compartments." Brad was ultimately an actor who varied his performance depending on the audience. The man that the public knew, that the studios knew, that even his closest friends knew, was not necessarily the man I knew. But that is the man I have tried to show here.

—Susan Bluestein Davis

After Midnight

CHAPTER

1

It all started with the letter, the certified letter that showed up that December in 1985, so casually on a Wednesday, a *workday*, that I thought nothing of it. I remember thinking "insurance renewal" or some other explanation as I flipped past the yellow Attempted Delivery notice tucked in amongst the Saks and I. Magnin catalogs and the cartoon-colored supermarket circulars that daily tumbled through our front door and that Doris, our housekeeper, dutifully retrieved and left tidied, like fresh laundry, on the kitchen table. It was almost always a benign pile. Never any overdue bills or IRS letters screaming for what was theirs and then some. Those would never reach us here. Not in our home.

That wasn't the way things were done out here. Not in Hollywood, where even the C-levelest of stars can get A-list protection, the phalanx of agents, accountants, and business managers whose job is to filter you from the world, protect you from bad news. And in the eight years since *Midnight Express*—years that had seen Brad go from hick unknown to a comer and down that path of excess that led, if you were unlucky, to exile and, if you were lucky, to rehabilitation—we had known our share of bad news.

So we had men, careful, exacting men such as Zane Lubin, our longtime friend and business manager, who put up that fat paper wall between us and those who thought less well of us and our credit than we deserved. That was the way things were done here and how they had been done for me almost since the day I arrived in Los Angeles almost ten years earlier, a scared, thirty-one-year-old émigré from Manhattan who was about to begin life as Mrs. Brad Davis.

So, the mail promised no threat that December Wednesday that found me as exhausted and preoccupied with work as any other day when I had a casting job to finish. For the past month, while Brad had been in Italy filming a four-hour miniseries, *The American Cousin,* I had been working on *A Different World,* a spinoff of the hit *Cosby* show—NBC's then signature sitcom—for producers Tom Werner and Marcy Carsey. Although Carsey-Werner were still a couple of years away from being the powerhouse producing team they are today—the creators of *Roseanne, Grace Under Fire, Cybill,* among others—*Cosby* had put them on the map, and that winter the pressure was on to create a new hit series for *Cosby* costar Lisa Bonet.

We were working out of offices in Westwood on the other side of the Hollywood Hills from where Brad and I rented our house. After several weeks penciling in wish lists on yellow legal pads and brokering with agents, my days were now filled with meetings and back-to-back auditions with actors all feverish and eager for a paycheck, actors to see and edit into their respective piles: yes, no, callback. This was my sphere of influence as a casting director, a job virtually unknown to the public and regarded even by the industry with only a certain obligatory enthusiasm. I was a helper to the *real* artists, the actors and directors, but still necessary, still needed in this town.

That describes my role in Brad's life: necessary. The necessary wife of the is-he-still-a-drunk and what-has-he-been-doing-since-*Midnight-Express* Brad Davis. I was the unseen ballast, a working mother, who with my stream of jobs and steady if unremarkable paychecks kept us upright and on track. After nine years of marriage, we had a house—rented, bereft of air-conditioning, and located in the Valley, but still it passed for home—too many pets, too much debt, and our daughter, two-year-old Alexandra. It was my job to keep it all together while Brad made movies and more frequently didn't. As they say about God, I was in the details, the pick-up-the-dry-cleaning, remember-the-birthday, call-the-accountant details. So an extra errand, a swing by the post office to pick up a certified letter before heading to the office, was all in a day's work.

"Tomorrow, I'll get the letter tomorrow," I thought, absently dropping the mail to the kitchen table, moving on to dinner, to Alexandra, the cats, and Sam and Alice, our husky and mutt, the real stuff of my life, never imagining that the silent papery pile already held the news, the secret that would change my life, the way a first kiss or a last glimpse of someone from an airplane can mark you without your even knowing.

When I think about it, though, my whole life with Brad had been marked with those kinds of unexpected but life-wrenching moments. *Scarred* might be a better word. Mention the words *Brad Davis* around town and what most people remember is a man infinitely talented as an actor, infinitely tortured as a human being. Drugs, alcoholism, promiscuity. Brad had worn all those labels and then some. But unlike a lot of Hollywood actors whose messy real lives often bore little resemblance to their carefully groomed public selves, he had worn them in public as if he were decked out in blazing neon.

From almost the moment he arrived in Los Angeles in 1976, a skinny, unschooled, but ambitious and rawly talented off-Broadway actor, Brad was the subject of stories—stories about Brad at parties, stories about Brad drunk or high, stories about Brad's various relationships—stories that were true or false, lurid or touching, depending on the tale and the teller. Like the one about Brad, in a drunken fit of self-loathing, shooting out every single photograph of himself that hung in our house. Or the one that had Brad smearing his own excrement on the walls of his hotel suite in a cocaine-induced blackout. Or the story about Brad digging an impromptu roadside grave for a dead bird and burying it with actual tears in his eyes. As everybody knew, or thought they knew, Brad was an incendiary mix of equal parts compassion and rage—a slim-hipped, green-eyed kid armed with a drawl and a talent for dazzling both sexes. Like James Dean sprung from the mind of Tennessee Williams.

It didn't help that Brad had arrived on fame's doorstep with something less than an altar-boy image. Although he had appeared off-Broadway in the early 1970s and had landed small parts in TV's *Sybil* and *Roots*, Brad had made his name playing real-life drug smuggler Billy Hayes in one of the more controversial films of the decade. Not an easy accomplishment when you consider that Hollywood in 1978 was a tough town to shock. But after its electrifying reception at the Cannes Film Festival, *Midnight Express* went from being a low-budget project from a bunch of then unknowns—director Alan Parker, producer David Puttnam, and screenwriter Oliver Stone—to the cinematic touchstone for the Woodstock generation.

The movie was based on Billy Hayes's graphic true-life account of life in a Turkish prison, and it achieved its notoriety by managing to tweak the zeitgeist twice—first with the film's unrepentant attitude toward drugs and secondly with what appeared to be an overly casual attitude toward homosexuality. Never mind that Hayes's book detailed at least one real-life homosexual encounter that occurred during his ten-year prison sentence, which the film's producers and executives at Columbia Pictures declined to portray. Typically, on-screen violence won out over on-screen sex. In the film's final cut, the controversial shower scene, which ironically involved Brad and his close friend actor Norbert Weisser, was edited to remain chastely unconsummated while Brad's infamous tongue-biting sequence—graphic even by today's standards—ran in all its grisly glory.

That was first real look the public had of Brad—a drug-imbibing, sexually charged, volatile outlaw. That image, however, would prove a mixed blessing. While *Midnight Express* won Brad a coveted Golden Globe Award as Best Newcomer and vaulted him from the rank of aspiring unknown to rising star, it was also the kind of notoriety that would dog him for the rest of his career. Indeed, it would be almost two years before Brad would begin to broaden his screen image with a second film role, as the editor of a college newspaper in the ill-fated *Small Circle of Friends*. Two years in which Brad continued to play the bad-boy role offscreen.

Like much of the film community, Brad jumped on the cocaine bandwagon with a vengeance. Life after *Midnight Express* meant scything through an endless round of Hollywood parties, the kind of jockeying, chaotic, drug-laden events that were endemic in Los Angeles during the late 1970s and early 1980s. I chose not to join—not out of prudishness, God knows, I had done my share of imbibing and ingesting back in New York. But as in many relationships where drugs play a role, I was the sober one.

Drug-taking, for a time, was a large part of Brad's life, and a large part of almost any successful actor's life in Hollywood in the late 1970s. Brad's easy attitude toward drug use had been fostered by his father, "Doodle" Davis, a semipracticing dentist back home in Tallahassee, who was in the habit of sending his oldest son his surplus supplies of Seconal and Tuinal. Hollywood in 1979 was only too willing to continue the parental tradition.

Although I was not a lightweight when it came to drugs, including alcohol, the savage free-for-all culture of Hollywood was alien, even frightening to me. Although I had spent several years working in New York as an assistant to Stark Hesseltine, one of the more prominent Broadway agents whose clients had included Robert Redford and Warren Beatty, I was largely unprepared for life as "Mrs. Brad Davis." It was one thing, I realized, to be one of the relatively faceless phalanx of businesspeople whom actors seem to gather around themselves, but quite another to be married to one of the more notorious up-and-coming stars. My penchant for keeping secrets, for lying even, came from the desire to keep at least part of myself out of the glare that seemed to follow Brad.

For even by Hollywood's normal standards Brad was an outsize personality. Kathleen Letterie, a casting director and one of our closest friends, used to describe Brad as a dangerous person. "You could just feel it when you met him," she said. And while Brad could be the quintessential Southern gentleman, well-mannered and soft-spoken, he also had a darker, more Faulknerian cast to his personality that erupted in self-destructive behavior with alarming frequency.

"He could be the best friend in the world," Stan Jones (not his real name), one of Brad's AA sponsors, once observed, "but you always felt that Brad was not the kind of guy who would live to be an old man." Or as Larry Kramer, the playwright and author of *The Normal Heart,* which Brad had starred in off-Broadway, once said, "Many people felt antagonism towards Brad because he wasn't the kind of guy who wanted you to love him."

Many times during those early years when everyone in town wanted to work with or at least meet the star of *Midnight Express,* Brad seemed to go out of his way to alienate people. Not only his friends—making scenes in restaurants, picking fights in grocery stores, driving home drunk to list just a few of his favorite ploys— but in key meetings with some of Hollywood's biggest power brokers.

His meeting with Mike Medavoy, the red-haired former Columbia executive who was then head of Orion Pictures, became legendary. Brad waltzed into his office, sat there with his sunglasses on, his feet on Medavoy's desk, ordered a drink, and went off on this riff about how he wanted to play Jesus in the film version of Nikos Kazantzakis's *The Last Temptation of Christ* or, barring that, Louis, the vampire hero of Anne Rice's cult hit novel. Medavoy threw him out.

It was the kind of performance Brad all but replicated at a dinner that Peter Guber, one of the producers on *Midnight Express,* hosted for Brad at Yamamoto's. Although Guber was some ten years away from producing *Batman,* which would lead to his appointment with Jon Peters as the head of Sony Pictures, the fast-talking producer was already someone to reckon with. That he was interested in Brad for a three-picture deal—including *First Blood,* the action picture that would launch Sylvester Stallone's Rambo— was obvious. What should have been an important but unexceptional meeting, Brad turned into another disaster by drinking too much and insulting almost everyone at the table.

Like any kid who came of age in the sixties, Brad was ambivalent toward authority figures. Some he loved, such as Wynn Handman, his old acting teacher in New York; Zane, our business manager; and Rick Rosenberg, a producer who would come to be Brad's closest friend during the last ten years of his life. But most others, whether they were directors such as Richard Heffron or just ordinary cops who hauled Brad in for being drunk and disorderly, were the enemy to him. Studio executives, even fawning ones, were no different. And given Brad's history of using alcohol to deal with pressure situations—he showed up drunk for his first audition for *Midnight Express*—it wasn't surprising that he took meetings with producers drunk. It was all a game to him then, as unreal and as lacking in consequence as his sudden fame.

Perhaps the most telling incident came at a post–*Midnight Express* party Brad attended. Brad was just getting his first taste of Hollywood celebrity. Typically, he threw himself into the melee with his usual lack of caution. In the middle of the party, Brad tore off his shirt and yelled, "Okay, who's got the drugs?" while a director muttered, "Well, there goes that career."

That is how Brad began what would be a twelve-year on-again, off-again career as a Hollywood actor. Looking back, I see now that his behavior was the kind that will, if unchecked, kill you one way or another. John Belushi and River Phoenix are just a few of those actors who could not handle the kind of success that only Hollywood hands out. Brad came close to joining their ranks. But if his substance-abusing behavior didn't kill him, his actions were, as those executives predicted, the kind that can terminate a career. As Brad himself said in one of his rare moments of introspection, "After *Midnight Express* I went from being 'Brad who?' to 'Look, it's Brad Davis and I think he's drunk.'"

It was, in hindsight, one of our first lessons: that Hollywood, like any organization, plays by certain unyielding rules, rules that are largely invisible to those outside of or unfamiliar with the group. It would take Brad more than ten years to learn how to control his behavior, to give up cocaine, his treasured bottles of chilled Stolichnaya, and his favorite early-morning ritual of cognac, espresso, and a pack of Camels. While he eventually got and stayed sober—resigning himself to such stimulants as sugar, herb tea, and the kind of high you get from baking yourself in a sauna for hours—to a very large extent, the damage had already been done.

By December 5, 1985, when I picked up that certified letter, we had already learned that Hollywood, for whatever else is known or said about it, is ultimately a club of nonvictims and that we were already on the outside looking in.

It was always easier when Brad was gone. Away on location, not home, underfoot, sleeping late, on the phone, making us both tense with worry, the way you worry out here, wondering when, how, the next job will arrive, the next check. I had enough to do without his usual insecurities. Christmas was only three weeks away and *A Different World* still wasn't fully cast. I'd already canceled the vacation we had planned for Alexandra and me to visit Brad in Rome—a city I was dying to see again—because I had too much to do here, casting the series while finalizing the arrangements for our trip to New York and Florida. Brad, God knows, always had to see his parents over the holidays. And there were still presents to get. I'd always been such a sucker for Christmas, probably because we had never celebrated it when I was growing up, but now with Brad and especially Alexandra, we went all out, as if our credit cards had any more give in them.

That was my frame of mind when I decided to swing by the post office on my way to the office and pick up the certified letter the mailman had tried to deliver the day before. I picked up the letter, noting the return address—Cedars-Sinai Medical Center—with only mild curiosity as I headed back to the car. I was used to checking Brad's mail whenever he was on location, and I knew he periodically donated blood at Cedars ever since Alexandra had been born there. I was pretty sure that he had just given blood before leaving for Europe. Some paper he forgot to sign or something, I thought, opening the letter with an impatience verging on annoyance.

It was a form letter, just a few brief paragraphs long, impersonal, matter-of-fact. I read through it once and then probably a hundred times more. "This is to inform you," it said, "that you have tested positive for antibodies to the HTLV-III virus." That's what they called it then, HTLV, or what is now known as the AIDS virus.

8

"The information herein is strictly confidential," the letter went on to say. "Your name and test results will be filed under the code number below." And, it stated finally, "it is important that you call us as soon as possible." It was signed by the hospital's head of Transfusion Medicine, a Dr. Goldfinger.

The heat of the car in the early-morning sun was suddenly unbearable. I rolled down the window and sat there for several minutes breathing lightly—too lightly—watching people walk in and out of the post office. People who were leading perfectly ordinary—stupidly, beautifully ordinary—lives of boredom and routine. People suddenly not like me.

I don't know how long I sat there, but looking back, I think it was only my ignorance that kept me from coming completely unhinged, my ignorance about the letter's full meaning. The blood test that screened for HIV had only become available earlier that year, and no one knew what exactly it meant for people who were discovered to be HIV-positive but who still felt healthy. AIDS was still vague to me, a headline or a report on the evening news, something I didn't pay much attention to. Now, I sat with a piece of paper on my lap containing those very words and my husband's name.

I canceled the drive to the office and turned back home to try to reach Brad. I made the call in what I realize now was that state of exaggerated calm following deep shock. It was nine hours later in Rome, already evening, when I reached him at his hotel, the Velabro, where he was making dinner for his Italian producer and director and their wives. He'd told me about this meal weeks ago, what a big deal it was for him and how he was planning it, the menu, shopping at the open-air markets. Now I was reaching him in the middle of it, and typically Brad was impatient.

"Can't this wait?" he asked, taking the call in an adjoining bedroom. I could picture him standing, running a hand through his hair, his nails bitten to the quick.

"No, it can't," I said, and insisted that he let me read him the letter.

Its chilly formality cut through Brad's impatience.

"It's a mistake, it's a mistake," he said after listening intently, then trying, I could tell, to shake it off. "Don't worry. Look, I'll call you later after everyone leaves."

I can't remember how I spent the next three hours, except making a cryptic call to the office to say I'd be late because of a family emergency. It must have been nearly midnight in Rome by the time Brad called back. He was alone now, quieter, and he asked me to read the letter to him once more, then again and again just as I had.

I think Brad was in as much denial as I was in shock. He wanted the name and number of the doctor at Cedars. It still was only afternoon in Los Angeles, and Brad wanted to reach him before the end of the day. "Don't worry," he kept saying like a mantra. "It's a mistake."

But I never believed it was a mistake, and, of course, it wasn't.

Brad eventually reached the doctor, who told him that as Brad's partner—"partner" was the word he used—I had to be tested immediately. My test was already scheduled for ten o'clock the following Monday. Only later did I realize how profoundly alone we were in the receipt of this information, how little we even guessed at all the changes we would go through and how alone we would remain for the next six years until Brad's death. So alone that we never even told our closest friends. Never even told our own daughter.

But that was yet to come. Today was only December 5, 1985. As they say, the first day of the rest of your life—the first day when my life as Mrs. Brad Davis, wife of the sobered-up, on-his-way-back Brad Davis, became a lie.

2

It would be easy to say that much of my marriage to Brad had its roots in my relationship with my parents. Too easy, perhaps. Yet like many women who find themselves married to difficult, demanding men, I realize now that I spent much of my childhood being groomed for just such a role. Groomed in the sense that I grew up witnessing in my parents' often fraught relationship the kind of skewed balancing act I would later re-create with Brad.

In my family it was my father, Hyman Bluestein, who was the rock of stability. A toy designer and salesman from the Bronx, he was the epitome of the stoic, self-made American male. He never talked about his life, he was too unassuming. Handsome, athletic, with piercing blue eyes, my father had played baseball in college and was a fine ice-skater, but he went through life self-conscious about his appearance because of his acne-scarred skin. He was the only one in his family who was really educated—he had dreams of becoming a lawyer—but he sounded like a truck driver with his strong New York accent.

He was also the complete opposite of my mother, Pearl Wiener. Voluptuous, pretty, vivacious, she was as demanding as he was giving, a woman with an almost compulsive need to be the center of attention. She was the youngest, the pampered, the baby, in a populous clan of Russian immigrants who had arrived in New York in 1916.

It was a role she continued to play even after she was married and the mother of two young children, a role that meant my father was the ballast of the family, the one who could always be counted on. He was the only security I ever had. When I went away to college, he was the one who asked, "Is there anything you need?" Around the neighborhood, Hy was the man who could fix anything. Everybody called my father if they were stuck. Maybe it was a huge burden. Maybe it was why he smoked so much—three to four packs a day of Luckys or Camels, always unfiltered until, as a concession to my mother, he switched to filters.

But my father was also what I came to understand as an enabler. He let my mother get away with so much, so much strange, even hostile behavior, either because he didn't see it or because he chose not to deal with it. She was tortured, emotionally fragile, battling both an eating disorder and agoraphobia, and addicted to tranquilizers for more than fifteen years.

Today, her depression would have been treated. But back then, we thought my mother was a self-pitying hypochondriac, with her closet full of wigs, her medical books and bulging medicine chest, and her talent for using all of us—first her sisters, then my father, and eventually me—as support systems in her increasingly unstable life. Such a household would now be tagged dysfunctional or codependent. But at the time, I didn't have the benefit of therapy, or even pop psychology, to help me through the emotional thicket that was, for more than twenty years, my family. For a long time I blamed my mother for everything. I even blamed her for my winding up with someone like Brad.

My earliest memories are of Queens, and our neighborhood at the corner of 174th Street and 69th Avenue. It was known felicitously as Fresh Meadows. My parents moved there in 1947 when I was still an infant. That they had fled the Bronx for the comparative exurbia of Queens and acquired their first house, a tiny brick duplex, had less to do with my birth on May 27, 1946, than with the death of my mother's mother that same year, which financially and psychologically liberated my parents from the city.

I was named after Susan Hayward, the first Susan my mother loved. Alan, my brother, was named for Alan Ladd when my mother realized "Tyrone Bluestein" was too much homage for her only son to bear. It all seems so typical now. Like Jews and their Chinese food; Jews and their Hollywood. . . . But for most of my childhood, the TV and its endless stream of old movies was my mother's closest companion. Eventually it became my only real connection to her, too, a shared late-night, vampirish fascination with television, with movies, with Hollywood. Movies, the never-ending tape loop on the Zenith, were our passion. Movies and the actors. My mother was the first to tell me that Rock Hudson was gay. "I read things," she said huffily, as if a housebound Jewish lady living in Queens would be out of the know. She knew almost as much about movies as she did about her pills, all the tranquilizers she took, searching for something, anything, to kill the nervousness she felt.

In our family, there were always secrets about my mother's problems, her behavior, her weight—which ballooned up and down—and her tendency to literally pull out her hair. For most of my childhood, I never brought a friend home without making sure my mother's door was closed and that her wigs were put away. Nobody ever just walked into our house and asked, "Is Susan home?" My friends always had to wait downstairs while I called out, "Is it okay to come up?" There was always some lie about my mother not feeling well or being tired. Before Brad, my mother was the first big secret I learned to keep.

But nothing calmed her like TV. My mother was addicted to TV. So I was raised on TV. Every day I rushed home from school to sit with her to watch the *Million Dollar Movie* at three o'clock. My favorites were *One Touch of Venus* and *Mr. Peabody and the Mermaid*. And then all night, we watched more movies— Humphrey Bogart, Peter Lorre—she and I sitting in the dark with the black-and-white images making shadows on the walls, on our faces. Every night I fell asleep to the TV. I still fall asleep with it on,

13

some late movie murmuring, rocking me to unconsciousness. I remember movies more than I remember the old television shows that most people remember. I remember movies more than I think I remember her.

That was how we lived—one parent who could fix the world's ills and another one who *was* the world's ills. We lived like that until I was twelve; a long time to be in one place where you know everyone and they know everything, or almost everything, about you. When we finally moved in 1958, I couldn't wait to get away from that sense of safety, that sense of suffocation that comes from so much familiarity.

It was better when we moved in 1958 to Spring Valley, a bedroom-community-in-the-making north of Manhattan in Rockland County. My father had a dream to own his own store, to be a local businessman in a small town. And in one sense, the move was a step up for us. We lived in the country and our house was much larger than the one in Queens, with a huge backyard and four large bedrooms. We also had a live-in housekeeper. As my mother liked to point out, we were upper-middle-class now. But living in Spring Valley was a disappointment to my father. Despite his long-held dreams about being a small-business man, it turned out that he actually didn't like having the store, didn't like dealing with the public and having to listen to all their complaints. He sold his business and went back to what he'd done before—designing and selling for a furniture company called Bassett.

It was hard to watch my father give up his dreams. Especially since for most of his life he had instilled in Alan and me that there were two things in life you didn't want to be, "a dilettante or a quitter," as he said. My father never cared if I was fat or thin or smart or stupid—all the things my mother cared about—but he did care about character. And in his eyes, I was a quitter. He never confronted me, never took me on in an argument, but one time he did tell me, "I see a lack of character in you." And he was right. I quit almost everything I ever started. I quit piano and ballet lessons. Later, I wanted to quit American University in Washington, where I was majoring in languages. But he wouldn't let me. School had never been my strong suit, but because my father had been the only one in his family to earn his degree, he insisted that Alan and I graduate. He also insisted we come home with degrees that meant something in the marketplace.

That's how I came to major in languages instead of music or literature, the two subjects that I thought I might excel in. So I studied Spanish, a major that was to steer me toward bilingual secretaryhood but instead led to a year studying in Madrid, where ebony-haired antifascist rebels amazingly enough found Jewish American coeds exotic.

But all of that paled beside my long-frustrated interest in music. All through high school in Spring Valley, I had sung in the school chorus. When I told my parents I wanted to learn guitar to accompany myself, they refused to buy me one because of my earlier failures, my "lack of commitment," as my father put it. So I decided to teach myself. Together with Marcia Inch, who was then my best friend and remains one of my closest friends today, we got Joan Baez records, sheet music, and some teach-yourself-the-guitar books.

We also got good enough to sing one night at the Bitter End, a New York nightclub, during my senior year in high school. It was the sixties and folk music was going to be my calling. Playing at the Bitter End, where the audience was largely working musicians and songwriters, was as close to a professional audition as I would get. But two well-known songwriters told me, "You have a beautiful voice, but you would have to get thin because we aren't in the business of promoting the next Kate Smith."

That cut like a knife. I knew I was overweight—I was extremely self-conscious about it—but that ended it for me. That and my father's discouragement. Not only did I give up any dreams of being a performer, but I decided to start taking amphetamines during my first year of college. By my second year, I was a lot thinner but I was also addicted to diet pills. For the first time I had a keen appreciation of what my mother had gone through with her own battles with her weight and tranquilizers.

Although I was taller than my mother, I looked exactly like her—dark hair, green eyes, and pale skin—and for most of my childhood she was on me about my weight. She had been the youngest and prettiest of her sisters—although none of them had had weight problems and neither did any of my cousins—and my mother was always comparing herself to her sisters, to the neighbors, to anyone. She did the same thing to my father, to Alan, and eventually to me.

Weight was actually the least of it. None of us was ever good enough in her eyes. It wasn't until much later, after therapy and oddly enough after reading *The Cinderella Complex,* that I realized my mother's endless criticisms were not constructive, that she was trying to cover up and make things look better. For her it was always about "Am I as good?" "Do I have as much?" "Are we successful?" Initially, her complaints were always about my father being successful, but later, after he died in 1967, it was about Alan and me. Were we doing enough? Eventually, she gave up on Alan when it became obvious that he would never do anything major and laid it all on me.

My mother wanted me to be thin and beautiful and successful and marry well and have lots of money and live the way our other cousins did. I wanted to live well, but the rest of it I could not have cared less about. I wanted to be an artist, a musician. But my mother wanted me to do something much more important because, I realized, she wanted to live vicariously through me. I grew up thinking that I was never enough. It's why I was so shy and why I had a problem controlling my weight. I never felt that it was all right just to be me.

Just before my college graduation in 1967, my father died of lung cancer at Ramapo General Hospital in Spring Valley in May 1967. He was there only a few days before he died—all of it in a coma. I had gotten a call at school to come home right away. I'm not sure he even knew I was there holding his hand. The way he died, drugged on morphine in a hospital room with strangers coming in and out. He had gotten his affairs in order, responsible to the end, but his death was so undignified, lying there unconscious in a hospital bed covered only by a sheet because the drugs they had given him made him hot. Even in his coma he would kick off the sheet, and I was embarrassed to have my father's thin, naked body exposed like that. I hated the whole scene, him lying there and the nurses coming in and out. I hated watching him die in a hospital.

Through that whole ordeal, my mother never made it to his bedside. Even though Alan kept insisting she had to go, for his sake, for her sake, she never did. So I was the one who was there the moment he died—just as I would be the one who was there when she died three years later.

After my father's death we sat shiva at mother's house for five days, which I mostly remember as a lot of eating. I was too young, only twenty-one, to cope with feelings of loss, which is why the next several months were a fog. I didn't work that summer after his death, after graduation. I stayed home with my mother, and the whole time she was putting pressure on me to live with her permanently. But I said no. I told her I had my own life now and I knew that that small spark of independence would be snuffed out if I lived with her again.

So I made plans to move to Manhattan that fall. I needed a place where I could recover from my father's death and get on with my life. But it wasn't as easy as I imagined. I still wasn't over my father's death when my mother got sick three years later. It was a heavy load dealing with the death of two parents. I was still struggling with that when I first met Brad.

3

It's funny what sticks in your mind, but coffee milk-shakes is what I remember about my first date with Brad. That, and an almost overwhelming sense that my life was about to change. By 1969, two years after my father's death, I had already changed a great deal.

For one thing, I had graduated, taken the train back to Washington a few days after the funeral, and, in something of a haze, picked up my diploma. I also had moved—against my mother's wishes—into Manhattan. I still had something of the Queens outsider complex when it came to Manhattan, but leaving home was far easier than I expected. I had inherited some money from my father's estate, most of which I was plowing into some overdue psychotherapy. But within a few months of my decision, I had landed a job as a secretary in the reissue division of RCA—later I would move to the rock division and work for Stephen Schwartz of *Pippin* fame—and a one-bedroom apartment in a new elevator building in one of the seediest blocks of Greenwich Village, which I shared with Monika Gardner, my old friend from college, who was studying film at New York University.

It was like any first-job, first-apartment experience: no money, boring work. But it was mine, and for the first time in my life I felt truly independent. Not that I felt I had a particularly bright future; I'm not sure I gave much thought to my future one way or the other. New York was just one big rabbit hole I'd chosen to fall down. But all that was about to change. Before I met Brad, I met Stark Hesseltine, one of the most influential men in show business at the time—Brad's agent and my first real boss—a man who would greatly influence both our lives.

Although few people would remember, or even recognize, his name today, in 1969, Stark Hesseltine was one of the biggest names in show business. Not only was he one of the most powerful Broadway agents—his client list ran from such up-and-comers as Michael Douglas, Christopher Reeve, and Susan Sarandon to the legendary Jessica Tandy and Hume Cronyn—but he was a partner at CMA, Creative Management Associates, the biggest talent agency of its day, the forerunner of ICM, which is today the second-largest Hollywood agency. Stark had started in the fifties, working at MCA for Maynard Morris, one of the legends of the business, where he developed a reputation as having a great eye for new talent, Stark's so-called "beautiful boys." Robert Redford and Warren Beatty were two of his earliest discoveries. He eventually started his own boutique agency, Hesseltine, Bookman & Seff, with partners Leo Bookman and Dick Seff. It was such a success that in 1969, Freddie Fields and David Begelman—the founding partners of CMA—bought Stark out.

But I knew none of this the day I showed up on a chilly April Monday at CMA's offices on Madison Avenue for what I thought was a pro forma secretarial job. I had left RCA in the fall of the previous year, mostly out of boredom, and spent four months just hanging out downtown where I dabbled in drugs—mostly speed and pot—spent my savings, and never went north of Fourteenth Street. I think it was latent grief over my father's death coupled with my feelings of being adrift after college with no real career goals in mind. I was only at CMA's offices because I was running out of money and needed a job again. I had also learned in January that my mother was diagnosed with terminal stomach cancer, and I knew I would be spending weekends with her up in White Plains. I needed a job, any job, for money and to get back to the city Monday mornings.

All of which Stark immediately sensed. He had that kind of imperious self-possession. Not unkind, just no bullshit. He was descended from a wealthy, old New England family and, in addition to his millions, had inherited a lot of old-money mannerisms. He was a Harvard graduate, forty, unmarried, and lived alone in a rambling duplex down in Gramercy Park with a library and walls covered in beige silk. He spent weekends at his country house in East Hampton, and every year he traveled to some exotic place like the Galápagos Islands or Machu Picchu.

We were definitely an odd match—him with all that Waspy taste right down to his frayed button-down shirts and aging tweeds, and me, a slightly overweight, insecure Jewish woman from Queens desperate for a paycheck and not really caring where it came from. Stark took one look at me and my résumé and in that pained, polite way of his told me he didn't think I would be happy as his personal secretary.

"I don't know why you want this job," he kept saying.

He liked the idea that I was educated because in truth Stark needed an assistant more than a secretary, someone who could handle his clients, actors who were just starting out and who needed a lot of hand-holding. He needed someone with a real commitment to him and the agency. "And I sense that lack of commitment in you," he said, sounding just like Father.

With visions of a life with my mother in Westchester dancing in my head, I vamped. "No, no, I really want this job," I said. "This is the business I want to be in. This is my career now."

"And what exactly do we do here?"

Well, he had me on that one. I just started laughing, and that's what ultimately landed me this job. "So, you're not afraid of me?" he said, peering at me in that imperious way he had.

"Why?" I asked. "Are people afraid of you?"

So, there I was, unexpectedly, in the thick of things. I was only a secretary, making a piddling $225 a week, but none of that mattered. I had no idea when I started that Paul Newman, Joanne

Woodward, Robert Redford, and Liza Minnelli would be the people whom I saw and spoke to on any given day. This was better than the legendary mail room at William Morris. I was working out of CMA's offices at 600 Madison Avenue, a new building with a classy Upper East Side address, where I thought my desk was the gateway to heaven. I sat just outside Stark's office, which was the closest to the front door, so whenever anyone came in, they asked me for directions. Paul Newman and Joanne Woodward coming in for lunch in their blue jeans: Which way to Freddie Fields's office? Christopher Reeve, Michael Douglas. Encounters like that day after day. I was too awed to realize that I was actually doubling as the agency's receptionist. Later, after I became an agent-in-training, it was aggravating playing the meet-and-greet girl, but in the beginning I was starstruck.

In truth, there was a lot to be starstruck about. In 1970, the entertainment business was far more fragmented than it is today, when Hollywood is all-powerful and agencies such as Creative Artists Agency (CAA) and International Creative Management (ICM) control the majority of talent deals from their offices in Beverly Hills. When I started at CMA, Broadway was a viable career alternative and New York was still the center of power. Out in Los Angeles, CMA agents such as Guy McElwaine and Sue Mengers, one of the first women in the business, were just beginning to build their reputations shepherding the nascent movie careers of Barbra Streisand, Candice Bergen, and Ryan O'Neal. But they were the exception. Many actors still based their careers in New York theater, either Broadway musicals or off-Broadway dramas. Not until the early 1980s and the rise of the so-called Brat Pack in Hollywood—that young crop of pouty, beautiful, and largely untrained actors such as Demi Moore, Rob Lowe, and Judd Nelson—did Broadway begin its surrender to Hollywood.

And agents were affected. CMA, which merged with IFA, the International Famous Agency, in 1975 to become ICM, moved its headquarters to Beverly Hills. Eventually, both Begelman and Fields, like many agents, left for careers as studio executives and producers. Fields headed MGM from 1981 to 1983, and Begelman was president of Columbia Pictures from 1973 to 1977, when he left after being exposed by actor Cliff Robertson in the infamous check-forging scandal. Later, he would resurrect himself as a producer of such films as *The Fabulous Baker Boys*. Failing upward is a great Hollywood tradition, and the town is filled with those kinds of phoenixes. It was a shock, in fact, when after yet another downturn in his career, David killed himself in 1995—an all-too-rare reminder that failure can have lasting consequences.

But in 1970, all of that was yet to come. All I knew was that working at CMA was like attending class. And I had a lot to learn. Although I had spent my childhood watching old movies and could bore anyone to tears with my knowledge of dead stars, I was naive when it came to dealing with live actors. I didn't understand about that peculiar clash of ego and insecurity that is at the heart of almost every star—that need for attention and love coupled with that omnipresent fear of not being "special." I was forever doing simple, mindless things such as telling Michael Douglas that he looked so much like his father, Kirk, which made Michael crazy because he was so sensitive to comparisons to his then more famous father.

Fortunately, Stark was happy to play mentor and father figure all in one. He was different from other agents that way. He wasn't secretive. He wanted to teach me the business from the inside out. And I was more than willing to learn. I would sit at my desk just outside Stark's paper-strewn, oak-paneled office, and we would shout back and forth to each other. Stark refused to shut his door or use the intercom. He wanted me in and out of his office all day. He would literally yell, "Susan!" and I would yell back, "Stark, I can't get so and so on the phone." It drove the other agents crazy. They'd all come flying out of their offices—Fields and the rest of them, Toni Howard, Jane Oliver, Arlene Donovan. "Can't you two talk on the intercom? What's with the yelling?"

I think that's one reason why Stark and I got on so well. Despite the vast differences in our backgrounds, we were cut from the same fast-talking, loud-talking mode. We also had complementary idiosyncrasies. I could never get through a letter without making a mistake, and Stark would never let me correct them. He was constantly writing over my errors in pen, even though his handwriting was illegible. I'd say, "Stark, let me redo it." But it was always, "Don't waste your time." That was Stark. Move fast, talk fast. His motto was Onward and Upward—even in the face of crushingly bad news for a client. I don't think I ever typed a letter of his that did not close with his scrawled "Onward and Upward."

Stark willingly applied this attitude to me. Within a few months of my arrival, he moved me into agent training, helping him cover off Broadway. At first he had to drag me to the theater, pointing out actors and performances he liked, asking my opinion, hauling me backstage to meet the stars. It was torture. He was the hottest theater agent in town, but I felt completely out of my element.

Eventually, I realized Stark was handing me the beginnings of my own career, and my self-confidence began to grow. Part of my job was to give the off-Broadway report in the weekly staff meetings. These were nerve-racking, ludicrous affairs with Begelman and Fields sitting there looking ice-cold and scary, while Sam Cohn, the legendary agent whose client list eventually included Meryl Streep and Mike Nichols, sat silently tearing up paper napkins, slipping the pieces into his mouth, eating them bit by bit. As bizarre as it was, this was all part of my training.

By the time Stark left CMA in 1975, jumping ship before the merger with IFA to form his own agency, Hesseltine-Baker, where I worked as a junior agent, I was regularly haunting theaters on my own. My usual stops were such places as La Mama, Circle in the Square, the Cherry Lane, even Yale Drama School up in New Haven. It was in these small houses that I was developing my own eye for talent, witnessing some of the first stage performances of actors such as Christopher Lloyd, Sigourney Weaver, and Christine Lahti—all unknowns back then and none of whom Stark wanted to sign. Like any agent, he had his blind spots. Sigourney and Christine? "Too tall," he said. Chris Lloyd? "Too much of an oddball."

I was also discovering that being an agent meant spending an inordinate amount of time on the phone. Not deal making—Stark still handled most of that—but just hand-holding with the actors. I had a knack, I realized, for making actors feel secure. Maybe it was because I was such a talker, or maybe all those years watching my father deal with my mother were paying off, because I could spend hours on the phone with actors listening to their fears about their careers, their lives. Similar to my protectiveness of Stark—no one could say a bad word about him to me—I was solicitous of his clients. Particularly the younger ones. I spent hours that spring talking with John Savage, who had a very troubled emotional life at the time. It was on the phone, in fact, that I first met Brad.

It was a Friday morning in September, just before Stark was heading out as he usually did for a long weekend in the country, when I took a call from an actor named Robert Davis, someone I had never heard of. I was surprised because I thought I knew all of Stark's clients by then.

"Stark, there's this kid on the phone and he says his name is Bobby Davis. Do you know him?" I yelled.

Stark just grabbed the phone. "Bobby! How are you?"

They must have talked for almost an hour. I hadn't seen Stark that animated in a long time.

"Who is that guy?" I asked him when he had hung up.

"Oh, Bobby's a little troubled, but he's very talented."

They had met the year before when Brad was finishing up his second year studying acting at New York's American Academy of Dramatic Art (AADA). The academy was something of a poor cousin to the more prestigious Juilliard, the place where Redford, Joe Regalbuto, and Kate Jackson studied. It was the first real training Brad had had, a long time in coming for the boy who had realized at the age of five he wanted to be onstage. His mother had taken him to see *Pinocchio,* and he had realized "I could play the puppet better than the cartoon."

Part of that drive was sheer physicality. Brad had great confidence in his body, not just sexually, but athletically. He was a gifted horseman, a fact not many people knew. He had owned a horse while growing up in Florida, a chestnut gelding named Flash, and he had won several trophies at local horse shows. Acting, I think, was another way for Brad to channel that intense physicality.

He did the usual student productions in school, and after graduating from Titusville High School in June 1968, Brad moved to Georgia, where he spent the summer working at the Atlanta

Dinner Theater. It was the only acting experience he listed when he applied to the academy that fall. In January, Brad took the train to New York, where he auditioned for Brynn Morgan, then the director of admissions at AADA. He performed a scene from Edward Albee's *Zoo Story* and the musical *The Fantasticks*. As Morgan wrote on his report, "Bobby Davis has good instincts and a sense of the dramatic; must learn to use them."

Brad's grades that first year were hardly an indication of his future. He earned Bs and Cs in movement, elocution, and scene study. Only in singing did Brad excel, earning an A. Still, he showed enough promise—and as the faculty evaluations pointed out, Brad was a well-liked student—to be invited back for the second year. It was almost entirely performance-based; Brad had roles in four productions, including *Philadelphia, Here I Come,* and *The Three-penny Opera,* which is where Stark first saw him.

Although Stark was the first to admit that Brad was very green, he was intrigued by his intensity, his rough-hewn charisma, a tough-guy/little-boy persona characteristic of many young male stars from James Dean to Brad Pitt. Not so much looks per se, since Brad was not yet really handsome, but that latent sexuality that Rodger McFarlane, one of Brad's closest friends, would later describe as an unconscious ability to turn heads. "Walking down the street with Brad was always an experience," Rodger would say, "because people, even kids, would just stop and stare, Brad was just so unbelievably sexy."

It was enough for Stark anyway. He had signed Brad, a huge stroke of luck for an unknown student. But within a matter of weeks, Brad abruptly left New York to go back to Florida. Stark never told me exactly why; I'm not even sure he knew. "Bobby went back home to have a nervous breakdown," was Stark's official, cryptic answer. But now, Brad had resurfaced. He was back in New York, living down in Chelsea. "He wants to try again," Stark said, sounding nonplussed. "Oh, God, just wait until he comes in, you're going to just lose it, Susan."

"Why?" I said.

"Because, he is just so insane."

Whatever I was braced for was not what walked in the door

when Brad came in to have lunch with Stark the following Wednesday. For one thing he was a boy, a kid really, and obviously just off the farm, totally unlike the elegant, polished actors such as Redford and Blythe Danner that Stark usually preferred. He was twenty-one, but looked more like sixteen, with buzz-cut hair, big ears, and a short, skinny body. He was five feet seven inches and must have weighed all of 120 pounds. I remember he wore one of those short-sleeved polyester shirts, and his jeans just hung on him. He didn't say much, just muttered, "Hi, I'm Bobby Davis," in that soft drawl he had, then Stark just grabbed him and took him into his office and shut the door.

I had been attracted to a lot of Stark's clients in the past—who wouldn't be—but this was hardly an introduction to set your heart on fire. My opinion of Brad didn't really improve in the weeks to come, weeks in which Brad called Stark again and again wanting advice about this and that audition. Even by the usual actor-insecurity standards, Brad was needy.

"Stark, that kid Bobby Davis is on the line again," I'd say, covering the phone. "He's such a pain in the ass." I didn't realize that Brad had an almost uncontrollable terror about auditioning, a fear that would dog him his entire life and eventually hurt his career. I just couldn't believe Stark was devoting so much time to a new, unknown client. I had never seen him treat any of his female clients that way, and I wondered if Stark wasn't actually attracted to Brad, if their relationship was, at least in part, an intricate game of seduction.

My opinion about Brad did not change until several weeks had gone by, weeks in which I spent hours on the phone with him myself. If Stark was busy or out when Brad called, instead of hanging up, he began talking to me. At first it was just work, jobs and auditions that Stark had sent him out for. Stark always had me reading plays, so I could talk to the clients about the roles they were going up for. Brad was auditioning for a new play called *Crawlspace*—to play a kid who actually lived in the crawl space of his family's house—a role I thought he'd be perfect for. That's how we started to become friendly. He called me a lot before and after the audition. Eventually, we talked more freely as I sensed a change in him, from trusting only Stark to recognizing that I could also be a valuable ally.

We couldn't have been more different, given my rat-a-tat New Yorkese and Brad's slower, softer rhythms. But I was also realizing that Brad was far more complex than the picture he first presented. Underneath all that Southern-boy sweetness and shambling insecurity lurked a surprisingly tough man, one with an ego, ambition, and—this was the surprise—a puckish and lethal wit. Whatever talents he did or did not have as an actor, and I had yet to see him perform professionally, Brad was a deadly mimic. He was like the proverbial bad kid in the back of the class who is sweet as pie in public but, when the teacher isn't looking, convulses everyone with his antics. He even captured Stark's manic verbal rhythms, a bit that became our private joke. It wasn't long before I found myself happy when I heard Brad's voice on the line, happy that he was calling *me*. But I am not certain that I would ever actually have gone out with him except for the situation with my mother.

That January, my mother had been diagnosed with inoperable stomach cancer—five years after she had battled back from a mastectomy. Now she was dying and the decision was made not to tell her. My brother and I knew the real situation, as did all my aunts, but it was somehow decided that my mother could not bear the news.

It all seemed like a bad dream come round again. Here I was living my high-powered days, or what seemed high-powered at the time, spending my weekends again caring for my bed-bound mother. It was like living my old life and my new life all at once. It was something of a shock after all this time on my own, especially since my mother had actually had a few good years after my father's death. At fifty, my supposedly helpless, hypochondriac, agoraphobic mother had come into her own. She had her job at Saks, which she had gotten as part of her recovery after the mastectomy—chose it over Lord & Taylor and Bloomingdale's because they gave the largest employee discount. She had sold our old house in Spring Valley and gotten her own apartment in White Plains. She had even traveled to Europe with friends.

But now, she was dying, and from January to November, when

she finally died, I spent virtually every weekend with her in White Plains, sitting with her, making her meals, slipping effortlessly back into our old ways together, never once mentioning her impending death. Even after we got a nurse to care for her during the week, I still made the trek up on weekends, more out of guilt than genuine affection. She was a difficult patient, never happy with anything that I or the nurse was doing. I couldn't even make her saltines with jelly the way she liked. I was Susan the inept once again.

By the end of October, she weighed all of sixty pounds. She had been in and out the hospital for weeks, undergoing various tests. But now it was obvious she had only a few weeks to live, and when she suggested she go back into the hospital, I refused. I had decided that my mother was not going to die in a hospital, cold and impersonal, like my father. It was the one thing I swore I would do for her. "Mom," I said, "I don't think you should go back in."

"Why?" she asked. "Am I dying?"

"Yes," I said, finally telling her the truth.

Whatever reaction I may have been hoping for, I didn't get it.

"Why did you tell me?" she said bitterly, turning her face to the wall. "Why did you tell me I'm dying?"

People do peculiar things in the face of death. It's like fate coming right at you: you can't stop it, so you find some way—even if it is irrational or goes against your better instincts—to assert your own will. That's when I decided to go out with Brad. It was a Tuesday afternoon. I even remember what I wore—a navy skirt and a knitted fuchsia top—while Brad sat on my desk in jeans and a T-shirt and a beat-up plaid wool jacket asking me to have eggs with him on Friday, November 6, 1970. I didn't know it was his birthday, that he was turning twenty-one. I just knew he seemed so funny and sweet and a little dangerous. Saying yes to Brad was like agreeing to a journey that I would never take on my own.

What I remember of that date is fragmented images, like a surrealist painting: the dangerous neighborhood around the corner from the Chelsea Hotel on West Twenty-third Street; his dark apartment; his husky named Sam; the slightly stale smell of a strange man's home; and the unmade loft bed where you had to sit if you wanted to sit anywhere. We had the eggs, scrambled as he'd promised. A bottle of wine, which I had brought, and the coffee milk-shakes that I'll never forget. And then we went to bed. Within an hour.

When I started dating Brad, I was living in a loft apartment down on Chambers Street, a netherworld at the time, located between New York's financial district and what would become TriBeCa. Monika and I and our third roommate, Ellen Goldberg, had moved there from the East Village. We had followed Monika's brother, an artist, into the neighborhood. It was the cutting edge of hip at the time: carving a home from raw commercial space with artists and wholesalers as your neighbors. I felt very bohemian living there, and I liked to think of myself in that vaguely schizophrenic way— uptown by day, downtown by night. As if I had a secret life.

And in a way I did. From the very first, my relationship with Brad was marked by secrecy. Not from my friends. They all thought I was nuts to spend time with this hick from Florida who was so different from me, who wasn't educated, who had no money, who couldn't even speak correctly, who wasn't even Jewish. No, Stark was the one who couldn't know about our relationship. I would be at Brad's apartment in the mornings having spent the night, and Stark would call to talk to Brad about auditions or some job, and then I had to roll into the office as if nothing had happened.

We kept our relationship a secret for all those months because dating Brad was more than an infraction of office rules; I knew Stark would be hurt by it, that he would feel betrayed by both of us. And I was right. When Stark got wind of it some months later, he confronted me. He felt, he said, as if I had stolen Brad away.

And maybe I had. But I didn't care. I was only dimly aware then of the sexual effect Brad had on both men and women, and Brad and I were each so used to keeping secrets in our lives, what was one more? That secrecy was, in fact, one of the reasons I was attracted to him. The slight aura of mystery that Brad cultivated about him reminded me a lot of my father. I felt comfortable being with another slightly distant but observant man who could sit in the corner of a room and watch everyone else talk. I felt comfortable because it was so different from me. I took after my mother: direct, loud. If you wanted my opinion about anything, all you had to do was ask. Not Brad. He never asked. He never probed into my life, my background. He just seemed to accept me. After all those years of not feeling good enough, and given all that I had been through with my parents—I was only twenty-four years old and both my parents were dead—it was a relief not to talk, not to have to justify myself. I was so happy with myself and with Brad that I even decided to quit therapy.

It was one reason why I didn't ask too many questions of Brad. Maybe I was simply returning the favor, or maybe I knew instinctively that he already harbored many skeletons in his closet. It was obvious that Brad came from a troubled family, although just how troubled I would not know for some time. I was content merely to be with him, this wiry, Waspy goy who seemed to like exotic women—Jewish women—and with whom I was having the best sex of my life.

On the surface, it must have looked as if I were Brad's superior. I was older, I had a steady, good-paying job. I had prospects and a career in the making. I looked stable compared to Brad in his scruffy jeans, his Gomer Pyle accent, and his skittish attempts to become an actor. But in reality, I was grateful to Brad. He was so knowledgeable and self-assured in areas where I was inexperienced. Being with Brad physically was totally different from anything I had known in the past. I hadn't dated many men, and most of my relationships had lasted just a short while and were sexually unfulfilling. I thought of myself as rather unattractive, depending on my weight, and felt that my prospects for marriage were not promising. Certainly I never thought I would have the kind of physical relationship that I had with Brad.

But that was another one of our secrets. In bed, Brad was a very different man from the insecure little boy he presented to the world. He knew exactly the right things to say and do. It was one of the reasons why it would never really matter to me what else Brad did sexually. Or with whom. I knew what the two of us had together. Perhaps I was naive. Looking back, I'm sure I was. But in the seventies, who ever suspected that sex would ever be lethal? It was still the sixties for all intents and purposes, the heyday of free love.

You weren't even supposed to get a bruised ego from casual sex. Being with Brad made me feel as if I had finally joined my own generation, that I was a full-fledged participant in the sexual revolution.

That was the backdrop for our courtship—the streets and cafés of New York during that social and cultural explosion. During the week, I worked uptown in a corporate world. Or as corporate as it got in show business then. But on weekends, I would shed that part of my life and assume a downtown identity that centered around Bleecker and MacDougal streets.

Like San Francisco, New York was a center of the sixties cultural movement, and in the Village there were something like five-hundred coffeehouses, clubs, and bars. Brad and I would hang out in such places as the White Horse, the Lion's Head, and the Bitter End. We were into music and would go to such clubs as the Village Gate, the Gaslight, and Bill Graham's Fillmore East. It was the hottest place in town for rock and folk music, and we heard people like Ravi Shankar, Bob Dylan, and Joan Baez. We moved in a loose circle of artists, up-and-comers whose names were just beginning to turn up in reviews—sylphlike ballerinas from the American Ballet Theatre and young actors such as John Cazale and Meryl Streep, who had just moved to Manhattan after graduating from Yale. These were the people we would see in the neighborhood and at parties, the best of which were held at K. C. Schulberg's apartment over on Twelfth Street.

K.C. was the nephew of screenwriter Budd Schulberg. He was also the stage manager of Joe Papp's Public Theater, New York's leading nonprofit theater, and was very plugged into the local scene. It was the beginning of the Public's heyday—just two years before the theater launched A Chorus Line, which would become the longest-running musical in Broadway's history. I knew K.C. from my work at the agency, and I knew, too, that K.C. hosted nonstop parties almost every weekend. Stark was always urging me to go to these, to chat up actors and find out about upcoming productions. But I just wanted to hang out at them with Brad and basically play. Still it was hard not to have a sense of history-in-the-making. I remember one party during the Public's run of Trelawny of the

Wells, sitting in K.C.'s apartment and marveling that I was in the same room with Kevin Kline and Meryl and John, who were just beginning to date at the time, and thinking, "This is the finest and best of what will come."

Dating Brad also meant that most weekends we got stoned. It was before cocaine dominated social drug-taking, so that usually meant taking mescaline or pot. I was not a natural drug-taker. I was terrified of hard drugs such as heroin and I had an aversion to needles. But taking soft drugs was considered as casual as drinking. Even I had spent most of my college years downing diet pills and powdered speed without much thought, cutting their aftereffects with Valium. Everyone used drugs and everyone seemed to have access to them. Even though I never loved getting high—food has always been my addiction—I joined in. And Brad seemed to enjoy it so much—certainly sex was better when we were both high. Years later, when we visited Brad's family in Florida, I began to understand how that part of his life fit into a larger pattern of out-of-control behavior that had its roots in his parents' alcoholism and abusiveness. But at the time, I never gave a thought to more serious consequences or what might lie ahead. Indeed, it wasn't until I discovered what would be the first of many instances of Brad's sexual infidelity that I had any misgivings about our lives then.

That July I had gone to Mexico, a quick vacation with Marcia Inch, my oldest friend, whom I had known since junior high school, to rest after my mother's death. I had only been dating Brad a few months, but already I missed him terribly. While I was gone, he decided to spend a night uptown with a woman he knew from acting class. I was away, so Brad was going to sleep with someone else. He only told me about it because he had taken my television set on the subway to her apartment and gotten off in Harlem by mistake where he'd been robbed and beaten up. At the police station, he had talked the cops into letting him adopt an abandoned puppy they'd found.

"Well, I lost your television, but I rescued this puppy just for you," Brad said later when I got home. I was completely nonplussed that my fantasized reunion with my boyfriend had turned into this scene, this betrayal that culminated in my feeling guilty about the little mutt shaking in my kitchen. You make those kinds of rationalizations when you're in love. Or maybe only I did. I didn't realize the whole scenario—the infidelity, the sorrowful confession, even the attachment to lost animals—would characterize our years together. I just took the dog—Alice became our first joint pet—and told Brad that I thought we should live together. At least that way I figured he would have fewer chances to sleep with someone else.

It also ended some logistical problems. Neither one of us had ever lived with a lover, and I was getting sick of shuttling between our two apartments and my long commute up to work, our lack of privacy, and Brad's sharing an apartment with Hal Truesdale. Hal was supposedly an actor, but I suspected he actually earned his livelihood as a transvestite. Later, I would realize that all of Brad's closest male friends were gay, but at the time the whole gay culture—and Brad's connection to it—was a mystery to me. Stark had introduced me to that world; he was the first gay man I knew who did not hide his homosexuality. But I had never encountered someone like Brad, a heterosexual man who had such a strong connection to homosexual men. I didn't know anything about this, so I didn't really question Brad about his friendship with Hal, or about his own job working at this seedy gay bar called the Glory Hole, where he used to step out back and literally feed the rats. It all seemed part of our life in the West Village, so I accepted it.

Besides, I was soon meeting very interesting people through Brad. Like Allen Ginsberg, the famous beat poet and one of the gay movement's earliest activists, who had come out in 1945 when he was just eighteen. Brad showed up with him one night when we were living up on Jane Street in the West Village. They had met at a bar in the Village and Ginsberg clearly thought he was coming back to Brad's apartment to get laid. But Brad had no idea who he was, that he had dragged Walt Whitman home. He treated the whole encounter like some big joke. Eventually we all wound up sitting on the floor in our living room, chanting and smoking pot and listening to Ginsberg read his poetry.

That was what it was like to be with Brad in New York in the early 1970s, and why I was anxious to move our relationship, or at least our living arrangements, forward. Our first apartment was a sixth-floor walk-up on Perry Street in the West Village near the Westside Highway, where we moved in 1972. It wasn't the greatest place to start out in. The neighborhood wasn't much safer than Brad's place in Chelsea—one night we saw a woman stab a man from out our window—and the apartment itself was pretty grim. The floors slanted, the bedroom was so small you had to crawl across the bed to answer the phone. Our friends had to shout to us from the street if they wanted to come up. But the rent was only $113 a month, ideal when we were living paycheck to paycheck.

We stayed there for two years, with Sam the husky and Alice, our mutt. During this time Brad landed a role playing a multiple-sclerosis victim on a new daytime soap opera, *How to Survive a Marriage,* in 1972. It was Brad's first regular paycheck, $600 a week, and it enabled us to eventually move a few blocks north to a larger one-bedroom apartment on Jane Street. The rent was more than double, $324, but 61 Jane Street was a brand-new luxury building on the corner of Hudson Street with a doorman and an elevator and relatively well-off gay tenants, the kind of guys who would come home in their suits after a day working uptown and then leave later in the evening dressed in leather or even in drag. By the time Brad left for Los Angeles, in March 1976, we had moved again, this time uptown to a beautiful prewar building on Fifty-eighth Street and First Avenue where we paid $450 a month—an enormous sum to us at the time.

If our move through the ranks of New York real estate was somewhat steady, Brad's entry into professional acting was by no means an assured ascent. But then it's a long way from Titusville High to Hollywood. My first involvment with Brad's career was his audition for *Crawlspace* that winter he returned to New York. Brad had never had a paying acting job at that point, only student productions and waiver theater. But both Stark and I thought he was perfect to play the part of a strange boy who observes his family while holed up in a crawl space. But Brad didn't get the job and I hounded Stark into phoning the casting director. "Brad was too green," came the word. "The kid was just all over the place."

It wasn't the first time Stark had had a client in need of help. He was in the habit of sending many young actors to his old friend

Wynn Handman. Wynn was a fixture on the New York theater scene, a veteran director who had worked with Sanford Meisner at Lee Strasberg's fabled Actors Studio and was then cofounder and artistic director of the American Place Theater, a relatively new off-Broadway theater where such writers as Sam Shepard, Joe Chaikin, and Steve Tesich were produced. Wynn, however, was even more respected as an acting coach. He had a reputation for helping launch several young stars; Steve McQueen, Dustin Hoffman, Joanne Woodward, even director Sidney Pollack, had all been Wynn's students. Stark hoped he could do the same for Brad.

"I really believe it's all there, but he's failing miserably in auditions," Stark told Wynn. "Take a look at him, listen to him read, and see if you can help him."

For the next two years, Brad studied with Wynn—at biweekly classes held at an old carriage house around the corner from Wynn's apartment on West Fifty-eighth Street and Eighth Avenue. Richard Gere was one of his classmates, something that would come to haunt Brad years later in Los Angeles when both of them were being considered for *Midnight Express*. Those years with Wynn turned the tide in Brad's career. He had always responded to strong male figures, and Wynn carried himself with authority. For one thing, he was rich—at least by theater standards—a successful, respected director with a huge apartment in the heart of the theater district. Wynn also looked the part with his tall, rangy frame, aristocratic aquiline nose, and flowing mane of hair. His wife, Barbara, was prominent in Democratic Party circles. At the time she worked for Sen. Eugene McCarthy, helping launch a series of political cabarets called "Eugenes." Later, she was a vice president at Norman Lear's liberal lobbying organization, People for the American Way. Wynn and Barbara also had two beautiful daughters, Laura and Liza. Brad and I weren't alone in thinking they were an interesting and exciting couple.

Wynn was one of the first people to connect with Brad professionally. He showed him how to focus in a role, to make clear choices when delineating a character and to stick to them. He also seemed to genuinely enjoy Brad. When he invited Brad and me to baby-sit Liza, his youngest daughter—something Wynn did to help his favorite students pay off their tutoring bills—Brad felt flattered. He was following in the footsteps of Dustin Hoffman and Steve McQueen, Wynn said. When Brad finally landed his first paying job in April 1973, the off-Broadway premiere of Brian Friel's 1958 drama, *Crystal and Fox,* Brad gave all the credit to Wynn.

It was the first of five off-Broadway roles that Brad would play before abandoning New York to move to Los Angeles three years later. But at the time, it seemed as if Brad were launching his career as an off-Broadway actor. He played Gabriel, the troubled seventeen-year-old runaway son of Crystal, an Irish housewife played by actress Rue McClanahan, who would later become famous on TV's *Golden Girls.* Although the play ran only twenty-four performances before closing at the McAlpin Rooftop Theater on May 13—it would be almost twenty years before *Dancing at Lughnasa* established Friel as one of the foremost living dramatists—it was a pivotal time for Brad. Not only did he become close to Rue, a friendship that would prove helpful in his move to Hollywood, but it was his first taste of what it meant to be a professional actor, the first time he had his own dressing room with the requisite flowers and telegrams.

It was also the first time that "Brad Davis" performed. Since Actors Equity already listed a Bobby Davis, Brad needed a stage name. I suggested Brad use his middle name—Creel, his mother's family name—as his surname. But Stark thought Bobby Creel sounded odd, not mainstream enough. "It has to be something Davis," he said. Eventually, I came up with Brad, which had been my cousin's name. Stark liked it and Brad didn't mind. So Brad Davis was born even though we all still called him Bobby—it would be years before I called him Brad—and I had named him.

Everyone seemed to agree that Brad Davis showed real promise. It was the first time I had seen Brad onstage, and it answered a lot of the nagging questions I had about his talent. Wynn told Brad it was the first time he had really seen him act. Even critics singled him out. Walter Kerr, then chief drama critic for the *New York Times,* praised Brad's performance, calling him "one of the most promising actors of the season."

Even with the play's early closing, Brad's life had changed. That summer he spent a lot of time with Rue at her house in New Jersey. Ostensibly, he was being paid to do odd, handyman-type jobs. But Rue was headed for California in August for her first TV role on *Maude,* and that summer they talked a lot about acting, New York theater, and the kinds of offers Hollywood could dangle in front of an eager, ambitious actor.

Although Brad would do four more off-Broadway productions, including two of Larry Kramer's earliest plays—the short-lived *Sissies Scrapbook* at the Playwright's Horizons Theater that November and *Four Friends,* which opened and closed on February 17, 1975, none of them were the kind of shows that convinced Brad he was going to have the kind of stage career he wanted.

There were some dark days from 1973 until early 1976, when Brad went to audition after audition but came back with no offers. It was his first taste of the kind of rejection that all actors go through. But Brad was not emotionally equipped to handle it with a sense of professional detachment. If he had started drinking during *Crystal and Fox* to celebrate his career, he now began to drink out of depression. Not every night, but enough nights Brad would go out before I even got home from work and not return until early the next morning. Here I was essentially a nondrinker who could hardly get through a glass of wine living with a man who loved to polish off bottles of Wild Turkey and Stolichnaya.

For most of the year we lived on Jane Street, that was the pattern of our days. I had known Brad was moody, even volatile, but I had never yet seen him in such black humor. But you rationalize. The next time he'll get the job, you think, and life will begin again. I think I only questioned my reasoning a few times. Like the day I came home from work to discover that Brad had slashed some paintings that I had from my mother. I was distraught, not so much about the pictures, but that Brad had done something violent in our home. I should have taken it as a sign of things to come, but Brad shrugged it off, insisted it was an accident of temporary passion. And I believed him because I didn't know then what I was up against and because I loved him.

By 1975, even Stark was beginning to change his tune about Brad and a stage career. After seeing him in several productions, he had started to think that Brad's intensity, his prettiness, were better suited to Hollywood and a film career. Although he knew Brad loved New York and the off-Broadway world, Stark told Brad that the camera would prove to be his ticket.

Although I knew Brad was ambitious and unhappy with his career, I didn't think he—let alone we—were prepared to make that kind of move. I was content, more or less, with our life in New York. Brad just needed to get more work. Besides, I was working as a full-time agent for Stark at his new agency. He had left CMA that year, just before the merger with IFA, to start Hessesltine-Baker. We worked out of his new offices on Fifty-seventh Street between Sixth and Seventh Avenues. Because I was making more money, we had also moved uptown to the apartment on Fifty-eighth and First Avenue.

But that delicate balance was not to hold. In October 1975, Brad landed the first film role of his career: an hour-long PBS dramatization about Walt Whitman's life, called *Song of Myself,* directed by Robert Markowitz. Brad played Whitman's ten-year companion and lover, Peter Doyle, while Rip Torn was cast as the legendary poet. The TV movie was set to air in January as part of the country's bicentennial celebration. Brad loved the whole experience, the difference between acting onstage and in front of a camera. He was completely up, his depression long since forgotten. Part of that had to do with his meeting Rip, a talented but difficult actor who had a reputation as something of a madman. Rip was married to Geraldine Page and was jealous of her success. His own career had been and would continue to be very mixed, right up until 1992 when he landed the role of the irascible producer on HBO's hit series *It's Garry Shandling's Show.*

Whatever difficulties Rip presented to producers, Brad, however, adored him, both as an actor and as someone whose personal life was flagrantly unconventional. His marriage to Geraldine was extremely odd, even for the times. He was intensely competitive with her, and he also had a lover, which he was fairly open about, as well as children from an earlier marriage. But neither Rip nor Geraldine seemed to care what anyone thought or said. Brad, of course, thought this was utopia, the life of a true artist.

Perhaps it was an omen. When *Song of Myself* aired in January 1976, Brad was praised in the reviews, especially the *New York Times*, where his picture ran with a story in the Sunday Arts & Leisure section. Ironically, it was Larry Kramer—ironically because Larry would offer Brad the biggest stage role of his life nine years later, playing Ned Weeks in the premiere of his seminal play *The Normal Heart*—who called. "You've got to go to California," Larry told Brad. "This is the kind of stuff that is going to get you work out there."

By March, Brad was gone, and his career as a stage actor and our lives together in New York were over almost before they had really begun.

CHAPTER

4

For most of 1976 after Brad left for Los Angeles, I continued working for Stark, still living in the apartment, now with an old friend, Erica Eigenberg, as my roommate, but my relationship with Brad consisted of phone calls. Late-night, early-morning calls. Brad at an audition. Brad at another audition. Brad landing a role. In *Sybil*. Then another. In *Roots*.

Brad's life seemed to be changing daily, but mine felt as if it were going backward—especially when I started to get the darker, more troubling calls. Brad out drinking all night. Brad at the emergency room. Brad in a car accident in another woman's car. Brad reprimanded on the set because the star smelled liquor on his breath. I was used to Brad's late-night habits, those nights when he came home at four or five in the morning stinking of booze as he crawled in next to me. It was one of the most troubling parts of our relationship, but at least he came home. This was different. We no longer had a home together. I wasn't even sure we still had a relationship, or if we did, what kind of relationship it was.

For most of that year, Brad lived in a spare room at Rue McClanahan's house in Studio City. Three years after they'd met on *Crystal and Fox*, Rue was a regular on *Maude*, the hit Norman Lear series that starred Beatrice Arthur—an auspicious pairing they would replicate a decade later on *The Golden Girls*. As with any actor with a hit series, money was no problem. Rue owned a big house in the Valley where she lived with her then husband, Gus Fisher, a real estate agent, and her teenage son, Mark. It was no problem to loan Brad a spare room downstairs. In exchange for his board, Brad was supposed to help keep an eye on Mark, who was something of a troubled kid at the time. But Brad's idea of helping out usually involved a bottle of his favorite chilled Stolichnaya. There were a lot of late nights when the two of them went out bar-hopping. Whatever Rue and Brad's relationship had been, I think she wound up being disappointed in him.

But none of that mattered to Brad. Almost from the week he arrived, Brad seemed to land on his feet. For one thing, there was more work. He was going to more auditions in one week than he'd had in a month in New York. And the reaction he was getting was good. He was twenty-six, handsome in a photogenic way, with solid television and off-Broadway credits. That Brad, at five feet seven inches, was on the short side—something that had hindered him in New York, where he was almost always cast as the male ingenue— wasn't such an impediment on film, not when you consider that non-giants such as Dustin Hoffman and Al Pacino have had thriving movie careers. Brad was what Hollywood has always craved, a new face. Especially when it is a variation on a tried-and-true face. And Brad fit the James Dean, rebel-without-a-cause mold well. That he showed up at auditions in jeans and a T-shirt looking as if he'd just rolled out of bed was considered all part of the image.

Not only was Brad an identifiable type, but he was represented by a new, aggressive young agent named David Eidenberg, a former stage manager at Joe Papp's Public Theater in New York, whom Brad began working with shortly after he arrived and realized he needed a strong Los Angeles–based agent—something Stark had never been.

Brad was scared by Stark's lack of muscle in Hollywood, especially since he had left CMA and its phalanx of high-powered West Coast agents the year before. As partners with Bob Baker in another small agency again, Hesseltine-Baker, Stark no longer had an official partner in Hollywood. Brad wanted someone on the ground with him in Los Angeles. But beyond that, he was worried that Stark and Bob weren't focusing on him the way he felt they should be. Typically, Brad acted out his fears at a party Bob threw at his apartment in Sutton Place. Brad got drunk and became obnoxious to the other guests. Whatever Bob had been thinking about Brad up to that point, he decided then and there that he didn't want Brad in the agency.

So Brad quit Stark—a departure that put me in an awkward spot and left Stark, that party notwithstanding, feeling embittered—to sign with Smith-Stevens, a small boutique agency headed by Clifford Stevens. Like Stark, Clifford ran an independent agency based in New York, but he had the foresight to have a strong West Coast partner, Susan Smith, who worked out of their offices on LaPeer in Beverly Hills, around the corner from ICM. Later, when Clifford and Susan parted company, he renamed the agency STE to reflect the addition of his new partners, including David Eidenberg. Clifford also sagely maintained a partnership in London, which helped him years later when he became the first to present to Hollywood such British stars-in-the-making as Ken Branagh, Ralph Fiennes, and Julia Ormond. Brad connected with Clifford, as he had early on with Stark, but he was less keen on Susan. So Brad really fell to David.

It was, initially, a fortuitous pairing. David Eidenberg and Brad were both young, handsome, and anxious to make Hollywood their oyster. If Brad was rough around the edges, David was polished, almost elegant, in his slim Italian suits. He was also enamored of Brad, and the two of them spent a lot of time together. Fortunately, David also seemed to be sending Brad out for the right jobs. Later, when almost two years passed before Brad got a second film after *Midnight Express*, David would not seem so prescient. But that spring, everything seemed to be moving in fast-forward. Quickly, Brad landed parts in two prestigious television projects—*Sybil*, the Emmy Award–winning TV movie that would launch Sally Field's adult career, and *Roots*, the seminal twelve-hour miniseries that won nine Emmy Awards and earned a notch in the TV history books.

It seemed like astonishing luck given Brad's less stellar years in

New York, and in truth both of the roles came about because of Clifford Stevens's connections—the agency represented Sally Field and Clifford's partner, Susan Smith, was close friends with Toni Howard, the casting director on *Roots*. But Stark and I didn't know any of this and we were rather nonplussed. Especially Stark. Whatever vindication he may have felt about plucking Brad out of a student production years ago, he was not thrilled to see another agent reaping the benefits. He was a fabulous man in many ways, but he did not forgive easily. In his eyes, he had been wounded once by Brad's and my relationship, and now he felt betrayed again.

And I had my own questions about Brad's loyalties. I still loved him—I certainly missed our life together—but I was less certain about what, if any, future we had together. Sharing the apartment with Erica was dull compared to living with Brad. My few attempts at dating other men met with predictably disastrous results. In the end, I'm not sure that undying love kept me involved with Brad as much as simple boredom with my New York life. It's easy to fantasize about someone when they are no longer a part of your daily life, and in the months that Brad was in Los Angeles, I did a lot of fantasizing.

Especially when Brad began to urge me to move out to Los Angeles with him. "You gotta get out here," he kept saying. "This is where it's all happening." I had reservations about uprooting my life, dull as it seemed, to move across country to keep Brad company. I still wasn't certain he could really make a go of it, and I was scared to be so dependent on him. But his entreaties were an enticement, certainly enough to see me through all those months when Brad called with his endless stories about auditions and parties. I told myself that at the end of the day, no matter whom he had been with or what he had done, I was the one Brad was calling. So I listened to him talk about crashing some girl's car after a late night of partying. I listened to him frantic after a visit to the emergency room where he'd gone to have his eye stitched up after some drunken brawl, where he'd convinced the doctors to set it with just a butterfly clamp because he had to shoot an episode of *Baretta*, Robert Blake's hit series, the next day. And I listened to him complain, bitterly, about Sally Field.

Brad knew when he was cast as Sally's boyfriend in *Sybil* that this was more than just an important role for him. It was a prestige film, one of the first made-for-TV movies about mental illness—Joanne Woodward was cast as the doctor—the kind of classy project Sally needed to vault her from *Gidget* and *The Flying Nun* into serious adult roles. Brad knew what was at stake, and he was, for him, on his best behavior.

But Sally didn't like Brad for whatever reasons. No matter that Brad and Joanne clicked, that she took a motherly interest in his career, urging him to return to New York and study theater again. "You should study Shakespeare," she told him. "It's the one thing Paul always wished he had done." Sally remained aloof during the entire shoot. Whatever her objections, they came to a head the day Sally took director Daniel Petrie aside and complained that Brad was coming to work with alcohol on his breath. Brad was livid, furious that another actor had complained about something he felt had no bearing on his performance.

That night, he complained to me for hours on the phone about Sally's unfairness, her "paranoia," as he put it. It was so different, he kept saying, from the way he'd worked in New York, especially his well-lubricated friendship with Rip Torn. Brad was like Stark that way, he never forgave a slight. But Sally's complaints were, in fact, the first time Brad had been criticized, in a professional capacity, for his drinking, and it really hit him—not in a shaming way, but making him resolve to do what he wanted to whenever.

He was still talking about it when I took some overdue vacation time and flew out to visit him two weeks later. It wasn't exactly an electrifying reunion. In New York, I was a successful Broadway agent, but in Los Angeles, I felt like a helpless child. I didn't have my license, so I spent most of that week waiting around for Brad, either holed up at Rue's or on the set of *Sybil*. I was uncomfortable at Rue's, and being with Brad on the set was completely different from attending one of his New York stage performances. You don't really know the meaning of superfluous until you hang around a movie set as an observer. I flew back to New York convinced I would never move to Los Angeles.

By July, *Sybil* had finished shooting, and Brad was working on

Roots. He'd been cast as Ol' George, the kindly sharecropper and one of the miniseries's few sympathetic white characters. For most of the summer, he was busy filming in Los Angeles or on location in the South. With the exception of my trip and a brief visit Brad had made to New York when *Sybil* had gone on location, I didn't see Brad for almost nine months. In our calls, he talked about new friends, people I didn't know. He even got his ear pierced. By fall, I was certain our relationship was over.

So it was a shock when after I agreed to spend the Christmas holidays in Florida with him and his parents, Brad suggested—actually insisted—we get married. "It's now or never," he told me. "Either we get married or we're splitting up for good and I won't see you anymore."

For most of our years together, Brad's family were an enigma to me—characters out of a Faulkner novel, mad gothic Southerners playing roles in black tales of alcoholism, incest, and suicide attempts. It would have been funny if weren't so tragic, if it weren't so true.

When I met Brad, I knew only that our backgrounds couldn't have been more different. I was from Russian Jewish immigrant stock, real Ellis Island material, while Brad was from one of the South's oldest and most respected families, descendants of Jefferson Davis, the president of the Confederacy. Brad was never very forthcoming about his childhood in Florida, his parents, Eugene Davis and Anne Creel Davis—Doodle and Annie as Brad referred to them then—and his younger brother, Gene, known simply as Brother. "We were the odd family on the street," he said. "We kept a monkey and we never cut our lawn. Our house looked like an abandoned rain forest."

When I finally met his parents during a first Christmas trip to Florida, the year Brad and I moved to Perry Street, they seemed to live amid relative placidity on three lush acres outside Tallahassee. Granted, they wore nothing but polyester and you could have blown their ranch house down with a feather, but that seemed the extent of the family's decline.

During that trip I first learned about the Davises, heard the story of how Brad's paternal grandfather had been one of the pillars of Tallahassee, how he had owned three brickyards, an extremely profitable business during the early part of the century when the state capital and most of the city proper were being built. He amassed a fortune, most of it in land, 2,200 acres inside the city limits. When he died, the trust of the acreage was left to his second wife and the nine children from two marriages, including Brad's father. Whatever affluence the Davis family had had, they were now a classic case of the land-poor gentry. The heirs owned a quarter of the city and stood to inherit millions the day the property was sold.

That day never came. At least not while Brad was alive. For most of his childhood, the family lived an unremarkable middle-class life supported largely by his father, a graduate of Emory University, a dentist with a modest practice who played poker on weekends and counted the mayor and chief of police as family friends. The family lived in Tallahassee for the first ten years of Brad's life, a comfortable household with a nice home in a good part of the city, two cars, and enough money to give Brad riding lessons. He was such an accomplished rider that he was known at local stables as a likely candidate for the Junior Olympic team. Even after Brad had left home, his parents kept a room displaying his riding trophies and ribbons.

That relatively affluent life, however, began to falter in the late 1950s. His father's drinking, never considered immoderate, accelerated. His dental practice suffered, a setback Brad's mother did not handle well. A strikingly beautiful woman who resembled Joan Bennett when she was younger, Anne Davis had always been high-strung and demanding. Motherhood was not her strong suit, and now with the added burden of her husband's financial problems, she was almost constantly depressed, medicated, and bedridden. In 1959, when Brad was ten, the family abruptly left Tallahassee and moved downstate to Titusville. Ostensibly, it was a financial decision, a move meant to capitalize on the booming local economy fostered by NASA's arrival at Cape Canaveral. But there was another, darker story, that Brad's father had been drunk while working on a patient and that something had gone horribly wrong with the drill.

If Titusville was meant to be the family's escape, it was hardly that for Brad. Although the family seemed intact to all outward appearances—Brad attended Kate Sullivan Elementary School and the local high school and he still rode and, in fact, had his own horse, Flash—the Davis household was increasingly dysfunctional. At one point, their yard was completely overgrown and there was animal feces in the house. They kept monkeys in cages, and one became crippled from the confinement. By the time Brad was sixteen, his mother was in the throes of a full-blown nervous breakdown.

Although his father would eventually get sober—in all my visits I never once saw him drunk—and move the family back to Tallahassee, it would take Brad years of therapy before he could begin to explore that part of his childhood, years when we were struggling to put our marriage back on track after Brad's drinking, financially difficult years when we had to bail out his parents, even buy their house to keep them from bankruptcy. Only then did I begin to put all the sordid pieces together, realizing that Brad's problems, his drinking, his drug abuse, his addiction to sex—and his darker secrets, his dabbling in prostitution when he first came to New York, and his suicide attempt when he fled back to Florida—were the direct result of his abusive childhood, his father's alcoholism, and even more damaging, his mother's incestuous relationship with her oldest, favorite son.

Today, the subject of incest is so common it is no longer considered taboo. But in the fifties and sixties, there was no enlightened media, no intervening social agency, to help a teenage boy forced to spend every night in his mother's bed. Whether this began innocently, the way mothers will sleep with their babies, or whether it was a way for an unhappy wife to punish a drunk husband, was immaterial. His mother's obsessive sexual attachment to her oldest son ruined the parents' lives and it nearly ruined Brad's.

It took Brad years before he could even acknowledge the abuse—he blocked much of it from conscious memory—and recognize that his relationship with his mother was the cause of his sexual compulsions, the self-confidence and confusion he felt in his sexual dealings. Brad told me, reluctantly and only years later, that he had supported himself during his first trip to New York by hustling in Times Square, an experience that I believe led to his abrupt return to Florida that year before we met, when he went back to "have a nervous breakdown," as Stark had put it. Brad told me that our relationship was the first sustained consensual sexual relationship with a woman he had ever had. I believed him. I also believed that his ease within the homosexual community, his sexual compulsiveness with women, even the rumors of bisexuality that dogged him his entire career, were the result of his having been an incest survivor, to having survived life with a sexually possessive woman who needed to be institutionalized when her sixteen-year-old son finally rebelled at sleeping in her bed, a woman who refused to attend our wedding.

But that Christmas of 1976, when Brad and I met in Tallahassee to talk about getting married, none of that was known to me. His parents were the least of my concerns. We were to fly in a few days before Christmas and leave the day before New Year's, barely a week together—all of it under the eyes of his parents—to figure out our future. When he met me at the airport, I hadn't seen him for almost six months, and I couldn't believe the changes in him. All those months in Los Angeles had given Brad a sheen. He had always worked out—it was one of the things he did to compensate for being short—but now, he looked almost sculpted. Sitting there in his sunglasses and his tan in his father's Oldsmobile, he seemed self-confident, self-assured, as I wandered out of the airport, squinting and hesitant in the blazing Florida sun.

We spent most of those first few days holed up in his parents' guest room. As happy as I was to be with Brad again, I was never able to relax around his parents. His father was affable enough, but I thought his mother was even moodier than Brad, and I suspected she had mixed feelings about our relationship. But Brad was uninhibited. He'd always been proud of his body in a slightly exhibitionist way, loved to joke around, shed his clothes, and pose for humorous erotic photographs. Being at his parents was no impediment. There was an old birdbath pedestal in their backyard, and he would cavort on it, naked, like some animated Greek statue.

Another favorite pose was to sprawl in front of their roaring fireplace, naked except for a live rooster placed crucially on his groin. I considered his antics sophomoric but also funny. I had never been comfortable with my body, and it was freeing to be with someone who didn't have my hang-ups and insecurities. I didn't know Brad's family history then, that he was probably acting out certain issues; I just assumed it was Brad's way of conveying his autonomy, his adulthood to his parents. I thought, too, it was why he chose his parents' house to propose.

He wanted me to move to Los Angeles. But I still had doubts about giving up my life in New York just to live with him. "So we need to get married then," Brad said, impatient as always. "We have to do this right now, or I'm going back and I won't see you ever again."

It was more of a threat than a proposal, what I would come to realize was Brad's bullying way of getting anyone to do anything. He wanted me with him in Los Angeles, and if he needed to marry me to do it, then so be it. But even a marriage proposal didn't resolve the reservations I had about our relationship. I knew that I loved Brad, that our sex life was the best I had ever had, and that on a good day, he was the most exciting person I had ever met. I also knew he could be moody, angry, even unstable. Artistic people are different, I kept telling myself, you have to make allowances. Right up to the day of our wedding, all during the drive to the courthouse in Cairo, Georgia, fifteen miles north of the Florida border where we were married in a civil ceremony, I kept telling myself, "You can always get divorced."

Maybe if my parents had been alive, I might have come to a different decision. But I was only thirty, alone in the world, and sitting there in the back of his father's car with my mother's wedding ring clenched in my hand and the windows down and with the warm, moist air pouring in and the trees wrapped in Spanish moss ripping by and Brad leaning forward to talk to his father in that twangy, intimate way they had, I thought, this is what my life is now.

So we were married on December 29, 1976, in Cairo, a town of barely nine thousand people, by a woman justice of the peace who had a bad stutter, with Brad's father and brother as the witnesses. I wore a white shirt and a black skirt—I had no other more dressy clothes with me—and we used my mother's wedding ring, engraved by my father so long ago. It should have been at least a touchingly ad hoc ceremony, but Brad and I were hysterical with barely suppressed laughter, what with the justice's stuttering and his brother standing there all solemn in a flak jacket and the tension caused by knowing his mother was at home in bed, sulking because Brad was running across state lines to get married, to "elope, just like white trash," as she put it. She was so angry she never got out of bed that whole week, never even came to the reception that their best friends, Mary and Roy Shuford, a local banker and his wife, gave us—presents, a cake, and a sit-down dinner set with Mary's family china.

Looking back, I think Brad's father must have been saddened by his wife's behavior, her refusal to attend their son's wedding. Or maybe, after all those years, he was beyond caring. It all felt familiar to me, living in the shadow of a weak and angry woman who tried to punish and control those around her with her moods and willful absences. Ironically, marrying Brad felt like freedom from all that. When we left the next morning, flying out to our respective cities, I wouldn't see Brad for almost five months, until my move later that spring, but I already felt different, as if I were another person, someone named Mrs. Brad Davis.

The rest of that winter, I got ready to move, an enormous undertaking it seemed now, since I was doing it all on my own. David had insisted there were too many movie possibilities for Brad to leave town, so I slogged through my last New York winter alone. My list of things to do seemed endless, from the mundane, taking my first driving lessons, to the daunting, informing Stark I was leaving. But first I had to tell him I was married.

He was stunned. Stark knew Brad was impulsive, but he had always considered me levelheaded, or at least a dyed-in-the-wool New Yorker. Moving to Los Angeles was unthinkable to him. "I know it's love, darling," said Stark in his usual dry way, "but to go and get married?" We talked halfheartedly about the possibility of expanding the agency, of my representing clients in Los Angeles, but it quickly became obvious that I would move on. In the end, I think, Stark was relieved. It would be the severing of his last link to Brad, a closing of the wound.

I needed a job that would get me to the West Coast. Although I had doubts about becoming a Hollywood agent, I didn't see that I had much choice. Brad was in no position to support us, and in any event I had no intention of giving up my career to become a full-time wife. Not to Brad. I made a few calls to the bigger agencies, but it was Mary Goldberg, head of the casting department at the Public Theater, who eventually put me on to Bob Gersh, the twenty-six-year-old head of the Gersh Agency, a small but respected agency in Beverly Hills. Bob and his older brother, David, had joined their father, Phil Gersh, who had been Humphrey Bogart's agent. Although Gersh would eventually become one of Hollywood's minimajors with such clients as Jennifer Jason Leigh, Juliette Lewis, and Ray Liotta, in 1977 Gersh represented mostly directors and writers. Harrison Ford, in his pre–*Star Wars* days, was one of the few actor clients. Bob was looking to expand the talent division and wanted someone with strong connections to New York theater.

"I want someone from New York who knows the ropes," he told me during the one and only interview we had in New York that March. "I need someone who can find talent."

I knew I could handle that part of the job. After six years with Stark, I had developed my own eye and opinions about actors. But I had never negotiated a movie or television deal, and I was nervous about my inexperience. "That's okay," Bob said. "You'll learn. Everybody does."

In hindsight, I should have been more cautious. That year would prove to be the most difficult of my career. I would make a lot of mistakes for a boss, who, despite being four years my junior, was not as indulgent a mentor as Stark had been. It would be my first look at Hollywood as an insider, a year that would ultimately cause me to leave agenting. But that spring I needed a job to get to Los Angeles. So I ignored my fears and accepted Bob's offer. My first day was to be June 20, 1977, which was also, auspiciously, the first day after *Star Wars* opened that weekend. I made plans to leave New York the Saturday before.

Buying a one-way ticket is always something of a mind-bender. After the flurry of getting out of New York, I spent the whole flight out thinking about what I was leaving behind—my beautiful prewar apartment, the theater, Stark, my friends, and Madison Avenue on a perfect June Saturday. Los Angeles was a blank to me—I had been there all of two times—and my concept of married life was hardly more coherent. When Brad told me he had found us a house to rent in the Hollywood Hills, I had no sense, other than the Hollywood sign, what that meant.

Whatever I was expecting from Brad by way of a reception was all but lost in our first few minutes together. He met me at the gate, and right away I could tell he was angry about something. I couldn't believe it. I had just flown nearly three thousand miles to begin our life together as husband and wife, and here Brad was, pissed off about some audition that he thought he'd blown. The whole way home, he kept pounding the steering wheel of his rented Ford. "I fucking blew it," he said. "I fucking blew it."

It was typical Brad, flying by the seat of his pants and blowing up when it didn't work out. But I was in no mood. I was exhausted from the trip and distracted by the drive, Brad's speeding, and the dogs, Alice and Sam, scrambling all over my bags in the backseat. I could not have cared less about another one of Brad's auditions that he had typically not prepared for. He hadn't even bothered to read the script, something that was immediately apparent to the director, an Englishman named Alan Parker, who was looking for a young, unknown actor to star in a film called *Midnight Express.* "It's based on this book," Brad kept saying, as if I should know something about it. "A true story about a drug dealer."

The name meant nothing to me. I was more concerned about orienting myself and the house he'd found us than some film about a drug dealer. The hills, I realized, were very different from the Valley with its long, flat boulevards and endless strip malls. I thought of Los Angeles as this undifferentiated sprawl, but here were hills, with curvy streets and little houses that looked more like cottages tucked back among the trees. The jacaranda was still in bloom—I had never seen a purple tree—and I thought I was coming to live in a fairy tale, especially when Brad pulled into the driveway of a little Spanish-style stucco house with a red-tile roof.

Whatever charm 3405 North Knoll Drive may have possessed, however, it belonged only in the eye of the beholder, not an actual resident. It had belonged to an elderly woman—Brad said it was some old silent-screen star, but we never knew for sure—who lived upstairs and rented out the basement apartment. She had recently died, and Gus, Rue's husband, was selling the house as part of the probate settlement. He needed someone to house-sit the property, so he'd talked Brad into renting the basement apartment—airless, dark, and dank—for $200 a month.

I couldn't believe this was to be our home, this hole with a painted concrete wall in the living room and one ratty old sofa. Brad, of course, thought the whole thing was hilarious. After dropping my bags and making a fast call to David Eidenberg, begging him to get him a second audition, Brad fished out a key to the upstairs. "It's haunted," he said, jiggling open the lock to the front door. "We're living in a haunted house."

Looking around, it was obvious the woman had only recently died. Her furniture was still in the living room and in the bedroom, her walker leaned in one corner, and her medications sat on the nightstand. There were even sheets still on the bed. "Look," Brad said, pointing to the pillow. "You can still see the indentation of her head."

If I had known then that I would live here by myself for three months while Brad was in Europe shooting a movie, I don't think I would have stayed that first night. In all our years together, I would be the one pushing us into better housing. Whether it was from Perry Street to Jane Street or from this dump in the hills to our next rented house in Encino and eventually to our own house in Studio City, I was the one who cared about making a home. Brad simply wanted somewhere to crash between movies and parties, a place with a phone and a sauna. He couldn't have cared less that we had nice furniture or china or a guest room.

We were still standing there in the bedroom when the phone rang downstairs. Brad was out of the room like a shot. "It's David calling back," he said, running out the door, leaving me standing there in the dead woman's house.

I suddenly needed to sit down. I looked around the bedroom, etched now in shadow, but there wasn't a chair I could bear to touch. Downstairs I could hear Brad murmuring on the phone and the dogs barking and then Brad yelling at them to shut the hell up when he was talking to his agent. I turned to look out the window, at the purple jacaranda nodding in the fading light, and I felt far from home and yet I couldn't even imagine, at that moment, exactly where my home was.

I stood there for several minutes, or until I became aware of Brad shouting, not at the dogs now, but at me. "It's okay," he said, his voice wafting up the stairs. "Susan, it's going to be okay. They think I can get another audition."

5

On October 5, 1977, during the filming of *Midnight Express* in Malta, Billy Hayes signed Brad's copy of his book. It was the same dog-eared, stained volume Brad had studied all summer while preparing for the role of Billy Hayes. "I feel a contact, a connection with you," Billy wrote on the frontispiece. "Stay on, stay strong." I always thought it interesting that Billy's maudlin inscription fell on the opposite page to Brad's own dry-eyed entries:

> Billy Hayes/Brad Davis
> July 20th, 1977
> Movie
> yes: O
> no: X

That was the question that plagued our lives that first summer in Los Angeles. Brad had his first audition the day I arrived in June, but it would take more than two months of Brad's reading and rereading Billy's book, Oliver Stone's script, and reauditioning for the producers before his contract was signed on August 19.

While Brad was obsessed with *Midnight Express,* I was facing my own challenges in learning to be a Hollywood agent, learning to drive around Los Angeles, and learning to live with Brad again. Much of that summer, it was a struggle just to get through the week—living in that awful rented house, making the long drive to Gersh every day, bluffing my way through calls with producers and studio executives. It was all so different from my life in New York. I was three thousand miles away from what still felt like home, I had no friends of my own, and I was lonely and, on many days, terrified.

But none of it really mattered, not when you considered the real event of my life that summer: getting Brad *Midnight Express,* the film that would turn him into a bona fide star.

By any standard, *Midnight Express* was a small movie. It was made mostly by unknowns and cost $3 million. Its impact, however, was far-reaching. Indeed, *Midnight Express,* Billy Hayes's story of his incarceration in a Turkish prison on charges of drug smuggling, hit a cultural nerve as few films had done. It took the Cannes Film Festival by storm in 1978 and was nominated for six Academy Awards in 1979, including Best Picture. During its theatrical release, the film made $30 million for Columbia—a profit margin that rivals that of such blockbusters as *Jurassic Park* and *Forrest Gump.* By 1992, a year after Brad's death, the film had played in Europe for fifteen years, grossing more than $60 million, returning royalties to even its lowly net-profit participants, of which Brad was one.

It was the kind of success that launched several Hollywood careers. *Midnight Express* turned newcomer Alan Parker into a bankable director, gave a little-known screenwriter named Oliver Stone credibility, and elevated the career of British character actor John Hurt. All of them received Oscar nominations. Stone won his. Although Brad received a single award for his performance as Billy Hayes—the Golden Globe for Best Male Acting Debut—it would be his career, more than any other, that would remain most identified with *Midnight Express.* Years later, after he'd made many other films, he would still be described as "Brad–*Midnight Express*–Davis." It would be the question on almost every producer's lips: "What have you been doing since *Midnight Express?*" It was the standard, for better or worse, that Brad would try to recapture and surpass for the rest of his life.

In hindsight, it all seems so logical for the true story of an American college student incarcerated in a foreign country for drug smuggling—a pawn really in the Nixon administration's international policies—to become the cinematic touchstone for a generation, while serving as the defining moment in many a Hollywood career. But on the day of his audition, the day I arrived at LAX, Brad only knew that he'd blown "the role of a lifetime."

He had gone to the reading that morning at the urging of David Eidenberg, who had heard that Peter Guber, an aggressive thirty-five-year-old producer with a three-picture deal at Columbia Pictures, was looking for an unknown actor to star in a low-budget film. Something about an American kid locked up in a Turkish prison on drug smuggling charges. "It sounds dark, depressing, and violent," David had told Brad. "Right up your alley."

Whether David didn't take the whole thing seriously or whether Brad was just being Brad—his old loathing of auditions and his competition with other actors—he nonetheless decided to go to the reading cold. Not only had David not gotten him the script, but Brad had walked into Guber's production offices, Casablanca Records and Filmworks down on Sunset Boulevard in Hollywood, knowing nothing about the film, not the story of the real-life Billy Hayes, or the filmmakers, two relatively unknown Englishmen, director Alan Parker and producer David Puttnam.

Not that there was much to know about any of them in 1977. That summer, Parker and Puttnam were simply a couple of ambitious émigrés from British advertising circles—a director of commercials and a photographer's agent—just two of a gazillion Hollywood hopefuls. Although Puttnam had produced something like a dozen small films in Britain, he and Parker had only one feature film—*Bugsy Malone,* a low-budget gangster spoof that Parker had directed the year before—that had proved enticing enough to open any studio's purse. It certainly didn't suggest their futures as two of the more creative, if controversial, footnotes in

Hollywood history. Puttnam would become the Oscar-winning producer of *Chariots of Fire,* in 1981, and the short-lived head of Columbia five years later, while Parker would be a leader in that new wave of British directors who descended on Hollywood in the mid-1970s, a list that also included Adrian Lyne and the brothers Tony and Ridley Scott.

On the morning of his audition, however, Brad only knew that Parker and Puttnam presented him with one of the more intriguing scripts he'd seen—Oliver Stone's adaptation of Billy Hayes's nightmarish account of his five years in a Turkish prison. The book, ghostwritten with William Hoffer, had just been published by Dutton, and Puttnam, anxious to make a bigger splash on his second film, especially one with a sociopolitical bent, had snapped up the rights.

Whether they found Guber or he found them, I was never clear on, but *Midnight Express* wound up under Guber's aegis at Columbia, headed by my old boss at CMA, David Begelman. Although Peter Guber, a former Columbia vice president distinguished by a slick ponytail and an even slicker way of talking, would become one of the more legendary Hollywood power brokers—the producer of such films as *Batman* and *The Bonfire of the Vanities* and the head of Sony Pictures from 1989 to 1994—he was, that summer, not so different from Puttnam and Parker, anxious to make some noise with a controversial hit film. Like his British partners, he had one movie under his belt—*The Deep,* a highly commercial adaptation of Peter Benchley's best-seller best known for the wet T-shirt wardrobe of costar Jacqueline Bisset.

Midnight Express intrigued Guber for several reasons. It was something of a political treatise on one of the sexier social issues of the day, but, more importantly, it was a blatantly sensationalistic story. Billy Hayes's book vividly chronicled his incarceration as a twenty-three-year-old student from Long Island who had been arrested on October 6, 1970, at the Istanbul airport for carrying 2.2 kilos of hashish. Sentenced to four and a half years in Turkey's infamous Sagmalcilar prison, Hayes saw his sentence upped to life as part of the Turkish government's response to the Nixon administration's foreign policy efforts to curtail poppy farming.

After enduring five years of prison brutality, Hayes escaped in October 1975.

Although his story had an upbeat ending—a requisite detail in Guber's and Begelman's eyes—Hayes's prison years were a graphic chronicle of brutal violence and homosexual affairs. Guber secured Columbia's involvement with a few conditions: the homosexual encounters would be eliminated from the film version—leading to a controversy that would later almost derail the film's release—and a star would be hired as insurance against the downbeat subject matter. Their first choices: John Travolta, star of the just-released hit *Saturday Night Fever,* and Richard Gere, one of Brad's old acting classmates in New York, who was earning a name for himself with the film *Looking for Mr. Goodbar.*

But Brad was unaware of any of this, that his audition was due to Parker's willful disregard for Columbia's directives, until his second meeting a few days later. Unbeknownst to Brad, Penny Perry, the casting director on *Midnight Express,* had telephoned David after that disastrous audition to suggest that Brad come in and try again—a call that coincided with Brad's own panicked message to David pleading for a second chance.

And by all accounts, Brad had "behaved badly," as David would later refer to that first meeting. Not only had he been unprepared and nervous, but David thought Brad had actually been drunk. "He was playing a very dangerous game even then," David would later recall. "He would do this 'Come hither' thing, that attractiveness thing that all actors do, but then he'd do something outrageous to put people off. Of course, Hollywood being Hollywood, people sort of respond to that, watching somebody on a tightrope of their own making."

It may have been one reason why Brad insisted that I accompany him to that second audition, dragging me along to Guber's Casablanca offices located in an old Spanish-style building down on Sunset Boulevard. Half of Guber's business was in music production, hence the company's Hollywood location and its hipper-than-thou record-company ambiance. It was my first time in a Hollywood production office and I was surprised, given my years with Stark, how out of place I felt.

Part of that had to do with all the intimidatingly chic women—girls, really—skinny and dressed in requisite black, milling around. But mostly it had to do with what I saw as a subtle but distinct change in my status. In New York, I had been actively involved in theater as well as Brad's career. But sitting in Penny's office cooling my heels for an hour while she and Brad disappeared down the hall, I no longer felt like a colleague. I could say I felt useless and in the way, except I actually felt more like a doorstop, holding something open for someone else.

I would know this feeling even more intimately later at Cannes—where Peter Guber would hustle me away from Brad when the paparazzi began snapping away and where Alan Parker behaved as if I existed simply to control Brad's drinking—and even later when I visited Brad on location shoots and discovered a new meaning to the word *invisible*. It was my first real brush with what almost every Hollywood spouse battles, that sense of feeling both special and second-rate, that as the wife of a Hollywood actor, my life was a distant second to The Career.

That summer, I realized that the balance in my relationship with Brad had shifted, that I was losing that sense of parity that I'd had with him in New York. It would take me years before I regained a sense of my own life. It was, in fact, that need to reassert myself—partly to Brad and our friends, but mostly to myself—that influenced many of my decisions for years to come, decisions about my career, about having a child, but especially what I chose to ignore about Brad's behavior in Hollywood, his drinking, his drug-taking, and his affairs.

It was why I decided, sitting there in Penny's office, not to read *Midnight Express,* neither the book or the screenplay. I told myself, as I would later tell Brad, that it was to keep me from influencing his decisions about the movie, about portraying Billy Hayes. But in truth, it was my way of keeping some distance, some independence, from Brad's career.

That night we went to dinner with Penny at the Imperial Gardens, a Japanese restaurant next to the Château Marmont that was to become one of our hangouts. Although this kind of fraternizing between an actor and a casting director seemed unusual compared to Broadway's more formal ways, I was grateful that Penny was taking such an interest in Brad. But casting directors tend to fall into one of two categories—overweight maternal types and intense, inscrutable ones—and with her bawdy mouth and easy manner, Penny was clearly the former. Not only was she actively lobbying for Brad, but she told us who Brad's competition was— Richard Gere.

"Your second reading was definitely better," Penny told Brad, "but there's a long way to go and Richard is definitely in the way."

While Penny told us she felt certain that Brad was perfect to play Billy Hayes, just what Parker was envisioning, a nonfamous face with plenty of raw intensity, she was candid about Begelman's all but insisting that Richard be given the role. For the next month, she added, she and Parker and Puttnam would be in New York auditioning more actors. The final decision, she said, would not be made until August.

For the next two months, Brad played the anxiety-inducing hurry-up-and-wait game that besets every actor hoping for a big job. I was used to Brad's mood swings when he had been up for off-Broadway roles, but this was a whole different league. He was obsessed with the idea of playing Billy Hayes, not just for the obvious reasons—that it was a leading role in a feature film, and a far cry from the nice-guy supporting parts he'd had on *Sybil* and *Roots*—but because the whole story, the drugs, the violence, the antiauthoritarian attitude, appealed to the rebel side of Brad. "It's me," he kept saying. "Don't you see how obvious it is?" Brad spent most of that summer holed up in our bedroom, reading and rereading the book and Oliver Stone's script, sprawled on the bed amid a sea of notes and script pages. The dark, repeated underlining in his copy of Billy's book, his scrawled notes—many of which already used the word *me*—showed an almost frenzied determination. On one page Brad wrote the word *Sagmalcilar* and illustrated the letters in red pen, dripping blood.

It was weeks of this, of me trundling off to Gersh every day while Brad stayed at home riding a roller coaster of emotions. He was dejected after a disheartening call from Penny in July when it looked as if they were going with Richard—a call that infuriated

Brad, who was deeply competitive with any male actor but especially one he considered better-looking than himself. Then he was ecstatic in early August, after another dinner with Penny at the Imperial Gardens, when she confided that Richard and Alan had met but that they hadn't gotten along, that Alan had essentially said no to using Richard. Brad was then back in the running and would be screen-tested with the rest of the final candidates, Dennis Quaid and John Savage, later that week—on August 9, the second date Brad logged in his copy of Billy's book. Puttnam and Parker wanted to get Brad on film because, as Penny said incredulously, Begelman thought Brad's eyes were too close together or something.

It was definitely good news, but I suspected some of Penny's cheerleading was due to her bias. Not only was she one of our close friends by then, but she was also involved with Gene, Brad's brother. Brad had fixed them up during her trip to New York in July. "Call him, he's trying to make it as an actor," Brad told her. "Maybe you can talk him out of it."

Brad had said it partly in jest. Gene had moved to New York during our last year there, ostensibly to follow Brad and get into acting. Although Brad never openly discouraged him, Gene's decision gave him some pause, especially when it fueled Gene's sense of competitiveness with Brad. Although Gene never abandoned his acting plans, that summer he was taking classes while supporting himself as a janitor at a church. He was hardly the most auspicious of dates, but Gene was, also like Brad, good-looking, and Penny had really fallen for him. It was the beginning of a relationship that would, much to Brad's and my shock, lead to their marriage a year later.

But that dinner with Penny in August was really the beginning of the end of that long, anxious summer. Within a few days of his screen test, Brad got the call from David. As he wrote in the frontispiece of the book: "Brad Davis/Billy Hayes—Sept 12, 1977: Start/Yes."

I don't remember our celebration. What sticks in my mind are the details of Brad's contract, that he would be paid $35,000— more money than either of us had ever made—and that he was to be in Malta for more than three months of filming starting Sept 12, leaving me in Los Angeles alone.

The weeks before Brad left, weeks of frenzied arrangements, phone calls, and last-minute celebratory dinners, I was torn about his going, especially his being away so long. It was exciting to think my husband would be shooting his first feature film, but I was nervous, and probably a little jealous that he would be in this exotic place while I was stuck at home. It was another difference from our lives in New York, where even a starring role off-Broadway permits you to sleep in your own bed. Now, I was facing the kind of schism that confronts almost every Hollywood marriage, how to keep a relationship intact in the face of repeated, lengthy separations.

I certainly didn't have an answer, at least not that summer. Even before Brad landed *Midnight Express,* I was having trouble adjusting to the new balance in our relationship. In New York, we had led independent but interrelated lives. I spent my evenings at the theater while Brad would be either in production, at acting class, or hanging out in the Village with our friends. But here, I didn't know half the people Brad knew, and I certainly didn't know the town as well. It wasn't unusual for Brad to spend his evenings out, where and with whom I didn't know. Now, with Brad to be away for several months, working with people and in a place I would never know, I faced an even greater sense of distance between us.

Brad, however, was adamant about going alone. It was his first big role, he kept saying, and he didn't need me around as one more worry. Besides, there was my job, wasn't there? Of course, my job. In hindsight, I think my resentment about Brad's departure had as much to do with changes in our marriage as with my slow but steady disaffection with agenting.

That summer, whatever satisfaction I'd felt as an agent working for Stark was quickly evaporating. In New York, being an agent was about getting the right actor to the right job. Money was secondary. In Hollywood, it was about getting the best deal you could get—a perception borne out later that year when the Begelman scandal hit Hollywood, when my former boss at CMA and the head of the

studio producing *Midnight Express* would be indicted on embez-
zlement charges.

This all added to my perception that unlike tradition-bound
Broadway, Hollywood was unsavory, that business dealings were
slippery, and people were not to be trusted. It was a big reason why
I would eventually decide to quit agenting and become a casting
director. Not only was I not the most accomplished deal maker—
but I was losing interest in the whole process.

I had started at Gersh when the lid was just coming off the
agency—when *Star Wars* was released that summer of 1977 and
suddenly we represented the hottest actor in town, Harrison Ford.
Now, with Brad landing *Midnight Express,* I felt like a helpmate to
everyone else's good fortune. I wasn't that interested in spending
my days trying to get actors exactly the kind of job my husband had
just been handed. I found it challenging enough to have my
personal life revolve around an actor husband, seeing him through
the cycles of insecurity and cockiness that came and went with the
various job offers. I didn't want to spend my days doing it all over
again.

It would be more than three years, however, before I would find
a way to leave Gersh. That summer, I was still struggling to establish
myself as an agent, something that was as difficult as I feared it
would be. Because I came from theater, I had a certain cachet at the
agency that nobody else had. Bob certainly didn't know enough
about theater. That was why he'd hired me. "Come meet Susan," he
would say. "She just came out from New York, where she worked
with Stark Hesseltine." I was the one who could supposedly talk to
the actors, many of whom had also come out from New York. I
knew where they had worked and had even seen some of the
productions. It was my job to say, "I saw you do Shakespeare in the
Park," or something equally "insidery," so Bob could brag, "Oh,
Susan can talk about the classics, she can talk about Shakespeare."

But that was as far as my influence extended. At least that first
year. Unlike New York, where Stark's name had been sufficient to
open all doors, in Los Angeles producers would not take my calls.
As a newcomer, it was my job to deal with all the casting directors

and producers who would no longer speak to anyone else at the agency. That was new to me, the animosity that springs up between agents and producers. I should have seen it as a warning sign about all the bad blood flowing through Hollywood. But at the time, I just thought it was a kind of hazing. Hollywood, I was only just discovering, functioned less along established professional lines than on a series of personal relationships played out on a shifting power grid of stars, producers, and directors. Not only was I having to learn who the players were—and get them to take me seriously—but I had to do it face-to-face.

Another big change was that in New York you could talk to colleagues for years on the phone without ever seeing them in person. Now I had to take people to lunch, something I had always hated. I was having to build my reputation while physically getting myself everywhere: to the office, to the studios, to production offices, to lunch. Just to get to work meant an incredibly complex commute from our neighborhood in Lake Hollywood Hills down into the Valley and up over the hills again and down into Beverly Hills. I was so frightened that I used to practice driving in the evenings on the twisty hairpin roads in our neighborhood. Many times I simply burst into tears sitting at a traffic light.

But Brad had little time for my fears. He was used to my confidence in New York, my connections through Stark. He thought I was being scared for no reason. "You're just making it harder than it has to be," he would say, grabbing the keys to our rental car when I came in, wrung out after a long day, while he disappeared for hours.

He had even less patience when it came to a discussion of the months-long shoot on Malta. Like most actors, Brad could be single-minded—even selfish—when it came to his career. He could also be willfully neglectful as the next several years would prove. But that fall, he was extremely protective of *Midnight Express*. There was simply no question of my going, not even for a visit, since we barely had money for a down payment on a car let alone a round-trip fare to Europe, and Brad didn't have enough clout to get a spouse trip written into his contract. "Face it," he said, clearly angry when I had pressed my case one too many times. "You're not coming." It didn't matter that I was unhappy about staying home, it was what was best for Brad.

So I stayed behind and he left, a first-class ticket to London and on to Malta, after a boisterous celebration dinner with Penny and David Eidenberg, where I tried to act as if I were as thrilled as everyone expected me to be. When Brad left for LAX the next morning, in the polished ebony limo that slipped into and then out of our driveway, leaving me standing there in that awful house, I comforted myself with the knowledge that while he was gone, I was to buy us our first car and find us a new house. It was another pattern in our lives that we would follow for years to come.

Now that Brad was out of the country, I had little choice but to throw myself into a job I was beginning to hate and watch our relationship revert to a series of long-distance phone calls. It reminded me of the year when Brad first moved to Los Angeles and lived with Rue in Studio City, while I stayed behind in New York. Once more I was receiving bulletins from the front—Brad's phone calls typically ran the gamut from manic excitement to fury, calls that fostered in me an equal range of feelings, and, for the first time in our relationship, supplied evidence that we had slipped, like so many Hollywood couples, into linked but separate orbits.

He was staying, along with the rest of the cast and crew, at the Grand Hotel Excelsior in Valletta, the capital of Malta, a fifteenth-century town carved almost entirely of limestone, with twisting cobbled streets and open-air plazas connected by steep wooden staircases. The hotel was situated on a rocky cliff overlooking the bay—Brad's room had a balcony with a view of the sea—about a five-minute drive from where they were shooting at Fort St. Elmo, the old English army casern. The crumbling stone barracks had been outfitted with a barbed-wire fence and a minaret to replicate Istanbul's Sagmalcilar prison.

It was Brad's first trip out of the country, and he was knocked out by how exotic it all seemed: the outdoor markets and cafés, the endless blue sea on the clear autumn days, the rawness of the whole island. The fact that Malta had an exceptionally rich history, dating to the Phoenician empire and up through almost two centuries of British occupation, mattered less to Brad than the fact that he was there in the company of a cynical, hard-drinking group of Europeans.

"They're great, great guys—you'd hate them," Brad joked in one of his first calls back home, rattling off names I only just recalled from the cast and unit lists. He was particularly excited to be working with two cast members—John Hurt, the veteran English actor from such films as *A Man for All Seasons,* who was playing Max, the sybaritic, opium-addicted English inmate, and Norbert Weisser, a young German-born actor who, like Brad, was making his feature-film debut, playing the philosophy-spouting Swedish inmate who becomes Billy's close friend and confidant. Both actors, but especially Norbert, who also lived in Los Angeles, would become among Brad's closest friends.

With Norbert, the friendship was formed from their on-camera relationship—one that culminated in the controversial seduction scene that would almost short-circuit the film's release—as well as a shared case of nerves that erupted in bouts of wild drinking after hours. As Norbert put it, "We were the young lions—and still young enough to get away with it."

Not that Brad needed to be encouraged that way. Increasingly, he seemed to turn to alcohol when dealing with pressure. Such as the day he met Norbert, a carefully staged meeting between the two actors who would be asked to French-kiss each other on film. As Norbert remembered it, "It didn't seem such a big deal that we had to kiss each other [in the scene], but I wanted to make sure the guy wasn't an asshole."

Typically, Brad was dressed in jeans, suspenders, and the pair of opaque granny glasses he liked to hide behind. He was nervous, not about the scene, but about meeting another actor who could become either a colleague or a competitor. Even Norbert noticed that Brad's "smiles were too controlled and his laughs too loud and that he was already a little tipsy." But after a few more glasses of wine, the two warmed to each other, and as Norbert would remember it, "pretty soon we were both blitzed."

As with many movies in the 1970s, *Midnight Express* was a

production where alcohol and, to a lesser extent, drug use were not only tolerated but expected. Even before shooting began, Alan and David habitually braced themselves for meetings at Columbia with a stop at a local bar in Burbank—an attitude that persisted when the group moved to Malta. "It's all so European," Brad said over the phone. "Everyone is drinking. John drinks wine all through his scenes. They just deliver it to you in the morning."

Although on *Midnight Express,* Brad never drank when he was shooting—except for one emotional scene that he chose to perform drunk—he, like most of the cast and crew, knew few limits after hours. The second night after Norbert's arrival, he and Brad went to dinner with John, whom everyone fondly referred to as "a professional drinker," where they got very drunk and Brad, typically, went after one of the waiters, yelling about some infraction and demanding to see a manager. Brad had a penchant for creating scenes in restaurants, whether he was drunk or sober, but his display of temper shocked Norbert and John. "Hey, take it easy," Norbert said. "This guy didn't fuck up, or if he did, what's the big deal?"

Norbert was only discovering what I already knew, that even more than alcohol Brad needed drama. He saw all people, whether they were colleagues or relatives or simply waiters, as either enemies or friends. It was what Brad had done with Rip on the Walt Whitman movie, with Sally Field on *Sybil,* and what he would continue to do for years, even after he got sober. Norbert said to me later, "It was like Brad needed to have both heaven and hell around him. He was unbelievably sweet and loyal to his friends, but then he'd find other people and then go for them, bad-mouth them, and just fuck with them."

While Brad quickly determined that Norbert and John, and to a lesser extent Randy Quaid, who played the fourth inmate, Bell, and crew members Caryn Picker, a production assistant, and Sarah Monzani, the hairdresser, were friends, Brad also decided that others—namely Irene Miracle, a first-time film actress who played Susan, Billy's girlfriend, and Paul L. Smith, the beefy, three-hundred-plus pound actor who was playing Hamidou, the brutal prison guard—were his enemies.

Some of this was the result of Brad's personality—"a narcissist par excellence," as Norbert once put it to me. "Brad was this voracious eater, drinker, smeller. It was all in, in, in for him, his needs were just much greater than everyone else."

But much of it was also Brad discovering what every actor discovers with their first leading role—that the ordinary rules no longer apply. Starring in a movie, even a low-budget film, is not an everyday occurrence. There is enormous responsibility in having your performance, your presence, carry a film. In many ways, the only way to accomplish that is to give full vent to your ego. Ideally, it is the kind of mind game that begins and ends with a performance, but in the pressure-cooker atmosphere of most movie sets, it is difficult, particularly for a young actor, to set those limits.

And Brad was no exception. It was obvious in his calls to me, and later, in the letters he fired off to Clifford Stevens, that he was feeling the pressure of his first feature film. He felt it so acutely that before each scene, Brad literally had to get pumped, stripping off his shirt, flopping down for a series of push-ups while the crew cheered him on. Conversely, there were days when Brad reached me in tears, exhausted by the long days of shooting and in physical pain, with the bottoms of his feet swollen and raw from filming the numerous torture sequences with Paul. It was the first time I heard Brad use the phrase *Gecmis olsun,* a Turkish expression meaning "May it pass quickly," which Billy had used throughout his book and which had become the buzzword on the film, the tag line on the daily call sheets and printed on the production T-shirts. It would become, in greatly bastardized form, what Brad and I would say to each other at difficult times. "Get Miss Olsen," we pronounced it.

If Brad was finding his first feature film physically taxing, *Midnight Express* proved to be a rough shoot in other ways. Not only was it a potentially explosive subject, one that had Columbia executives increasingly on edge, but like many films it was also a proving ground for several conflicting egos, those of David Puttnam, Peter Guber, but mostly Alan Parker, a young but strong-minded director who made no bones that *Midnight Express* was *his* movie.

Although Brad respected Alan, like most of the cast he had some difficulties adjusting to the street-smart cockney, a wholly self-made, enormously ambitious man who did not suffer fools and who preferred to spend his time in the company of his crew, a tight bunch of working-class Brits, many of whom he'd first worked with on *Bugsy Malone*. It was telling that Alan wrote a lengthy welcome-aboard note to crew members—his intention "to make a very violent, uncompromisingly brutal film" was a signal of the controversy to come—that was not sent to the cast. Indeed, Alan's attitude toward actors was far less comradely. Cast members, for instance, were banned from viewing the daily rushes while Alan and the crew sat and joked about all the bad takes. Alan also had a habit of running the actors credits at the end, rather than the opening, of his films—something that would infuriate Brad later when his name never appeared in any of the film's posters or promotional ads.

It was Brad's first real look at the kind of behind-the-scenes life that actors can expect—a far cry from the so-called star treatment—and the kind of resentment it can foster among a cast. John and Randy, two actors with long credits, were particularly annoyed with Alan, eventually wreaking their revenge with a couple of well-executed practical jokes. John hired some local prostitutes to crash one of Alan's cliquey crew-only parties, while Randy showed up at lunch one day with a cast on his arm and his face black-and-blue. Alan went pale at the thought of losing one of his principal actors and spent more than an hour trying to rearrange the shooting schedule. Finally a production assistant figured it was a hoax and Randy confessed. But Alan was so angry that he picked up a plate of food and threw it at Randy's face before walking out.

It was all part of Alan's habit of playing bad cop to David's good cop, another facet to the production, the close but competitive relationship between the director and the producer. Although David was another self-made product of Margaret Thatcher's Britain, he chose to play the erudite, aristocratic role—a posture that came in handy when he had to soothe the increasingly unhappy Columbia executives. David spent weeks flying back and forth to meet with Begelman and Dan Melnick, Columbia's head of production, who objected to what they considered the film's excessive use of violence and homosexuality. As Brad and Norbert referred to the situation, "some of the old guys who were disgusted about having faggots in certain scenes."

What was at issue were two key scenes, both of which involved Brad: the seduction scene between Billy and Erich, which included a chaste or obscene kiss depending on your view—Brad's note on the scene in his script read, "a chance to touch another human being and to be touched"—and the scene in which Billy violently confronts the prison guards and literally bites out the tongue of the chief warden. From the very first draft of Oliver's script, with its graphic descriptions of inmate sexual practices—"the nuthouse is a whorehouse!" he described it in a letter to Alan—Begelman had worried that the prison scenes would play as overly gay. Alan had tried to head off the fear. He was more interested in making a film that exposed the political hypocrisies of drug sentencing than inmate sexual peccadilloes. He had no compunction about modifying Oliver's script—possible largely because Oliver stayed behind in Los Angeles—and took a personal hand in such seemingly mundane issues as supervising Norbert's costume, rejecting clothes he thought were too suggestive. "No, too tight," Alan would say, tossing aside certain trousers and shirts. "Looks too much like a buggerer."

Still, it was months before Begelman and Melnick were persuaded to leave the film as Alan had shot it. In the end, it was still a hilarious reversal of Billy Hayes's actual incarceration. He never killed anyone in his book, but he did have a homosexual relationship, but this was switched for the film version.

Ironically, neither of these scenes was as challenging for Brad to shoot as the scene he had with Irene Miracle. It was a highly emotional exchange, which required Brad to fake masturbation after asking Susan to expose her breasts to him during her lone prison visit. As Oliver's overheated prose put it, "her breasts spring free, quivering, full and ripe."

Whatever Brad's fears were, he decided he needed to be drunk to film the scene. "It's the only way I could do it," he told me later. It would be months before I would see it on film, a scene that I felt, as many others felt, was one of Brad's best pieces of work—an opinion Alan perversely refused to share. "You know, you didn't have to be drunk to shoot that scene," he told Brad later at a lunch at the Beverly Hills Hotel. "You could have done it without it."

But Alan didn't know how resentful Brad was about working with Irene, an anger that had more to do with Brad's feelings toward David, who was spending so much time with Irene, and to a lesser extent Alan. Brad felt that there had been better-qualified actresses up for the role, but that David—a devoted family man who would later publicly upbraid Hollywood for its lack of morals—may have cast Irene for selfish reasons. Whatever the reality was, Brad and the others on the set believed that David and Irene were romantically involved. Whether they were or not, their closeness led to gossip about how she got the role. "It's such a fucking joke, but I'm the one who has to work with her," Brad said over the phone.

It was Brad's first up-close look at the kind of double standard that often prevails on film shoots, the collective sense that there are two sets of rules: one for home and one for the set. It was an attitude that Brad, ironically, adopted himself.

What bothered me most was that the news didn't come from Brad, but from Penny, who called me that fall ostensibly to let me know how well Brad was doing, but actually to let it slip that Brad was having an affair with a production assistant. "Of course, I assumed you knew," she said.

Of course, I had half-expected something like it. All those months of Brad's being on his own in Los Angeles when I had stayed behind in New York had not left me unprepared. What I hadn't expected was that it would be my sister-in-law, one of Brad's and my closest friends, who would break the news. After all Penny's help in getting Brad the role, I was furious at her disingenuousness. I hung up feeling intense shock and anger—at her, at Brad, and at myself—as well as an incredible calm, as if I had passed some sort of test, some rite of initiation. Or maybe it was just my realization that there was already nothing I could do.

When I reached him a few days later—his return call after my series of messages at the hotel—he erupted in anger at me. He was furious, he said, that I would bother him about something like that. "I'm in the middle of the most important role of my life and you call me with this!" he screamed into the phone. I knew Brad well enough to know that I could either let him vent his anger or, as was becoming increasingly common in our relationship, I could scream back. Despite the long-distance and the bad connection, I gave in to my rage.

"I don't care," I yelled. "You left me here when I wanted to be with you and now you're screwing somebody else. I hate this. I hate my life, I hate this kind of marriage."

But there was nothing I could do. Nothing except listen to his rantings, absurd as they were, his dismissal of this woman—"she's nothing to me and you should know that"—and his fury at Penny. "That bitch," he said, outraged by what he saw as a clear act of betrayal by someone he'd considered a friend. "I can't believe she would do this to me."

It was Brad's way of dealing with any of his wrongdoing: turn it into someone else's problem, someone else's failing. It was a pattern of denial that would plague our marriage for years, denial that in hindsight I realize I was also guilty of. I thought I was facing one of the hardest facts to confront a Hollywood marriage, even the supposedly solid ones. But in reality, I was buying into that schism between the public and private selves. I could live knowing the worst about Brad as long as I didn't have it thrown in my face. It was like his abusive childhood, an incident best left unexamined, unspoken. Besides, I already knew that beyond his compulsions, his affairs, his addiction, really, to sex, that Brad would never leave me. If I couldn't always trust him, I could at least trust that.

So I made a pact with myself during those long weeks alone. If Brad was going to be a star, then I would be a star's wife. It was that simple, and it's what sustained me those weeks and later in the years to come.

"Gecmis olsun," I said to myself naïvely, because, of course, none of it passed quickly.

If the filming of *Midnight Express* was a watershed in Brad's career as well as our marriage, the weeks following his return were just as pivotal. Whatever I may have fantasized about his homecoming, I soon discovered it had no basis in reality.

I had made some changes while Brad was gone, changes that reflected my desire for a more ordered, less chaotic life than the one I led when Brad was around. Rue's husband had found us another house to rent, an unremarkable tract house in North Hollywood that Brad insisted I take out of some sense of obligation or desperation. I had also gotten us a new car, or rather a new used car, a Volvo I bought off the lot in cash for the asking price. I just wanted us to have one thing that was our own. My days, too, seemed to be progressing, or at least attaining a rhythm of their own. I still wasn't crazy about being an agent, but I was no longer terrified of working at Gersh. Even driving was easier. Los Angeles was beginning to seem like home.

But within days of Brad's return, I felt as if we were back where we had started—or worse. Instead of seamlessly fitting back together as I had hoped, there were fights, screaming matches, as we readjusted to our life together. Some of it was the fallout over Brad's affair, the anger I had and the guilt Brad was feeling. But a lot of it was Brad's general depression that the whole shoot, that exciting, private part of his life, had ended. Those first few weeks with Brad were like living with a child sulky at being hauled home after camp has ended. A child, that is, who had a drinking problem.

Whatever the reason—John's influence or the pattern of life on the Malta set—I soon realized Brad's drinking had increased about tenfold. Within a matter of days, a new pattern was established. We were back to sharing the car, but now Brad insisted he needed it during the day. I'll never forget sitting at Gersh that first day that Brad didn't show to pick me up, sitting at my desk as everyone left while I waited and waited. "See you tomorrow," I said as blithely as I could, because it mattered to me that I hide whatever fears, whatever problems, I had. Finally at nine, Brad showed up. He'd been at Barney's Beanery in West Hollywood getting drunk with Norbert. And he'd driven drunk to pick me up.

In the next several weeks, it got to the point that I was scared every day how and when and even if Brad would come get me. It was all so different from how he'd been before Malta, so focused on getting the part, so disciplined about working out, about taking care of himself. It took me a while to realize that underneath all the drinking was Brad's struggle to readjust. I didn't yet know that it was a pattern that he would be repeat after almost every film—the decompression that any actor undergoes when he is no longer on a film set, when his every need is no longer catered to, when the focus is no longer always on him. It was that odd down period that every actor faces after filming has wrapped but the movie is not yet released. You're exhausted but you have no evidence, no sense of closure, about your work.

In that regard it was a tricky time. Brad was anxious to do something, anything to get on to the next project, but David Eidenberg wisely wanted Brad to wait for the film to be released. The early word we were hearing was good, and David thought that Brad would be in a different league once *Midnight Express* was released. Although Brad was offered a TV movie, David turned it down. He did, however, let Brad go to New York to do a small play, *The Elusive Angel,* at the Marymount Manhattan Theatre.

It was not until months later, in March 1978, that Brad finally got a look at his work. Alan had spent the winter editing the film in London before flying over with a print for Begelman and Melnick. It was a tense screening, given all the disagreements, but when the lights went up, everyone was deeply moved. Brad had seen a rough cut in London when he'd flown over for looping, and his strongest reaction then had been relief that his performance "was not an embarrassment." It was at his second screening later with Norbert, a viewing they celebrated by getting royally drunk, that he had a more articulate response to his work. When it was finished, Norbert turned to Brad and asked him his reaction. Brad's answer struck Norbert as apt commentary on the role of the actor in any film.

"It's the first thing I ever did that is completely the director's movie," Brad said. "There's so many things that I did that Alan used in a completely different way. It's nothing like I thought it would be even though I was the one doing it."

Midnight Express was not scheduled to open until the fall of 1978, almost a year after filming had begun—scheduling that frustrated Brad and David Eidenberg. But it was obviously not a summer film, and Begelman and David Puttnam wanted to build word of mouth by entering it at Cannes that May and holding a London premiere the following month. Whatever else was to come—the American premiere, the Golden Globes, the Oscars—there was, at least for Brad, nothing like Cannes, where in the space of a single screening at the Grand Palais, Brad went from an unknown to a star.

If Brad was anxious about the festival, I was ecstatic. There was no way I was going to miss it, and Brad was actually pleased I was going. I had seen only a rough cut of the film, in a tiny screening room with just a handful of Columbia executives and Norbert and his wife, Tandy Parks, but I had a sense of what might happen in France.

Not that I was prepared for any of it. Although I had spent that year in Spain during college, I felt about the Riviera how Brad had felt about Malta—that I was in this unbelievably beautiful and exotic place that was even more unbelievable because I was seeing it as part of the whole Hollywood machine. In Cannes there were huge posters of the film, posters featuring Brad's photograph, lining the Croisette, as well as in the lobby of our hotel. We were booked into the Hôtel Carlton, the best hotel in Cannes, with the whole Columbia contingent, as well as Peter and his wife, Linda, John Hurt and his girlfriend, Marie-Lise, and Billy Hayes. It pleased Brad no end that Alan and David had been booked into the Hôtel Mas Candille outside town, forcing them to drive in for every press conference, every screening, and change into their tuxedos in the men's room of the Carlton.

That week was like a nonstop party, an endless round of screenings and receptions and dinners, a festive ragtag group—Rue McClanahan was somehow there, along with Clifford Stevens, who'd flown over—at the center of which was Brad, almost always drunk but incredibly happy and ordering more champagne, more caviar, for more and more people and throwing it all on Columbia's tab. It was amazing to be in the midst of all of it, the parties and the crush of the press and the hordes of photographers and all the businessmen and stars tooling around in their limos, and I actually had a reason to be there. It was one of the first times in my life that I felt at the center of things, when I didn't have to look for someone to talk to or worry about planning the next day. People just came up to us, and everything was always arranged.

Even having to borrow a dress from Rue for the screening of *Midnight Express*—some beaded, turquoise thing since I had brought nothing dressy enough with me—and running into Brad's production-assistant lover, who was, I was happy to see, extremely glum, didn't dampen my spirits. She was angry that I was there, but Brad's attitude was 'Fuck her. She knows I'm married to you, that you're my wife, and if she's mad, then so be it." None of this mattered.

Later, there would be controversy and the hostile mixed reviews—mostly directed at Alan about the film's excesses—and the tension at the press conference the morning after the screening when the press turned suspicious because the word had gotten out that Billy Hayes was not quite the innocent victim that he had portrayed himself in his book. Alan and David had reason to believe that Billy's trip to Turkey had not been an isolated incident, but one of many trips he'd made running drugs out of Turkey. They were in a panic that Billy, never given to immodesty, was going to shoot his mouth off at the press conference. It wasn't Brad's fight, so he mostly sat there in his jeans and suspenders, and for once he was sober, which was helpful.

But none of it compared to the night of the screening, when we all limoed down to the Grand Palais and stepped out onto the red carpet, made our way past the flanks of photographers and into the cavernous auditorium. Brad was decked out in an awful burgundy velvet tuxedo, and it took forever for everyone to find seats and stop talking and for the lights finally to go down so I could stop feeling so nervous and relax in the dark.

And it was great. Whatever I had seen in that tiny screening room in Los Angeles had not prepared me for the impact *Midnight Express* had in that huge auditorium. Brad kept elbowing me through the whole thing, right up until the lights went up and everyone in the auditorium turned to us and after a moment of silence erupted into cheers and applause. I have a photograph of Brad looking awed and thrilled and extremely young; Alan is next to him and his face is a mask, unreadable.

It took forever to make our way out of the auditorium. In the crush of people we made our way to the lobby, where the photographers started screaming Brad's name and I began to lose sight of him because of all the flashing lights, and suddenly Peter was grabbing my elbow, screaming into my ear, "We have to get you out of here, we have to get to the reception," and he literally pulled me away from Brad and into the car and I was whisked away—it was hours before Brad showed up—and I didn't know why he did that, why, when I had wanted to stay with Brad and watch him, just watch him have his moment in that horrible red tuxedo, a moment that he would never have again.

6

After Cannes, the rest of that year into the winter of 1978–79 was like a wave, this *Midnight Express* wave that swept us along with it. In June, it was the British opening with the torrent of self-righteous, breast-beating reviews—"a national-hate film," said the *Times*—the Turkish embassy's protest, and the botched Amnesty International benefit. Then, in the fall was the American premiere, October 27, at Mann's Chinese Theater in Hollywood with the whole nine yards, red carpet and paparazzi and Peter Guber doing his glad-handing thing—all of it hilariously apolitical after London.

Apolitical until the reviews rolled in, that is. Richard Schickel weighed in in *Time:* "What we have here is one of the ugliest sadomasochistic trips with heavy homosexual overtones that our thoroughly nasty movie age has yet produced." *Variety* was only slightly less shrill: "sordid and ostensibly true . . . once you swallow the whole specious and hypocritical story." The *Hollywood Reporter* was one of the few positive reviews, describing it "as harrowing yet filled with hope."

Parker got the worst of it—Brad had been right in his assessement that it would be seen as Alan's film—criticized for directorial excesses and exploitative violence, accusations that would eventually have David Puttnam tap-dancing his mea culpas to Hollywood's powers that be. But Brad also got nailed by the critics, particularly by the caustic-tongued Pauline Kael and Andrew Sarris, who were noticeably unimpressed with Brad on the big screen.

It was the first time Brad had really been reviewed, and given all his insecurities, he wasn't thrilled with most of it. But none of it mattered, not the losses in Cannes—where the Grand Prix award went to Italy's *Tree of Wooden Clogs,* the Best Actor went to Jon Voight in *Coming Home,* and *Midnight Express* made do with a special jury prize—not the brittle, accusative reviews. None of it made a dent because *Midnight Express* was a hit and audiences loved Brad, loved him to the point of filling movie theaters and standing and screaming, "Go on," when Brad/Billy Hayes bites off the tongue of his captor.

Columbia could not contain the fame, Brad's fame—he would receive fan mail about *Midnight Express* until the day he died—any more than they had been able to contain Brad at Cannes, where it had quickly been determined that the star of *Midnight Express* was no longer an asset but a liability—too many late nights on Columbia's tab—and Brad was bundled off to London.

Given his propensity for "behaving badly," to use David Eidenberg's coy phrase, Clifford Stevens had known Brad would need chaperoning on what would be his introduction to the international film community. When David Eidenberg refused to play baby-sitter, Clifford had gone to Cannes. Not that his presence had any discernible effect on Brad, who simply waited until "the old duenna" retired before sneaking out to party the rest of the night. When Columbia decided to send Brad packing a few days after I had left for home, the decision was ostensibly about money, the oceans of Dom Pérignon Brad was going through every night with John Hurt and anybody else who happened along. But in reality, it had more to do with the growing sense that Brad was out of control, that he needed to be put under wraps.

Brad would unwittingly cultivate this perception for the next two years when he found himself, as the star of that fall's hot movie, at the top of Hollywood party circuit, wined and dined by producers, executives, other actors, anyone anxious to get close to the new heat source in town.

It's an old ritual, no different today than it ever was. Except 1978 was the height of the era of cocaine use in the industry—an era that would not end until Belushi's death in 1982 when AA and coffeehouses would become the centers of celebrity chic. But that year, as the star of a hit film hailed by a new generation of moviegoers as an homage to sixties counterculture, Brad was right at the apex of Hollywood's endless fascination with celebrity and its then equally insatiable appetite for drugs.

If Brad had increased his drinking tenfold during the making of *Midnight Express,* his use of drugs took a similar leap in the movie's aftermath. Like any hot actor, Brad had an aura, a frenzy about him, and wherever he went, people feted him with cocaine. At parties, meetings, dinners. The drug was everywhere and used by everyone, from stars and directors right down to the lowest grip. Everyone had it supplied. Meetings would be taken and cocaine was part of the refreshments. It was on every set, often written in as a soft expense on the film's budget. And not just for people you read about in *Variety,* but friends, agents I had known in New York who were now out in Los Angeles setting up their own agencies, their own production companies—these people used it as if it were nothing.

It's hard to remember now in our pious, politically correct times that cocaine once didn't seem so terrible. Not then. Unlike marijuana, psychedelics, or, especially, heroin—the drug that had killed Janis Joplin in 1970 and Jim Morrison in 1971—cocaine was considered a risk-free drug, nonaddictive, an aid even to the frenetic, workaholic pace that Hollywood prides itself on keeping. I had friends who were doctors who actually said that cocaine is good for you, it gives you energy. Even I, a dyed-in-the-wool nonuser, believed it. Of course, Brad never gave it a thought. That fall he went to an endless round of parties, one or two almost every night, where he snorted coke and got drunk as a matter of course. It didn't seem to matter that Brad got sloppy, out of control at high-profile parties. I have pictures of him meeting Gerald Ford at one party. Bianca Jagger. Sandy Gallin. A whole raft of jet-setters who welcomed and wooed the latest hot ticket.

And for several months, *Midnight Express* was a hot ticket, not only in the United States but in Japan and Europe, where it would go on and play in theaters for years. The film opened in the United States in October, and by the time the excitement of the opening cooled, it was time for Oscar talk, the drumbeat that begins every year around Christmas and does not let up until the actual awards ceremony in March. This was the world that Brad was suddenly plunged into, a world that was essentially closed to those on the outside, but a world with its own radar where the word was already that Brad was a comer, but also trouble.

That scenario was perhaps best captured at a party Brad attended that winter, a party attended by several influential directors as well as studio heads. Brad was already drunk when he showed up, and after a few minutes of surveying the scene, he plunged into the crowd, tearing off his shirt, yelling, "Okay, who's got the drugs?" He was already too out of it to notice over in the corner two studio executives riveted by his performance. "Oh, my God," said one. "He's an addict." A director was overheard muttering to himself, "There goes that career."

By the time the Golden Globes came along in January—less the precursor to the Oscars that they are now than a well-lubricated, untelevised beauty pageant hosted by the otherwise toothless Hollywood Foreign Press Association—Puttnam and Parker had their eyes on Brad. He'd been nominated for Best Male Acting Debut—a nomination tempered a bit in Brad's mind when Irene Miracle got the nod in the female category—and given the film's British pedigree and the whole controversy surrounding the film, he was considered a shoo-in.

It was also considered just as probable that Brad would get stoned at the awards dinner. And on January 27, 1979, in the ballroom of the Beverly Hilton Hotel, with Chevy Chase as the emcee, you could score an ounce of cocaine in the bathroom. That, in fact, was where the real party was.

Out in the ballroom, Brad and I were seated at the official *Midnight Express* table, down in front by the dais and next to the

Coming Home table headed by Jon Voight and Jane Fonda. Brad and I were squeezed between Alan Parker and David Puttnam. Both of them were so petrified that Brad was going to get high in the bathroom that they simply refused to let him leave the table. Literally, he was not allowed to go to the men's room and was given only water to drink. It was touching, in a way, how they were looking out for him, except I knew they were only concerned because they wanted to avoid any more negative publicity for the movie. But they acted as if they cared. David made a toast to Brad that "forever and for all time" he would be known for *Midnight Express*—a chillingly accurate prediction in hindsight—then he leaned over to me and whispered, "Brad's really got to watch it tonight." I murmured some bland thing in return, but I couldn't help noticing that in their paranoia about Brad, they were completely ignoring Oliver Stone, nominated for Best Screenplay, getting completely bombed next to Peter Guber across the table. Oliver sober was bad enough, but when he was high, as he was that night, there is no stopping the fevered ramblings.

It was a long, chaotic dinner. Then suddenly Brad's name was announced. He'd won, everyone turned our way, and Puttnam twisted around in his seat and pulled on Brad's scarf—he'd worn this white silk scarf over his tuxedo—like a father straightening his son's tie. Brad was clearly nervous, smiling in that awestruck way he had when he jumped up onstage, but he managed to give a lovely speech. He didn't thank me, but he did remember to thank everyone else at the table, which was politic. It was all very nice and unembarrassing, especially compared to Oliver's speech, a drunken political diatribe about drugs and cover-ups and governmental hypocrisy—themes he would come back to again and again in his career as a director—a speech in which he managed to thank no one while making a complete fool of himself.

Afterward, it was just a blur, Brad hugging Jon Voight, who, as at Cannes, had won Best Actor, and then a rush to the bathrooms, which of course no one cared about at that point. Later, we all wound up at the *Midnight Express* party at some other restaurant where, irony of ironies, Peter Guber was to accept an award on behalf of the film from the Federal Drug Enforcement Agency.

Brad, Norbert Weisser, and Billy Hayes logged most of that party in the men's room snorting coke. A lovely scene into which wandered the DEA officer, still holding his cocktail. "Is he a cop?" Billy whispered to Brad, which of course the guy overheard, because he turned around and just laid them out. "Yeah," he said, "as a matter of fact, I'm the head of the DEA, you fucking assholes, and we're about to give you an award."

The thing about having a hit movie, especially when it's also your first film, is that the pressure to get a second successful film becomes almost unbearable. You must prove that you're not a fluke or, worse, merely lucky.

There is some give to that rule, for some people, mostly actors with a proven track record of several hits, at least one of which has passed the magic $100-million mark. Kevin Costner entered the big leagues with *Dances with Wolves,* an Oscar-winning hit, which gave him protection for his next several failures. Jack Nicholson is another star who's managed to hang on to his status through good films and bad. He even had a theory worked out that he shared with Michael Keaton when they were filming *Batman:* "With one hit movie, you can weather three failures before your career is in trouble."

But for an actor such as Brad, just starting out and with only one feature film to his name, the months following *Midnight Express* were a much more unforgiving scenario. As Clifford Stevens said to Brad, "The time between your first and second films is crucial, it's a very fragile moment." Or as Alan Parker put it, in his inimitably blunt fashion, "Listen, you just gotta do it," he told Brad one afternoon when they had bumped into each other about a year after *Midnight Express.* It was a somewhat awkward meeting—Alan was already at work on *Fame,* while Brad had nothing coming up—but it underscored Brad's situation. "You've got to just make a movie," said Alan. "It's not going to get easier, or better, you just have to make the choice."

But it wasn't that simple. Not in Hollywood, where the majority of working actors laugh at the idea of "choosing" how their careers will go. Most of the time, they simply scramble after those jobs that manage to come their way, usually after somebody with more box-office clout has beaten them out. That's the sad reality for much of Hollywood's talent pool. It was that situation that Brad faced after *Midnight Express*. The movie had opened a door, but it was up to him—as well as his agents, David Eidenberg and Clifford Stevens, who had formed STE—to figure out how to capitalize on that.

Not that either of them was particularly suited to dealing with Brad's career then. At the time, STE was still very much an agency that catered to its more established, New York–based clients, actors such as Jason Robards, Lauren Bacall, and Colleen Dewhurst. Shepherding a young up-and-comer film star was not Clifford's strong suit. So it was left to David, still something of an up-and-comer himself, and Jeri Scott, an even newer new agent Clifford had hired, a former model booker and producer of commercials in New York, to keep Brad's career on track.

Or rather, to keep Brad, period. Because if Brad ever had an opportunity to leave STE, this was it. Typically, several powerful agents came sniffing after Brad after *Midnight Express,* powerful people like Sue Mengers and even Bob Gersh, who joked to me after my return from Cannes, "So, when are you going to bring Brad to us?" That kind of poaching goes on in Hollywood all the time— when careers are on an upswing and even when they are on a downswing—but at the time I thought I was being used to get at Brad, and it was one of those incidents that made me think about quitting agenting altogether.

But Brad was, if nothing else, loyal to those he considered loyal to him. Although he and David would eventually part company— part of Brad's larger exorcism of the whole *Midnight Express* segment of his career—that year he was still close to David. He felt David had been instrumental in getting him his first jobs in L.A., and they were also close in personal ways, spending many evenings together eating at the Imperial Gardens.

So with David's guidance, Brad began to make the rounds. Producers, directors, studio heads, whoever wanted to meet the star of the hot fall movie. And people were intrigued with Brad. John

Frankenheimer came calling with a project. Peter Guber wanted to sign him to a three-picture deal. Orion's Mike Medavoy took a meeting with him to explore what, if anything, he could do for the studio. It was exciting for Brad, and for those first weeks after the opening, Brad was really upbeat—taking meetings during day and then making the rounds of parties at night.

But for a young, inexperienced actor, this can be a deceptively heady time. All the attention and flattery helps ease the what-do-I-do-next jitters. Unfortunately, most of it is all talk. One of Hollywood's hardest facts is that 99 percent of what is discussed never comes to pass. A job will never appear. A check will never cross the table. Weeks, months will go by with the illusion that things are happening, that your career is going forward. Then gradually a new feeling begins to kick in, a gnawing anxiety that something, anything, had better happen and soon—a sense of panic that occurs about the time the money runs dry. With Brad having been paid only $35,000 on *Midnight Express,* that didn't take long.

Maybe with better, more experienced agents, this crucial time in his career would not have been wasted. But in hindsight, the ups and downs of Brad's career had as much to do with Hollywood's shifting priorities as it did with his talent. Like Alec Baldwin, Brad was really a character actor with leading-man good looks. Playing Billy Hayes had been an attention-getting part, but it was not the classic hero role that most studios wanted. I've often thought that if Brad had come along a decade earlier, in the sixties, when tough, gritty antihero films were still being made, films such as *Easy Rider* and *Midnight Cowboy,* he would have met with more consistent success. But by 1978, *Midnight Express* was really a coda to that era, which had effectively ended with the release of *Rocky* in 1976. That movie, relentlessly sentimental, manipulative, and a smash hit, changed Hollywood overnight. Upbeat replaced downbeat. Whatever you wanted to say about Brad's image, it wasn't unremittingly sunny.

So he went to his meetings with producers and studio heads with his studied insouciance masking growing insecurities. No one really knew what to do with him. Producers weren't sure how to cast him, and unlike some actors, such as Tom Cruise—who showed up in my office that year, a handsome, serious kid new to town who was making the rounds of casting directors as if he were getting out the vote, literally toting a briefcase and almost eerie self-possession— Brad didn't come in with a plan for his life. He had never been very good about the details of the acting business, the hows, whys, and wherefores of a role, the kinds of questions that matter when you are planning a career for the long haul. He had left New York on the slenderest of pretenses, that the camera rather than the theater was his ticket. But now, Brad's mantra was "Just get me a job."

Because he didn't really want to think about his career, it sort of fell to me to talk to David Eidenberg. More and more, I noticed I was spending hours on the phone with him, talking about Brad, about the business. Because I was also an agent, I knew what movies were being cast and who was being sent out for what roles. By default, I was becoming Brad's manager. Later, I would back off from this role when it became clear that I would quickly have no life of my own, but at the time it made sense.

So I was the one who screamed at David about the billing on *Midnight Express,* what I considered Alan's sadistic practice of throwing all the actors credits at the end of the film. I was the one who urged Brad to meet with Medavoy, Guber, and especially Frankenheimer, who wanted Brad to star in *First Blood,* an action film about a vengeful former Green Beret. It was the first of what would become the lucrative Rambo franchise, and Frankenheimer was keen enough on Brad to suggest he actually get hair plugs. Brad wasn't even thirty, but his hair was already thinning, and Franken-heimer wasn't thrilled with the idea of Rambo wearing a rug. But like so many Hollywood deals, the film never came together. When it resurfaced years later, it was at Carolco, Frankenheimer was gone, and Sylvester Stallone was attached to star in it.

There were other offers, ones that David and Clifford decided Brad should turn down. The biggest of those was *Alien,* the role that was eventually played by John Hurt. Who knew the sci-fi thriller would be such a success, a movie that would launch Sigourney Weaver as the most unlikely of action heroes? But at the time, David felt that playing a crew member who is killed off before the film's climax was simply too small a part for Brad to play after starring in *Midnight Express*.

But all of those deals were nothing compared to the ones that Brad just blew on his own. Blew, because ultimately an actor has to sell himself. Beyond an agent's pitch and strategizing, beyond a studio's wooing and coddling, an actor has to sell himself, because, whether he admits it or not, he is up for sale. And that was the one thing that Brad could never do.

The first of those disasters was his meeting with Medavoy. Orion wasn't a large studio, but it wasn't on its last legs; that came in 1990 when it declared bankruptcy. It was known as a haven for iconoclastic artists. Woody Allen, for instance, was the best-known director at the studio. So when Medavoy invited Brad in for a meeting, he might have expected a polite audience for less-than-mainstream ideas.

And Brad had them in spades: film adaptations of Nikos Kazant-sakis's novel *The Last Temptation of Christ* and Anne Rice's cult hit *Interview with the Vampire*. Already, he had a taste for charismatic, sexually seductive martyrs. But playing one in the office of the studio executive was out of place. Brad was much smarter than he pretended to be, but he enjoyed playing the Southern rube, the gothic artist, as a private joke, a way of manipulating his audience with a bit of chamber theater. Within minutes of his arrival he'd asked for a drink and went off on one of his rambling, pugnacious tirades about eroticism and artistic integrity. On one level, Brad was simply ahead of his time. Both films were eventually made, and *Interview,* which starred Tom Cruise and Brad Pitt, was a success. But at the time, Brad came off as too off the beam, personally and professionally, even for the indulgent Medavoy, who quickly invited Brad to leave.

But that meeting was nothing compared to how Brad behaved at dinner with Peter Guber some weeks later. It was a key meeting, six of us—Brad and I, Peter and his partner Bill Tennant, and their wives—dining at Yamamoto's. Since *Midnight Express,* Peter had been trying to come up with a script for Brad that would be the first of a multipicture deal. And of all the offers Brad entertained that winter, it seemed to make the most sense. Peter and Brad knew each other, *Midnight Express* had benefited both of them, and my wariness of Peter notwithstanding, he was the kind of producer who got things done.

It seemed like a fortuitous pairing, except for one small detail: the film Peter had developed, a sort of James Dean–type movie about a gang who raced cars on Mulholland Drive, was awful. Even Brad knew it was a piece of junk. So, at the dinner, admittedly a key step in the Hollywood mating dance, Brad got drunk and let his opinions fall where they may—a real scene, with him raving, yelling at waiters, at Peter, even insulting Linda, Peter's wife.

It was bad enough to see Brad make scenes in restaurants with our friends, but it was quite another to see Peter and Bill and a clutch of waiters muscling Brad out to the curb. Not surprisingly, Peter backed out of the deal shortly after that. The movie eventually got made, *King of the Mountain* with Harry Hamlin, a complete bomb that did nothing for his career.

These two disastrous meetings should have raised a red flag—with me, with David Eidenberg, with Brad himself—about his drinking and self-destructive behavior. But at the height of Hollywood's cocaine era, Brad's drinking did not seem so crucial, and none of us fully understood the damage he was already doing to his career. Some of this had to do with my sheer ignorance of how much Brad was drinking, how much coke he was taking. I didn't know his drinking buddies, his dealers, the little network of cocaine suppliers that Brad had assembled, guys who operated out of otherwise ordinary-looking houses in our neighborhood. I didn't go to the parties, so I didn't see how Brad behaved with his peers. All I knew was how much praise and recognition Brad was getting on the street.

But I also didn't realize how quixotic Hollywood could be, how ephemeral success can be, and how seemingly small things, such as a meeting or a dinner, can hurt you. It was still a few years away from a time when actors such as James Caan and Don Johnson would lose jobs because of their drug and alcohol problems. It was still a few years before Brad's reputation would almost cost him his career.

As Brad put it later, in notes for the writing of this memoir, "I'd achieved my greatest ambition and I was still only twenty-eight. How did I follow that success? I got high and I stayed high. What did I want to do next? Well, there wasn't anything I wanted to do. Not a thing."

That Brad did *A Small Circle of Friends,* a coming-of-age story about a group of Harvard students in the sixties, as his first film after *Midnight Express* was pure happenstance. Like most films, it simply came together at the right time and at the right price. Rob Cohen, a Harvard alum and an early producing partner of director John Badham, had written it as a roman à clef about his undergraduate days. He'd written it, he said, with Brad in mind to play his alter ego, the editor of *The Crimson,* the student paper.

Neither David Eidenberg nor I were particularly keen on it. I thought the script was weak, and I was concerned that Brad was making his all-important second film with a first-time director.

The film had been stuck in development hell at United Artists at the time when the studio bosses were preoccupied with *Heaven's Gate,* Michael Cimino's mega-western that would bankrupt the studio the following year. *Small Circle* had languished despite producer Tim Zinnerman's efforts to move it along. David thought that Rob's biggest reason for pitching it was his infatuation with Brad. But in one of his better moves, David capitalized on that. He knew the film was small enough so that if Brad actually signed, Tim could get the studio to green-light it. So David forced their hand with a clever pay-or-play deal. To our amazement, they actually coughed up $25,000 a week, up to $250,000, for Brad, almost ten times what he'd been paid on *Midnight Express.* Included in the cast was Jameson Parker in his pre–*Simon & Simon* days and Karen Allen, fresh from *Animal House.* Brad's contract was finalized on February 15, with the film's start date in Boston set for March 26, 1979.

That was an added bonus, as the shoot took Brad out of town during the Oscars. Ever since his win at the Golden Globes, he'd been hoping for a Best Actor nomination. It was a long shot given the competition that year—Jon Voight in *Coming Home* and

Robert De Niro in *Deer Hunter,* to name just the most obvious two. Voight eventually won it, as he had at Cannes and the Golden Globes. But still, when the nomination didn't come that falsely sunny February morning, it was a blow, the first touch of that chill wind that can sweep across a career without warning. It was especially tough since the film earned six nominations, including nods for Oliver, John Hurt, and the film itself. Even Giorgio Moroder's score was nominated. Brad felt as if he'd been specifically snubbed. Although I wanted to go as part of the *Midnight Express* support team, there was no question of attending the ceremony after that. Brad was happy for John, but he was never anybody's idea of a good sport.

So, conveniently, he left for Boston a couple of days before filming began and before Hollywood became completely besotted with itself as it does every Oscar season. Clifford Stevens remembered thinking *Small Circle* was not a bad solution to the "What next?" problem, probably "not a breakaway movie, but a sweet film." I remember it in far more graphic terms—the only movie where you can actually see the effects of Brad's drug use, the $2,000 worth of cocaine he was doing every week.

If *Midnight Express* had been about Brad's bonding with Europeans over drinks, *Small Circle* was about nothing but cocaine. It was Brad's way of controlling his drinking: to snort coke instead. Brad always considered himself a drinker rather than a drug user. It was his demented idea that if he only did drugs, he wouldn't drink and he would be fine. But Brad on cocaine was much worse than Brad drunk. With alcohol, Brad got bigger; he became voluble and obnoxious. But on cocaine, he shrank into this paranoid, nasty thing, like some wounded animal who bit anyone who dared come near. During the filming of *Small Circle* he lost twenty pounds, so much weight they had to redo his costumes and beef up his makeup to cover the dark hollows in his cheeks and under his eyes. I still can't look at the film, he is so obviously stoned. I didn't know it then, but he looked worse in *Small Circle* than when he died.

Even before shooting began, the film seemed to go off the track. The first night Brad spent in Boston, at the Copley Plaza Hotel with the rest of the cast and crew, there was a terrible fire. Four people on the floor above Brad died, and many of the crew went to the hospital suffering from smoke inhalation. Ironically, one of those hotel guests who survived by dangling from a window ledge was Sumner Redstone, the owner of a local chain of movie theaters and the future head of Viacom, the parent company of Paramount.

Although Brad wasn't hurt, the traumatic experience, a literal trial by fire, brought the company closer together. Brad was always one for cliques on films, his usual list of enemies and friends. And on *Small Circle* Brad quickly became tight with a group that included Nitro Glassman, a local kid who had been hired as Brad's assistant, and the two hairdressers on the shoot, Lynda Gurasich and Joey Tubens, who had been Lauren Bacall's hairdresser on Broadway's *Applause* and *Woman of the Year.*

It's a natural link on a movie set, that connection between actors and hairdressers, for the simple reason that they are among the privileged few allowed to see a star before he is camera-ready. It's one of the rare points of vulnerability for an actor—the early-morning hair-and-makeup call—a time when the previous night is still written in his face. You either like and trust your hairdresser or you don't. Even by that standard, Lynda and Brad became especially tight. Not only had she worked on *Coming Home* and known Jon Voight, who Brad knew from Cannes and the Golden Globes, but Lynda was the one who saw firsthand how much pain Brad was in from his hair transplants.

Even in New York, Brad had joked about his thinning hair, another lovely trait he said he'd inherited from his mother. But after Frankenheimer flat-out told him to get transplants to be considered for *First Blood,* he had gotten completely paranoid. Right before Christmas, Brad flew to New York to have it done by one of the legends in the business, Dr. Orentreich. It's a horribly painful experience at best, but in Brad's case it was a disaster when Orentreich inserted the plugs like rivets across the top of his forehead. It ruined Brad's hairline. Even he knew it was mistake, although I suspected that Brad had, in his bullying way, told the doctor to do it that way. For months, he had to comb his hair forward à la Richard Burton's Julius Caesar to cover the line. It was only the first of what would be several more transplants during his career, including one operation where, in an act of desperation, the doctor simply cut away the center of Brad's scalp and pulled the sides together.

If nothing else, it was a handy excuse for more painkillers, Brad's usual cocktail of Tuinal and Demerol—he was allergic to codeine—and cocaine. It was another reason for his friendship with Joey—both were into cocaine and, for some ghastly reason, Peter Allen. Brad would get in these phases about people—it was the height of Peter's career—and since Brad liked to get pumped up before shooting his scenes, he carried a boom box to the set blasting out Peter Allen songs.

As annoying as that was, it was nothing compared to what Brad was doing off-camera. Like Hollywood, the rest of the country was in the grip of the cocaine epidemic in the 1970s. And Boston was no exception, not with its liberal reputation and enormous student population. Lynda remembers seeing people openly smoking dope or snorting cocaine on the street. It wasn't hard to find a local supplier. On the set, Saturday was the official shopping day, when everyone got their weekly per diem checks and, with the exception of people such as Karen Allen, who wasn't into drugs at all, blew them on drugs.

But even in this atmosphere, Lynda was amazed to see how much cocaine Brad was doing—never freebasing or using needles, but snorting it and rubbing it over his gums enough to draw blood. It's hard to know exactly how much Brad was actually using, because, as was well-known, if Brad had drugs, everyone had drugs. As much as Brad loved to spend other people's money, particularly a studio's, he was a notorious soft touch that way—a gratis dealer who was going through $2,000 worth of cocaine a week, most of it sent to him FedEx from one of his suppliers in Los Angeles.

I knew Brad was doing cocaine on the set. How could I not know given what he was doing before he left? But nothing prepared me for what met me at the airport when I flew east for a week in April. After not making it to Malta for *Midnight Express,* I had been determined to visit Brad on location in Boston. But within minutes of my arrival at Logan, I regretted my decision. Brad and Nitro had driven to pick me up, but they were both obviously high, laughing and talking a mile a minute in that jittery, hyper way. I was furious and Brad knew it. I had wanted a nice week with my husband, but I realized I had walked into a private, ugly party.

By the time we found the car—parked in a tow zone, of course—the cops were already there writing up a ticket. We stood there dripping in a freezing rain while Brad tried to talk them out of the ticket. "I'm Brad Davis and I'm starring in a movie here," he kept yelling, as if it mattered. The next thing I knew, the car was on a hoist and Brad and Nitro were in the cop car on their way to jail. "Go get Rob and tell him to get us out," said Brad as they pulled away.

I had no choice but to take a cab to the hotel and try to find someone to get them out. It was hours before they got back. Fortunately, the hotel let me into Brad's room, where my worst fears were confirmed. He'd pasted a note on the door, "Maids Do Not Enter," with a skull and crossbones drawn below. And with good reason. Inside was like some DMZ. Everywhere there were bags and pouches of cocaine, scales and mirrors, razor blades—he clearly wasn't attempting to hide anything—a lethal obstacle course, which Nitro, the threadbare black cat Brad had adopted, was nimbly navigating.

I was convinced Brad was dealing. How could one person go through this much cocaine? I didn't want to touch anything. I sat on the edge of the bed in shock. How could they not know? I wondered. How could Tim Zinnerman, how could Rob Cohen—how could the hotel?—not care that the star of the movie was an addict? Even by the liberal seventies standards, it seemed completely out of control.

And I was right. The stories that came out of that movie were some of the worst that were ever told about Brad, stories that were true and false, but stories nonetheless that got passed around Hollywood, largely thanks to Tim's gossiping, that really came back to haunt Brad. There were benign narratives from Larry Kramer, who would be wakened at four in the morning by a phone call from Brad. He was in New York for the weekend, on a break in the shooting schedule, down with Lynda and Joey. "I need drugs, a place to sleep," he would say. But Larry, a well-known straight arrow, had no patience for Brad in that mode. "Pull yourself together," he told him. "You're not doing yourself any favors like this."

Then there were other darker, almost surrealistic stories from the shoot. Stories about Brad disappearing for hours from the set, holding up filming, then reappearing, bloody after having been in a fight somewhere with someone. The worst tale had Brad blacking out and smearing his own excrement on his hotel room walls. But the worst of all to my mind was that everyone on the shoot, from Rob and Tim down to the lowest grip, seemed to know exactly what Brad was doing. I never knew whether they couldn't stop it or whether they simply chose not to. But that was one of the mysteries of the movie business that I was only beginning to understand, the protective layers that can descend around a star—the enabling that goes on when you're hot, so anything is made availabe to you—and can just as magically lift when you are no longer considered indispensable.

I was so disgusted, with Brad, with Rob, with the whole scene, that I stayed just three days, mostly fighting with Brad and then shopping on Newbury Street as revenge. During those days, I crossed a line in my mind. If being married to an actor meant living a schizophrenic life—one kind of relationship at home and another one during production—then I needed to make some adjustments. I couldn't stop Brad from going on location, at least not when a ten-week separation meant more than $200,000. And I certainly couldn't control his behavior. But I could mentally separate myself from him. I flew back to L.A. determined to make changes in my life, starting with an all-out, spend-the-bucks trip to Europe that I had planned that spring, with Marsha Kleinman, a casting director over at NBC whom I had become friends with through the agency.

Marsha had invited me to go in with her as partners in an independent casting agency, Marsha Kleinman & Associates. For months, I had been seriously thinking of quitting Gersh. All my fears about being a Hollywood agent, the agressive deal-making, the cutthroat competition, had become realities. After almost three years in Los Angeles, not only was I tired of feeling so responsible for a bunch of actors, most of whom were unemployed at any given time, but I realized that being an agent wasn't just about getting actors work, it was about jockeying and sparring with the other agencies. A real cock-measuring thing that had nothing to do with talent, only ego. I simply didn't care that much, not about the power plays and mind games I was supposed to be playing. I just wanted out.

I thought at first I would simply go out on my own and become an independent agent. In New York, it was quite common for an agent to be on his own. But that scenario is far less feasible in Los Angeles, where relationships are everything, where you need connections with your fellow agents' clients. Fortunately, Marsha called with her offer. She wanted to leave NBC and the whole network bureaucracy to set up her own shop. She had enough contacts and years in the business to make such a move possible. But I was less sure about myself. Although I knew Marsha well, I hadn't considered casting as a career. In Hollywood, it is regarded as a woman's job, neither prestigious nor a stepping-stone toward something larger. But the more I thought about it, the more it seemed like the best alternative. Going in with Marsha would get me out of agenting, but without the burden of having to start from scratch on my own.

If I hadn't completely decided to accept her offer before I left for Boston, I had certainly made up my mind on the flight back. I was going to become more independent, starting with our first joint venture, our European trip, which we had planned for the following week. Marsha had carved out some time during a lull in pilot season, and I had planned the vacation knowing Brad would be gone for weeks. Now, with his cocaine use fresh in my mind, I was determined more than ever to enjoy myself. My attitude was unrepentant: "I'm going to spend this drunk's money." And I did, packing my bags and flying to Paris, Rome, Florence, and Venice, where we stayed in the best hotels and just ate and shopped our way across Europe.

It took almost another year, or until the following February, before Marsha and I would finally break free and set up shop together. But that trip was the start of a new phase in my relationship with Brad. He would go off and make movies and get high and screw around, and I would just spend money on what I wanted, clothes, jewelry, travel. Whatever. It almost didn't matter. It was something just for me.

However misguided, it was my way of dealing with Brad's drug use. And even he seemed to recognize something had gone wrong during those months. When he got back from *Small Circle* in June 1979, he swore he would never do cocaine on another film. "You know, I did a lot better drunk," he would say.

Brad wasn't the only one who was concerned. Although neither of us was aware of it, stories about Brad from the shoot were already beginning to circulate around town. David Eidenberg heard them, and so did Zane Lubin, our business manager, who had been with us since before *Midnight Express*. Zane called me one day shortly after Brad got home to tell me he wanted to commit Brad to a detox program at St. John's Hospital in Santa Monica.

I was stunned. I knew Brad had a problem, but I hadn't actually considered that he needed medical help. But Zane was adamant, and of all the people who knew Brad, Zane was one of the ones I trusted most. He is a big, bearlike man. You just didn't mess with him, and indeed, Zane was one of the few people that Brad was never abusive toward. He respected Zane, partly because he had been with us longer than almost anyone, and unlike agents, a business manager has a far less predatory relationship with their clients. Brad looked up to Zane and I trusted him more than I have trusted most therapists.

So, if Zane was concerned, I knew I should pay attention. I knew he was no alarmist nor a Pollyanna. Before he had become a personal business manager for people such as Brad and bigger stars such as Henry Winkler, Zane had spent years working for several record companies—Decca, A&M, Warner, and Elektra—in the sixties. Zane had gone to meetings, conferences, where it was expected that a pile of cocaine would be in the middle of the table for everybody's dipping pleasure. But more importantly, Zane knew the kind of money that drugs can eat through. He had known Ike Turner during the height of his drug problems, and now he knew how much of our income was going to Brad's habit.

Not that it was hard to spot. Our fixed expenses were ridiculously low given Brad's income. We had no car payments, no furniture to speak of, just the $1,000-a-month rent on that awful house we leased on Biloxi in North Hollywood. But somehow we were always short of cash. Zane knew that almost all of Brad's *Small Circle* money, his $250,000 fee as well as his per diem, had literally gone up his nose. He knew it because at one point, Zane had stopped billing us because we were almost $30,000 behind in our payments just to him.

"At first they've got guys on the set who supply it," as Zane explained it to me. "Then pretty soon you're buying, or in this case, Brad is buying, and everybody wants to get close to the star, but suddenly you—Brad—are the bank."

But if Zane was concerned about the impact of Brad's drug use on our finances, what pushed him over the edge was an accident Brad had just a few days after he returned to L.A. from Boston. They were doing some final interior shots for *Small Circle* on a local soundstage, and somehow Brad managed to fall against a dolly and rip a gash in his leg. It was bad, blood everywhere, and Brad wound up going to the emergency room, where Zane and I picked him up.

Zane was convinced Brad had been high at the time. "It's only going to get worse," he said to me while we sat there under those icy fluorescent lights waiting while Brad had stitches. "You know you're going to have do something, don't you?" Then he told me about the detox program at St. John's, how Brad could voluntarily sign himself in for basically three days of supervised bed rest. After that, Zane said, Brad and I could decide if he would stay with the rest of the twenty-one-day rehab program. I think Zane knew that neither Brad nor I was ready to do anything like that. So when he called a couple days later, asking me to meet him and Brad in his offices on Forest Lawn in Burbank, I suspected what he had in mind.

We got Brad over to St. John's largely because Zane literally picked him up and carried him out to his car. Brad hated hospitals, but even he knew at that point that he was physically sick, so he went along with it, walking into St. John's at 5 P.M. on June 13, under his own power. To this day, I can't believe that I let Zane sign his name on the admitting forms. He even hired the shrink, Dr. Gerald Levin, to see Brad while he was there. It was something of a risk on Zane's part. When he called Brad's lawyers to tell them what had happened, they went berserk. "You took on an incredible liability," they told Zane. "You should have let Susan do it, because you have no idea what he can legally do to you." But that was all part of my attitude then, that this was Brad's problem.

The hospital records, signed by Dr. Franklin Dines, the admitting physician in the chemical-dependency unit, show a twenty-nine-year-old white male, weighing 131 pounds, living on Forest Lawn—typically your business manager's offices serve as your address—having ingested large amounts of cocaine and alcohol over the last three to four months, including a quarter ounce of cocaine a day plus Percodan, Demerol, Valium ("to come down from coke"), and "yellows," Nembutal amyl nitrate. The report listed blackouts, but no DTs or seizures.

And in the coolly dispassionate medical terminology, it was easy to think that Dr. Dines assessment was no more serious than a weather report:

> The patient states he has used Cocaine up to four and five grams per day over the past several weeks to several months and has been using Cocaine on a regular basis for the past couple of years. He also states that he had been drinking up to a fifth of Vodka a day over the past several weeks.

You had to read further to get the really sobering stats:

> The patient states that his father was "alcoholic" and that his mother had "severe emotional problems" requiring multiple psychiatric hospitalizations and electroshock treatments. The patient has one younger brother with "many problems . . ." The patient states that he has seen many different psychiatrists and psychologists since he has been thirteen years old, when "I was different from other people." The patient has been hospitalized once in a psychiatric facility approximately nine years ago in Florida. At that time, he took an overdose of Thorazine "to get

the attention of my father." The patient was briefly hospitalized and given a series of six electroshock treatments.

I knew about Brad's troubled past, his mother's problems and even about Brad's suicide attempt during those months when he had left New York and gone back home to his parents. But I had been unwilling to see the relationship between those events and Brad's behavior now. I didn't see what those reports spelled out so clearly: "The patient's significant drug abuse appears to be related to his ongoing depressive personality."

Now, I wanted to believe that a three-day hospitalization would fix Brad's problem. His medication was certainly low-tech: multivitamins, folic acid, Librium, Dalmane, and bed rest. The nurse's log of Brad's behavior during those three days suggested a compliant response: "Asleep." "Sleeping." "Lying quietly in bed." "Sitting in dayroom alone and in dark glasses and headphones." "Refused dinner." "Asleep."

Zane and I visited Brad each of the three days. Usually we came with sushi or some other treat to entice Brad to eat. The second night, one of the hospital administrators stopped me in the hall. "I want to talk to you," she said. "I think you should start coming to some of our meetings, and I think you should join Al-Anon, because this is partly your problem, too."

It was the first time anyone had suggested that Brad's drug use was also my problem. At that point, Alcoholics Anonymous was still the province of the unwashed, a cliché of bums drinking coffee and smoking endless cigarettes. Al-Anon, the support group for the relatives of alcoholics, was even less well known. I couldn't see how this had any relation to our lives as part of the Hollywood community. A quiet little hospital stay was one thing, but a lifelong commitment to meetings with ex-drunks? I flat-out refused. "No thanks," I said. "This is not about me. This is his problem and I'm sure he will take care of it."

It was my attempt to contain the problem. I was trying to make it smaller, not larger. But if I was busy fooling myself, Brad had already fooled most of the hospital staff. Not only did he hold some impromptu acting classes for some of the other patients, but he completely bullshitted the psychiatrist. When Zane met with Dr. Levin, he told Zane, "Yeah, his nose is a little bad, and, yeah, he's got a little bit of a problem, but he's not out of control." Zane exploded. "Not out of control? He's an actor!"

In the end, it did nothing. When Brad was released on Wednesday, I picked him up, and we drove straight to Norbert and Tandy Weisser's to celebrate. On the way, Brad had me make one stop, a head shop in Santa Monica where he slipped into the back, past the madras curtains, where he scored cocaine. Within minutes of his release from detox, Brad was high. As if nothing had ever happened.

CHAPTER

7

By the time Brad had landed his next job—the CBS miniseries *Rumor of War,* based on Phil Caputo's acclaimed Vietnam memoir—it was clear that he wasn't going to have the kind of movie career he wanted. In just over a year since the release of *Midnight Express,* Brad had gone from being a rising young star to a troubled working actor—an imperceptible change in the public's mind, perhaps, but a crucial distance in Hollywood.

That summer of 1979, after he'd finished *Small Circle* and his blink-and-you'll-miss-it stay in St. John's, Brad resumed his drug-taking, partying ways with a vengeance. Although, unlike his behavior in Boston, he was careful never to let me see drugs at home, it was obvious I was living with a completely drugged-out husband.

Roommate was more like it. Except for our fights, we lived almost completely separate lives. We hardly ever saw each other, and our sex life was nonexistent. Not only was Brad never home in the evenings, but I had drawn my one line in the sand: I refused to have sex when he was drunk. It disgusted me to be awakened almost at dawn when Brad finally came home, stinking of booze, falling into bed. I was angry enough that he was out running around, but I couldn't bear the thought of being touched, like some coda to his private little evening. It made me feel used. On those nights, I would get up and literally vomit.

So I began to separate myself, psychologically as well as physically, from Brad. I spent my days at the office, working and plotting my escape from Gersh, while Brad spent his days at home, sleeping late and talking for hours on the phone, then visiting the gym, Vince's over on Ventura Boulevard. In the evening, when I would get home after a screening, Brad would be out, having dinner, the one meal a day he allowed himself, and running around the city, to parties, clubs, whatever, until four or five or whenever he deigned to come home. He'd bought himself a new Jeep with some of his *Small Circle* money, and for all intents and purposes, that was his home.

Now that Brad was back in Los Angeles, the search for the all-important next project started up again. Although David Eidenberg and Jeri Scott kept pursuing various possibilities, it was quickly becoming evident to all of us that Brad had a problem landing roles. After three years at Gersh, I knew there were few real secrets in Hollywood. Although I didn't directly hear the rumors about Brad, I knew that David and Jeri did, and I was shocked at the speed with which Brad's reputation seemed to be plummeting. I mean, *Small Circle* had just finished shooting, it wasn't going to be released until the following spring, but already that film seemed to have damaged Brad. Whenever David or Jeri mentioned Brad to a producer or a director, there was always some objection. Sometimes it was couched as "He's not really right for this." Other times, it was a more frank admission: "I heard he's trouble on a set." Sometimes, it was simply "Isn't he an addict?"

But as David explained it to me in one of our few meetings that summer, "It's Tim [Zinnerman], it's what he wakes up for in the morning—to get on the phone and tell these stories about Brad." I thought Tim was less interested in getting even with Brad than he was in using him as scapegoat for a film that looked to be a sure bomb. I was proved right when *Small Circle* opened the following April to a torrent of ridiculing reviews—which also rightly nailed Brad's stoned performance—and sank without a trace. Small comfort, however, when the damage to Brad had already been done.

That he even landed *Rumor of War* was actually something of a lucky mistake. Jeri had a few connections in television, one of which was David Manson, a young TV producer who had just been hired by Chuck Fries and Dick Berg, two big executive producers who were working on the TV-movie version of Phil Caputo's novel. Jeri knew Chuck, and although she shared David Eidenberg's less than complimentary views, she liked David Manson. When she heard he was looking for an actor to star in the film, she suggested Brad. To her surprise, David loved the idea, as did Chuck and Dick. None of them had heard the gossip about Brad. In their eyes, he was still a hot young star, someone who could easily headline a TV movie.

That was another fact of Hollywood, that film and television are separate camps and never the twain—or the gossip—shall meet. It was something I would learn firsthand when I made my transition from agenting into casting, casting TV movies and series primarily because of Marsha's contacts at NBC, and discovered movies were no longer considered my province. Actors face a similar Berlin Wall when they attempt to jump from one medium to the other, seen as either slumming or reaching above their station. However, that is less true today, when stars increasingly use TV as both a launching pad and rest stop in their film careers. Still, witness the breast-beating that attended David Caruso's decision to quit ABC's *N.Y.P.D. Blue* for films, and the speed with which Michael J. Fox returned to television after less than spectacular film careers. In Hollywood, those kinds of shifts are akin to changing your citizenship, not something that is done easily or lightly.

So when Brad got the offer to do *Rumor of War*, Clifford voiced some hesitation. "It will look as if you are taking a step backward," he told Brad. But Brad didn't care. He was desperate for a job—David and Jeri knew that better than Clifford did, a continent away in New York—and when the offer came with an astonishing $300,000 fee attached, there was no question in any of our minds that Brad was taking it. We told ourselves that *Rumor* was a prestige project, an adaptation of an acclaimed book and one of the first TV movies addressing the Vietnam War.

And it was an ambitious undertaking, nearly three months of filming on location that winter, two weeks at Camp Pendleton outside San Diego and the rest of it in Mexico, in Villahermosa and Puerto Vallarta. Chuck and Dick had hired two dozen Marines out of Pendleton—kids eighteen and nineteen years old—to play the extras. Although Brad had missed the war thanks to acting school and a high lottery number, he approached the role as he had with *Midnight Express,* as a hard-bitten coming-of-age story. As Caputo put it, "I went to Vietnam a boy and came back a man."

With filming scheduled to begin on December 17, 1979, Brad was gone most of that winter, and my life settled back into a calmer routine. The first order of business was finding a new house. I was sick of living out in Encino, where we'd moved after North Hollywood, and now that money was coming in again, I wanted a larger, more expensive house in Studio City. The one I found, three bedrooms and a pool on Teesdale, just north of Ventura Boulevard, ran $1,000 a month. I didn't blink, just had Zane write out the check and called the movers.

It was the first house I felt was actually a home. It was also convenient to Sunset Plaza over in West Hollywood, where Marsha and I had found office space. February was our target date for the debut of Marsha Kleinman & Associates. By the time I gave Bob Gersh my notice in December, he wasn't exactly crushed, not after all my ill-concealed unhappiness at the agency.

While I was determined to change my life, Brad was simply repeating his. I knew that physically *Rumor of War* was a rough shoot, with days of filming outdoors with equipment on the base and in the Mexican jungle. But it quickly seemed to escalate into another *Small Circle* debacle. Brad was doing his best to outdo the Marines, who saw *Rumor of War* like some overdue spring break, a chance to play war, drink, and chase women. "As long as I'm supposed to be a Marine, I'll do what they do," he said. In fact, Brad began drinking so heavily that one of the other actors on the film tried to intervene with some advice from Alcoholics Anonymous. Brad thought it was bullshit. And by January, I got the call from David Eidenberg saying that Brad had run into real trouble.

Beyond his carousing, Brad had unwittingly stumbled into a minefield of production politics that involved last-minute script revisions. It had been years since Brad had worked on TV, and he was growing increasingly irate with the rushed shooting schedule and what he saw as David Manson's last-minute meddling. Many days, Brad simply refused to film the revised script. By the time David Eidenberg determined that he needed to fly down—"Just what I need, to baby-sit in that hellhole"—Brad and David Manson were no longer speaking.

But David Eidenberg correctly saw another *Small Circle* in the making. He spent three days in Villahermosa trying to patch things up, to at least get Manson and Brad talking again. "I think I've made some headway," he said to me over the phone. "We even had a victory dinner tonight where everyone got high to celebrate."

But it wasn't the end of it. That night, David Eidenberg was awakened by Brad in one of his usual fits, banging on his door at three in the morning. There was a virtual riot in one of the bars, "a real donnybrook," as David put it, between the Marines and some of the local men. Latin machismo had finally had it with Marine machismo. None of it was Brad's fault, but it was the last straw in a fraught situation. Chuck Fries had to fly down and made the decision to move the whole company to Baja. Amazingly enough, they finished shooting only a few days behind schedule.

And compared to *Small Circle,* it all seemed pretty tame. Clifford, however, had a vastly different impression. He felt that *Rumor* did more to kill Brad in Hollywood than any other single event. Despite the classy nature of the project—when it aired that September, Brad made the cover of *TV Guide*—Clifford saw it as a public admission that Brad wasn't getting the right kind of movie offers. Or that STE wasn't able to get him the right kind of movies. In fact, the very next job Brad took—a quick role in a film adaptation of James Thurber's short story "The Greatest Man in the World"—was for PBS-TV. "The perception is that Brad has taken a step to the side," Clifford explained to me during one long phone call. "Once it's done, it's hard to get the momentum back." Clifford also felt that Brad's culpability aside, he had become the patsy on *Rumor of War* as on *Small Circle*. "He broke the one cardinal rule in Hollywood: he cost the production money."

And Clifford was right. A year later, Chuck filed suit against Brad for almost $250,000 in cost overruns. Brad was owed an extra payment after the movie had aired theatrically in South America, but in typical Hollywood fashion, Chuck sued Brad instead. Eventually, some settlement was made, but the damage had been done. "There isn't an agent alive who is going to be able to help you out of the hole you're digging for yourself," Clifford told Brad. "I feel less like an agent than an accomplice."

"Accomplice?" said Brad. "That suggests a crime, doesn't it?"

"Yes," said Clifford. "Because it's criminal what you're doing to yourself."

If Brad's name had lost almost all its value in Hollywood, David Puttnam hadn't heard about it. That spring, he called Brad personally to ask him to play a cameo in a new film, *Chariots of Fire*, a low-budget movie about the 1924 Paris Olympics. Although the film was budgeted at a mere $6 million, David was having trouble raising the money. It was directed by a first-timer, Hugh Hudson, another refugee from British advertising circles, and the cast was exclusively English stage actors. David needed "two American names" to secure financing, and he wanted Brad to play Jackson Scholz, one of the American track stars. It wasn't a big part, it wasn't even an interesting part, and David could only afford to pay $15,000 for what would be a month's work. He also told Brad of the need to train for the role because the budget didn't allow for any stunt doubles. "It's a favor," he said. "I did you one on *Midnight Express,* now I need you to do this for me."

David Eidenberg and Jeri Scott were dead set against it. Even if Brad was desperate for work, a low-budget, low-profile foreign film was the last thing he needed. Especially when there was no money in it. "This isn't about favors," David said to Brad, "it's about your career." But Brad didn't hesitate. He felt he owed David Puttnam, and a job, any job, was better than sitting around watching your career grow totally cold. And it was a small thrill watching the financing and a U.S. distribution deal fall into place once Brad had signed on.

Nobody, including David Puttnam, had any idea that *Chariots of Fire* would do what it did. Not only was the film a huge hit, the dark-horse Best Picture in 1981, but it became a moral flash point in the film industry. With its evocative Vangelis score and the haunting image of the English track team running through the gray English surf—not to mention its themes of self-sacrifice and duty—*Chariots of Fire* arrived in Hollywood like a gauntlet thrown down. None of the excitement rubbed off on Brad; nobody seemed to notice that he was even in the film, his cameo was so insignificant. But it did effectively launch Puttnam in all his self-righteous glory in Hollywood, eventually paving the way for his much heralded, if short-lived, appointment as savior of Columbia Pictures.

Brad was to spend all of June 1980 filming in London and Liverpool. That spring, he spent two months preparing, training, and working out with a coach. He spent hours running around the track at Harvard-Westlake, a prep school on Coldwater, a few blocks from our house. For two months, Brad trained and he stayed sober. I was stunned at the change in him, but I never thought that the nightmare of Brad's using drugs was over. For one thing, *Small Circle* came out in April, a very public reminder of how bad Brad could get.

And in fact his sobriety was temporary. When Brad flew to London in June, he quickly resumed his old ways, drinking and using and generally tearing up the town. His partner in crime this time out was Dennis Christopher, the star of *Breaking Away*, whom Puttnam had cast as the other American track star, Charles Paddock. Eventually, I got the inevitable phone call from David Eidenberg: Brad had gotten so out of control that Puttnam had resorted to separating him from Dennis by putting them in different hotels. I hung up the phone feeling like a dead weight had settled back on me. I simply dreaded Brad's return.

At the same time Brad's career was in a free fall during those two years following *Midnight Express,* our marriage went through some of its darkest hours for the simple reason that his drug and alcohol abuse were at their height. Our house was a battleground. Years later, friends would confess in that apologetic way people have that they couldn't imagine how I put up with the abuse. I had no answer. My memory of those months, those years, is lost in a haze of arguments, slammed doors and broken windows, and inevitably the sound of Brad's Jeep pulling out of the driveway, leaving me alone in the angry silence.

Since I was never present, I could only imagine how effortlessly Brad had joined the omnipresent round of Hollywood partying— the endless dinners out for sushi with friends such as Norbert or John Hurt or those hangers-on whom every celebrity attracts, then Brad announcing, like a battle cry, "Let's go," and everyone piling into the Jeep or a limo and Brad ordering the drugs by phone, to be bought only in someone's house, never in a parking lot like Belushi, and on into the night, the parties, the friends, or simply strangers who just came up to you asking, "Aren't you Brad Davis?" In this seductive life nothing seemed to mean anything except your celebrity, the value of your face. You are traveling so light, just your face, you don't even carry money, because you are a star and things are handed to you, arms reach across your shoulders, people you don't even know, faces you don't recognize but that recognize you. And always there is another party, at the Château Marmont or the Holiday Inn or another and another and another. What there is not is any reason to stop, not a reason in the world to come home to your wife, who grows angrier and angrier as she realizes that stardom is not a shared activity, that the light only reaches so far.

Perhaps I stayed to get even. Several times during those months I came close to leaving. Certainly, there was never any question of Brad leaving. He might be gone for hours, days even, but I knew in Brad's cockeyed mind that I was his home. Looking back, I am less amazed at his actions than my own—my refusal to accept what they told me at St. John's, my almost obsessional focus on my job, my decision to have an abortion that first winter when I accidently became pregnant. My life was as much of a nightmare as Brad's and I didn't even know it.

Not that I knew that much about Brad's life. Or perhaps, I should say, I *chose* to have little knowledge of his life. I say that because

Brad never lied to me. His deceit was always by omission. If I didn't ask, he didn't tell. I always asked myself, "Do I really want to know who his dealers are? Do I really want to know how much coke he is doing? And with whom?" My answer was always no. My ignorance was my protection, I told myself, in the event of some legal problems, in the event that Brad should ever be arrested. It was my protection, period.

During those years, but especially in the months following *Rumor of War* when it seemed as if Brad would never get another job and the whole promise of *Midnight Express* seemed like one cosmic joke, Brad spent more and more time with people like Norbert, who'd stayed friends with Brad since they'd worked together on *Midnight Express,* and in the company of another little group made up of Monty Christianson, a writer Brad had met at a party, Dee Archer, an aspiring singer à la Janis Joplin, and Brad Wilson, a bartender and would-be actor. These people knew more than I could ever know, the intricacies of Brad's life, and they saw how low he could go.

Brad Wilson had been our neighbor when we lived on Biloxi in North Hollywood, or as he and Brad called it, Rancho Biloxi Estates. They had met one night at three-thirty in the morning when Brad literally leapt the hedge separating the two houses, holding out his bloody palm and telling a rather startled Wilson, "My fucking dog bit my hand." It was the spring after Brad had filmed *Midnight Express,* and Wilson, a bartender at the Victoria Station at Universal Studios, had no idea who the guy demanding bandages and peroxide was. Wilson let him in, and Brad stormed into the bedroom, threw open the closet door, grabbed Wilson's only good shirt, wrapped it around his bleeding hand, and asked, "Do you have vodka or pain pills?" When Wilson happened to have both, the friendship was cemented.

It was one of the classic Hollywood pairings, the wanna-be and the celebrity of the moment. Wilson ran with a crowd of stuntmen, crew guys, and some aspiring artists such as Dee and Monty. They all hung out at the old River Botton Inn on Barham Boulevard across from the Warner lot in Burbank. It was a dark industry hangout for "below the line" people, those nonstar workers who live on union salaries. In the Hollywood caste system, below-the-line is one step above civilians. Wilson and his gang met at the bar once a month to drink their paychecks. They called themselves the Once a Month for Lunch Bunch, and Brad was their celebrity. "I was proud to be seen with him," as Wilson put it. "I was proud to be seen as Brad Davis's friend."

And they were an odd bunch, Brad and his court—he was known as Bobo to them—the lanky, courtly Monty, "the only guy who looked shitty in a tuxedo" as Wilson loved to put it, and Dee, the earth mother with the flowing hair and raspy Janis Joplin voice. Like Wilson, they all aspired to more than they had. Dee dreamed of a recording contract and Monty was that only-in-Hollywood phenomenon, a writer who lived comfortably penning unproduced screenplays. They also shared another trait: they were all alcoholics who would, except for Monty, wind up in AA. Wilson would show up alone at our house with a couple of six-packs of Löwenbräu and a fifth of Jameson Irish whiskey, ostensibly to watch Brad mow the lawn, and in less than two hours it would be gone.

But if drinking formed their initial bond, their relationship quickly escalated into a much tighter and more complex one that centered on Brad's daily use of cocaine. Or rather, his willingness to drop thousands of dollars on cocaine that they all used. Zane estimated that from *Midnight Express* until he got sober in 1980, Brad spent nearly half a million dollars, before taxes, on cocaine. Almost his entire fees from *Small Circle* and *Rumor of War* went up his nose. And Wilson's nose. He had been using cocaine since 1970. He even dealt on occasion to make ends meet. During those years, he saw Brad's drug use as much as anyone, and he knew his suppliers: Wilson himself, out-and-out dealers such as Lizzy Morgan (not her real name), who lived in Studio City, and people holding legitimate jobs in the film business but who moonlighted in the industry's lucrative drug trade. Wilson saw how Brad would order seven and eight grams at a time and knew that Brad could go through a gram in less than fifteen minutes. Wilson would eventually see Brad so strung out that he would fish a vial of cocaine, dripping wet, out of a urinal and pack it into his nose.

Wilson knew about Brad's drug-induced behavior, his food

binges, his scenes in restaurants, his total lack of decorum. Wilson knew, for instance, how after snorting cocaine Brad would blow his nose with just his fingers and let the snot congeal on the window of his Jeep. He knew how Brad would roll into restaurants, nice places such as the Italian restaurant in Toluca Lake, dressed "like he hadn't bathed in a week," with three or four days' growth of beard and in some old T-shirt and jeans. He saw him order everything on the menu—iced platters of oysters, steaks, bottles of wine, and send it all back. He saw how Brad literally picked the fish off Wilson's plate one night, announced that "this is unacceptable," and handed it to the waiter.

But Brad was a star and he got away with it, got away with ordering bowls of chocolate mousse and quadruple snifters of Rémy and launching into his favorite postprandial ritual, rinsing his mouth with water and then spitting it right into his plate—that got everyone's attention—then taking a spoonful of mousse and then a slug of Rémy and, with chocolate rolling down his chin, a puff of the French cigarettes he was smoking at the time, Balkan Sobranies, and then just breathing it all in, oh, fuck yes. "Oh, fuck, is right," Wilson thought, going along with it because he just wanted to get Brad out of there because the captain was already hovering by their table, gold epaulets glinting on his jacket, as Wilson said, "It's okay. It's Brad Davis, the actor."

That was the kind of license that Brad had in those days. Wilson saw it, as he saw the quick-fix sex Brad needed once he was high, the casual affairs. He knew, for instance, that Brad was having an affair with Dee, that she had gone to be with Brad in Mexico when he was filming *Rumor of War*. He knew that Brad had also been spending time with Bianca Jagger shortly after the release of *Midnight Express*. Wilson accompanied Brad to most of those parties, parties where they didn't even know the host and regular tight little gatherings such as the ones agent Joel Dean threw at his house, the "sanctuary of debauchery" as Wilson called it. Wilson was also with Brad at Rod Stewart's house the night Brad was arrested after fighting with Bianca—a stupid, petty, but telling argument over her refusal to return his *Midnight Express* jacket—

the night that Brad wound up playing matador with the cars along Benedict Canyon until the cops picked him up.

So it was also Wilson who sat with Brad in the backs of cop cars, in jail cells, waiting for Zane or David to bail them out after being thrown out of parties or restaurants or after having been picked up for driving drunk. To this day, I'm amazed that Brad never lost his license. Many nights Wilson and Brad would greet the sunrise parked somewhere in his Jeep, sharing a bottle of vodka or ouzo and talking in that drunken intimate way about where the fuck their lives were going. "And somehow you just knew," Wilson said to himself, "this was a guy who wasn't going to live long."

It wasn't much different from what Norbert saw in Brad's life at the time. Except maybe the drugs were a little rougher. Although Norbert prided himself on being a binger rather than a daily user like Brad, he was also a heroin user and their drug-taking centered on Lizzy Morgan's house in Studio City.

Lizzy was one of Brad's big coke suppliers, but was unusual by the normal standards for "not being strung out, but very languid, very fuckable looking," as Norbert put it. She lived in this unremarkable tract house in Studio City, where she kept a nasty little pit bull who eyed the goings-on from the corner of the living room. She also had a heart condition, and one night, like some hilarious, horrific scene out of Quentin Tarantino's *Pulp Fiction*, she collapsed and Brad had to jam her with a hypodermic full of adrenaline to keep from her dying right there on her own floor.

It was at Lizzy's that Norbert first freebased with Brad, compliments of John Holmes, the porn star who later died of AIDS, who was one of Lizzy's main suppliers. He arrived on the doorstep one night, armed with his briefcase. It was the only time Norbert and Brad met John, and his presence struck Norbert like "Hades, just a whiff of cold air." He set up shop in the kitchen, like a caterer, cooking up the freebase, which they all smoked.

In Norbert's eyes, Brad was strictly a coke and alcohol abuser. There was always a lot of speculation, including my own, about whether Brad ever used a needle. I knew he didn't like heroin, and I had doubts about whether he actually injected himself with cocaine, or a speedball, the cocktail that killed John Belushi. If any of his friends had seen Brad with a needle, it would have been Norbert, and he maintained that he never did. "He told me he'd used needles," Norbert remembered years later. "In New York with someone, but I never saw it. And maybe he had. That was always a big thing with Brad, secrets and compartments to his life."

Although I was ignorant of that part of Brad's world, I had my own encounters with his drug-taking, three incidents that pushed me, finally, toward the realization that Brad needed professional help—and that I needed it as well.

Shortly after Brad finished *Rumor of War*, he hit his lowest ebb. Clifford had been right, that movie did Brad in. It was obvious now, even to Brad, it would take a miracle for him to get another film role. His reputation was in tatters. The drinking and using that had begun as a celebration of his stardom with *Midnight Express* had become his escape from the reality of his stalled career, the endless days when Brad woke up in a tangle of sheets, hungover in an empty house, the silent phone a constant reproach to the night before and all the nights before that.

It was a marked contrast to a year earlier, the days filled with meetings, scripts to be read, his daily trek to Vince's, and then dinners, endless dinners. And the homecomings from shoots, like Napoleon back from the wars, the noisy arrival of the limo, piles of luggage that seemed to burst once in the house, clothes thrown everywhere, the bedroom, the living room, piles on the floor; just to get to the kitchen required navigation, and the phone constantly rang with friends calling to set up lunches, dinners, meetings, and the boom box blaring and Brad yelling from another room, always needing, wanting something. It was like being at Cannes so long ago; it all came at you because they wanted you. Maybe that's why Brad was willing to have a weekend away that winter after he was back from Mexico. Because the Hollywood river had stopped flowing toward him.

We had booked a room at a hotel in Ojai, a small town about an hour north of Los Angeles that we had visited a few years earlier on a day trip with Rue and her son, Mark. Brad had liked it. Its rural, farming nature reminded him of Florida. I thought a return visit might give him, us, a break.

But within minutes of our arrival, Brad began drinking. Stolichnaya and Rémy Martin. He'd brought a bottle of each with him. And he sat in that room and drank until he was blind drunk. Brad never passed out, his stamina was amazing, he only blacked out— yelling, screaming, completely out of control, and he would remember none of it. As if it had never happened.

I had learned to live with it, but the manager of the Ojai Motel had not. After several calls to the room and a polite tap at the door, they gave up and called the police, who took Brad away, dragging him screaming down the hall. "Get me out of this, Susan. Get me out. Call Zane and get me out."

I just wanted him to shut up, to please just shut up so this nightmare could end. But he didn't. He fought with the police. So they beat him, right in front of me; they hit him until his face was bloody and he stopped screaming and they led him away in handcuffs.

I didn't call Zane. I didn't call anyone. I let Brad spend the night in jail. It was the first time I saw him in custody. And while I felt trapped at the hotel, I also knew Brad was trapped. There was nothing he could do. So I let him sit it out until he was sober. And he wasn't sober at seven the next morning when I drove to the station. Brad was furious, his eyes were swollen and his face was cut. He wanted me to get him out. But I didn't take him until after ten, when he finally sobered up.

Standing there, in the sheriff's office, watching them uncuff Brad, it suddenly seemed so unbelievable to me, almost as unbelievable as it had been sitting next to him at Cannes, at the screening of *Midnight Express*. And just as then, I had to go back to work as if nothing had ever happened.

The second incident occurred shortly after, on a flight home from New York, an Easter trip we had taken to see my family and some of our old friends. Brad had been drinking on the flight home, first the airline's liquor and then his own, for the whole six hours, so by the time we landed he was completely drunk, berating the first-class stewardess about the flight, his luggage, their refusal to serve him more booze. He had drawn some line in the sand and he refused to get off the plane. Again, I felt trapped, publically humiliated by this drunk. And again, the police came and literally dragged Brad off the plane and through LAX, where people parted like waves, people who I could tell recognized Brad.

We had a limo waiting and the cops just shoved Brad into it and told the driver to keep the doors locked. It was like looking at an animal behind glass, Brad screaming and pounding on the window. The driver didn't want to take us, but I insisted it was all right as I slipped in the front seat.

But it clearly wasn't all right, with Brad screaming the whole way, demanding to be let out. Before we even got halfway up Sepulveda, I told the guy to pull over. "He wants out, we're going to put him out."

The driver didn't want to do it. "We just can't leave him here," he said. But as in Ojai, I'd had it. Brad wanted out, so let him. He had a million friends. Help was as far away as a pay phone. It just wasn't going to come from me. I didn't care what happened, I just wanted him out of the car, out of my life. I just wanted away from Brad.

So we stopped. The guy popped the locks, Brad sprang out, and we pulled away. It was that simple. We pulled away. In the side mirror, I watched Brad growing smaller and smaller until I couldn't see him anymore.

But as bad as those two incidents were, they didn't compare to the night I woke up to the sound of a gun being fired somewhere in the house, that sickening pop and then the sound of glass shattering. We were still living in Encino, before he'd left for *Rumor of War*, a night that had typically ended with Brad coming home at four-thirty in the morning after a three-day cocaine binge. Brad Wilson had actually driven him, he was in such bad shape, and then Wilson had passed out in the spare room while Brad, in a coked-up rage, had gone into the den and taken the pistol he kept in the house, an old .22 of his dad's, and begun shooting out the pictures of himself taken from *Midnight Express*. We had three stills from the film framed. He lay on the daybed and shot himself, in the face, three times.

It was the beginning of Brad's anger toward the movie he now saw as a cheat. I was furious and terrified that Brad was actually going to kill himself or me. I blamed the only person I could at that minute, Wilson. I marched into the guest room and just started screaming. "Your friend is in the other room and he's trying to kill himself," I said. "Your goddamned friend is trying to kill himself."

I don't really know what I expected Wilson to do, I just wanted to stop it. We ran back to the den where Brad was lying on the bed with the gun in his mouth. "Will this kill me?" he said, removing the barrel and laughing.

"Yeah, it'll kill you," said Wilson calmly. "Is that what you want to do?"

I got hysterical. All I remember is Wilson shoving me out the door, telling me to get dressed and leave, get in the car and leave, and that he would handle it. But I was really panicked. I hated Wilson right then, so I called David Eidenberg, who showed up looking disheveled and as scared as I felt. Meanwhile, Wilson somehow got the gun away from Brad and threw the clip out the window. I don't remember what happened to the gun, but I know that it left the house and nothing like that ever happened again.

Those three incidents finally got me to do what I had been resisting for so long: get some help. To quit thinking, to quit actually saying to Marsha and my friends, "Well, every day he tells me he's not going to drink anymore. And this time, I think he actually means it."

I had been working with a therapist, Howard Parad, a kindly older man whom I started seeing after Brad got back from shooting *Small Circle*. While I never found Howard particularly crucial to my own therapy—not like Claude, a psychiatrist whom I had worked with in New York after my mother died—he was the first person I talked to about Brad. He was the one who told me, "You're living with and married to an alcoholic." Howard was the one who pointed out the patterns, the codependent patterns Brad and I had, his denial and my denial. He was the one who pointed out that Brad's drinking and my weight problems were not unrelated. It was Howard who recommended to me that I investigate

Overeaters Anonymous, or OA as it is known. It was Howard who finally said, I had to make my own changes.

I hadn't listened at the time, but now I realized that Howard and that administrator at St. John's had been right. That *I* had work to do. As Brad was bottoming out with his drinking, I had been bottoming out with my weight. And while I wasn't ready to hear about OA—I was still a few years away from really confronting my own demons—I did feel braver about trying to deal with Brad's. I decided to take the plunge and investigate Al-Anon. So that spring, just about year after Brad's visit to St. John's, I went to my first meeting, a tough group, way over in Hollywood in a broken-down area near Las Palmas.

It was difficult at first, but the more I went and the more I talked to people, the more I realized that I did need to be there. That it was a relief, finally, to be able to talk about all the lies that I had told people at work, told my friends, told myself. There were many women there whose husbands and boyfriends were practicing alcoholics, and like me, they had had to learn how to live with and handle a practicing alcoholic. And I began to learn as well. Simple but obvious things, such as simply getting out of the car if he was driving drunk, or getting him out of the car and leaving him. I learned to leave the house if he started to throw things, that he would eventually stop if he didn't have me to rail against. I learned some practical lessons. It wasn't about psychology then. It was about survival. You want to kill yourself? Okay, but you're not going to kill me.

And so I made changes. When he started to go crazy, I would leave—the house, a restaurant. I would just get up and leave. If he would get crazy in the car, I would leave him. I left Brad many times, all over Los Angeles. I left him one night after we'd gone to dinner with Marcia Inch, my old high school friend, and her husband, Tony. They were in town and we'd gone out to Carlos N' Charlie's on Sunset where Brad liked to go, and he'd gotten drunk and I said, "We're leaving."

Marcia was stunned: "You just can't leave him." Tony wanted to stay with Brad: "You go on ahead and I'll stay with him." But I was firm: "No, it's what we have to do."

So we left. It was the beginning of my not being embarrassed, of being able to say to people, "This is what it has been like." To begin to reach out to friends for help: Marsha Kleinman at work, and Kathleen Letterie, our old friend from New York who was now living in L.A. and working as a casting associate with us. People I could call and say, "It's starting again. Can I come over or can you meet me for coffee?"

It didn't happen right away. I was a tough case. I had what-ifs for everything. But the women at Al-Anon nailed me. They'd heard it all before, and in this particular group, they really laughed at me. I had all these reasons why Brad was different, that he needed to be protected, that his drinking needed to stay a secret. I wasn't like them, living with a truck driver or a waiter or whomever they were living with. My life, Brad's life, depended on maintaining this image, this star image.

But they nailed me. "You can take your fucking high-minded reasons to the grave, girl, because that is where you are going to be." That's how they talked to me. They didn't have money and they were disdainful of me. In their eyes, I was this rich, white Jewish girl who had plenty of options, options that they didn't have. "God, you have a career, you have your own money," they said to me. "You could be self-supporting. You are putting up with this because you are choosing to put up with it."

And that got to me. For so long, I had thought there was nothing I could do away from Brad, away from Zane and our checking accounts. And some of my hesitation was practical. Marsha and I had done okay at first, but we weren't constantly busy, and the money wasn't coming in right away. But as the work began to flow, and I began to realize that even my small salary was more than a lot of those women had, I saw that I could pick up and go.

So I began to actively think about leaving. I began to think about living away from Brad. I didn't know for how long or really even where. But I did go so far as to get some brochures from the Château Marmont, about keeping an apartment there, a toehold really, because it was so close to work.

I never really felt that Brad got sober because of me, because of my growing independence. I think it was a combination of things:

my changes, Zane, David, everyone telling him the obvious, that he was about to lose everything. And he was. Certainly, he had the arrogance to say, "Fuck it, someone will hire me. I'm still a star." It's what he'd been saying for more than a year. So I don't know, the way no one ever really knows, why someone finally makes a change, why they begin, at last, to strike out for shore.

But it was on November 28, 1980, after Thanksgiving, in our house on Teesdale, in the den with the horrible rust-colored shag rug, that Brad told me he'd been to his first AA meeting. I'll never forget that moment.

He had disappeared until about ten, and he came in and stood there leaning against the fireplace proud as a peacock. "I went to an AA meeting," he said. And I hadn't seen his face like that in a long time. And he wasn't drunk. That was another thing. It was ten at night and he wasn't drunk.

CHAPTER

8

Now that Brad was sober, or rather trying to become sober, because he did slip that first year, our lives began to change. Some of it was virtually overnight. The partying, the out-all-night binges, the where-is-he-and-whom-is-he-with fears I had at three in the morning—all that ended with Brad's first visit to AA that November.

For the next several weeks, our house was more like an infirmary than a home. Brad spent most of those days holed up, like a wounded animal, in our darkened bedroom. When he wasn't at home, he was at AA meetings, sometimes as many as three a day. It felt odd to come home at the end of the day and know exactly where Brad was. For years I had felt so separate, so cut off from his life. Now I felt as if I had a sick child, he was so needy, so there.

But that was only part of the transformation. And in many respects, the easiest. The day-to-day nightmare had ended—for the first time in more than two years, I was able to sleep through the night—but our real problems remained unresolved. For Brad this meant confronting, for the first time in his life, his self-destructive behavior and the reasons behind it, namely the abuses of his childhood. For me, it meant walking a ridiculously complex line in my own mind, balancing the relief I felt with the anger that I also had. Anger at Brad for what he had put us through, the drinking, the using, the lying, the affairs. And anger at myself for putting up with it, for lying to myself as much as Brad had, for eating my way to solace. I honestly didn't know whether I could forgive either of us. On those nights that I went with Brad to his AA meetings, we could hardly look at each other. Sitting there amid all that confessing, all that "I'm so sorry, I could die" testimony, I could hardly listen to it, because my own voice, my inner voice, was raging so.

But my anger notwithstanding, I knew those days were difficult for Brad. At that first AA meeting, the Monday night after Thanksgiving down at the Big Book Study in Hollywood, he had been so shaky as he walked in with his sponsor, Molly, a local gallery owner he'd met through friends. It was that moment of utter horror that every substance abuser knows, the first steps in the long march in the chilly gray dawn of sobriety where your comforts are so few and so paltry—sugar, coffee, and meetings and more meetings. Like living in an unheated room with no furniture. For Brad, there was the added terror of being recognized, that when he stood up and said the requisite words, "I'm Brad and I'm an alcoholic," he was finally conceding that Brad Davis, the actor, was a drunk.

He was thirty-one. And for the next nine months, Brad didn't .work. He couldn't get a job. He didn't want a job, he said. Certainly not a film job. Maybe some theater. In a little while. Instead, his life consisted of trying to stay sober, detoxing, and going to AA meetings and getting involved in that whole life. Writing inventories. Being sponsored. Talking to people. Making amends. It was twenty-four hours a day, and for those first few months, he couldn't see any life beyond going to AA meetings seven days a week. He was already going three times a day. He'd get up around noon and head out to the meeting closest to our house, over on Radford across from the CBS lot in Studio City. He'd meet people afterward for coffee and then go to another meeting down in Beverly Hills on Rodeo Drive. Or the one in Hollywood. His entire day was spent in AA.

That was the framework, but in many ways Brad's life was just as difficult as when he was drinking. Only now he was cognizant of it—his tattered career, the financial hole we had dug, the DMZ state of our marriage. That's what happens when you get conscious: you start to realize what you've done and you just want to crawl into a hole. That's what Brad did. When he wasn't at AA meetings, he holed up at home.

Some of it reflected that he simply had a lot of time on his hands now. He wasn't out running around and he didn't have a job. But a lot of his reticence was because he was sick. Literally. After that first AA meeting, I told Brad he should go back to a hospital to detox. Zane and I both felt he needed medical supervision, since his addiction was far more pronounced than it had been when he had gone to St. John's the year before. I was frightened of caring for Brad in that state. What if something happened, what if something went wrong? "Just go back for a week," I pleaded with him. "Just go where there are people who know what to do."

But he refused. "I'm not going to a hospital where everyone will know my business," he said, as if everyone didn't already know.

So he treated himself. For the three weeks after that first meeting, almost until Christmas, Brad spent hours at home, in bed with the shades drawn. He had always loved the dark. He'd painted out the windows on our Jane Street apartment to keep out the light. Now, day after day, he lay in our darkened bedroom, sleeping or staring at the ceiling, with only a fan flicking the air from the corner to break the silence. Many times I would come home from work and find him lying there in a fetal position, like a baby, damp, with his T-shirt sticking to his back from sweat. Except for the meetings that he dragged himself to, he was too sick to go out, and he didn't want to see people. For the first time in our lives, Brad didn't answer the phone, just let the machine pick up, the impatience of his voice in the message a painful contrast to the still figure in bed.

And it was a bad withdrawal. Not with hallucinations or the shakes per se, but a lot of physical pain, cold sweats and pains, he said, pains in his scars. Brad had a lot of scars, most of them from accidents when he'd been drunk. Now, he would call me into the room and point to them—the one over his eye he got that first summer in L.A., the one down the back of his leg from falling over the dolly on *Small Circle,* and others, the long gash on his arm when he'd put his fist through a window during one of our fights, the other smaller nicks up and down his forearms, and the pits on his face from a shingles attack a year or so ago—he'd point to them and tell me that they all felt fresh, like fresh cuts all over his body, and that they were going to bleed. "Watch," he would say, pointing to one of the raised, white lines, "it's going to bleed."

I knew this was part of his physical withdrawal, but I also knew that it was the beginning of the emotional pain he was feeling now that he was sober. Pain about the past, his past, as a sexually abused child in Florida, his early days in New York when he hustled to make ends meet, but also our past, when we began living together in New York, when I saw—but refused to really see it—the nightmare that was coming, foreshadowed by those isolated, scary incidents. That was pain that his scars were living proof of. Because if there were any secrets that Brad and I kept, one of the biggest was that he mutilated himself. Again and again. With razors.

Now, sitting in our darkened bedroom, running my hand up and down his scarred arm, just to calm him, the way he asked me to, I could see for the first time what should have been obvious in New York on all those nights when Brad had wrestled with what he called "his demons." The nights he drank himself into a blackout and then lashed out. The night he slashed my mother's paintings with a kitchen knife. The night he had painted a floor-to-ceiling mural in our Jane Street apartment, a self-portrait, a grotesque figure, done in thick green and blue oil paint that you could never wash off. And the windows, painted out in red, so the whole room glowed with an evil, hot hue. When we moved, we left the building secretly in the middle of the night because of the damage he'd done.

And there were worse nights, the ones when Brad started cutting himself. It started with his hair. If he was having a bad day or night or he couldn't get work, he would cut off his hair. Just grab a pair of scissors and, in a fury, hack off his hair, and it would seem to calm him. But then he began to cut at his skin. I'll never forget the first night. During the run of *Crystal and Fox,* when Brad started drinking more than he ever had, in the middle of the night I woke up to find him in the bathroom, drunk, slashing at his forearm with a razor blade, the white of the sink, the white of his arm, bright with blood.

Now I know that is a classic sign of an incest survivor, self-mutilation, inflicting pain on yourself just to feel something, anything, because you are so dead inside. And while Brad cut himself, he talked in a stream of consciousness about mothers and children and mothers crawling over their children and taking advantage, sexually, of their children. But I didn't really see it. Not then. I just knew that he never cut very deep, just surface scars, and he never touched me or cut his face, and that in the morning, when he awoke with his arm bandaged, the blood dried on the gauze where it had soaked through, we never spoke about it. But there were the scars, like notches on a tree, a record of all the secrets we kept.

How can you look at your husband slashing himself and think it's okay? Or that it's a phase? And I sat there in our darkened bedroom with Brad finally asleep, running my hand over the tiny raised lines on his arm, and I wept for what he had done.

For those first nine months of his sobriety, that was the tenor of our life. We were like two walking nerve endings. It took a month or so, but gradually things began to improve. Brad stopped being sick and, typically, threw himself into AA. Now he spent hours on the phone again, talking to other AA members, as well as old friends, Norbert, Monty, Kathleen, and Brad Wilson, bullying them into joining AA. It was Brad's usual myopia. Now that he no longer lived for drugs and alcohol, but for meetings, Häagen-Dazs ice cream, coffee, and hours in the sauna in our house, that had to be everyone else's agenda as well.

But Brad was the first of his group to get sober. Or as he put it in AA parlance, the first "to get sobriety." Belushi's death, the de facto death knell for overt drug use in Hollywood, was still a year away. In that regard, Brad's sobriety was slightly ahead of the curve. It would be months before the rest of his friends joined him on the wagon. Meanwhile, Brad was making new, sober friends at AA, such as Eddie Bondy, an agent at William Morris who would soon represent Brad, and Stan Jones, a screenwriter who would become his AA sponsor and one of his closest friends during those months.

Stan was a Yale grad, a writer who had studied with Robert Penn Warren and who later attended UCLA film school with The Doors' Jim Morrison. He was five years older than Brad, but short like him, and something of a hell-raiser even when sober. He had a few years on Brad in AA—he'd joined in 1977—but after they met at the Book Study meeting that fall, they became close, almost like brothers.

With Stan, Brad found the next in the series of tight, male friendships that colored his life. He also began to revert to many of his old ways. That winter they spent hours down at the Old World on Sunset, a restaurant they liked to hit after meetings where they smoked, drank coffee, and just hung out. Or Spago. They loved to go to Wolfgang Puck's Hollywood eatery after their meeting at the Book Study and gorge on pizza among Hollywood's beautiful people. It was with Stan that Brad also resumed his penchant for making scenes in public, although now this was less about him losing his temper than simply embarrassing others. Like the fights he staged in grocery stores, petty domestic arguments amid the vegetable bins as if he and Stan were lovers. Or that evening at Spago when Brad burst into song, a rendition of "People" that had Stan under the table. "Shut the fuck up," he hissed at Brad, who had a clear view of Barbra Streisand at a nearby table.

It was inevitable that they would begin to collaborate on projects, two scripts that Stan wrote with Brad in mind, *Devil in a Blue Dress* and *September Song*. Neither script went anywhere, although producer Steven Reuther, now partnered with Michael Douglas, bought *Devil*. Stan was trying to access whatever clout Brad still wielded. Brad simply needed a way back to work. Hardly an atypical friendship in Hollywood. Their first meeting had been that kind of careerist cock-measuring, AA meeting or no AA meeting. Stan had recognized Brad and introduced himself. "Yeah, hey, what's going on with your career?" Brad had asked, to which Stan thought, laughing to himself, "Sure, pal, what's going on with *your* career?"

The short answer was not much. Now that he was no longer drinking, Brad had to face that his career was in real trouble. That winter, he had a number of long, painful calls with Zane—we were already in debt to him in excess of $10,000—as well as his agents, David Eidenberg and Clifford Stevens. It was clear something had to be done. We had virtually no money coming in other than what I was making, and our debts were out of sight. But Brad's prospects, even in television, were slim. Whenever his name came up, the response inevitably was "The network won't have him."

Brad had burned his bridges, that was obvious. Brad was no longer a star, but a working actor and a troubled one at that. "Putting Brad into a movie is not like putting, say, a Kevin Kline in a movie," Clifford explained to me. "He isn't a pearl beyond price, and there isn't a reason to hire him over somebody else." Not only was Brad damaged goods, but he was rapidly achieving the most dreaded status of all. He'd become passé. Clifford spelled it out: "People don't want to fall back on an actor who's been around the track a couple of times and hasn't quite run the race."

The only thing Brad had going for him was his looks. Now that he was no longer drinking and using, he looked better than he had in years. He was working out and eating healthier. He had gained weight and lost his boyish cuteness and become, in my eyes at least, an incredibly sexy man. The way Sharon Stone has aged, going from being just another cute blonde to becoming a truly striking woman. So when David got a call that May from an Alan Shallcross, a relatively unknown British producer who was looking for a sexy American to costar in a BBC film, *Mrs. Reinhardt*, it seemed like a gift from heaven.

Europe, I thought, thank God. None of us had really considered that market. Europe wasn't the hotbed of small independent films that it would become in the 1990s with such movies as *Four Weddings and a Funeral* and *Il Postino*. But Brad's name still had some coinage there because of *Midnight Express*. All of us breathed a sigh of relief except Brad, who was torn about the film.

A low-budget adaptation of the Edna O'Brien short story, *Mrs. Reinhardt* told a dark tale about an unhappily married English-woman who becomes sexually involved with an attractive but pathological American during a holiday in Brittany. Brad didn't think much of the part. "The guy's a psycho," he said, and he had no idea who Edna O'Brien was. Nor had he heard of Helen Mirren, the acclaimed English actress who was cast in the lead. Although Helen would eventually become well-known as the hard-boiled Detective Tennyson in PBS's popular series *Prime Suspect,* at the time she had only a few films to her credit. Even David's claim that, given her reputation for playing sexy roles, Helen was something of an English Jane Fonda failed to impress Brad.

Beyond what he saw as drawbacks to the offer, Brad was terrified about getting back in front of a camera. Not only was he scared to act again, but the idea of being on location, away from the safety of his AA routine, alarmed him. It wasn't until Brad phoned John Hurt to ask his advice about the film and got an earful about what a fabulous actress Helen was that he agreed to the role. "Well, I need a job," he finally conceded. "And I guess I could use a trip to France." It would be his first job sober, and the first since *Chariots of Fire* more than a year before. It was also the last job that Clifford Stevens would get him.

By Fourth of July in 1981, Brad had left for two months in Brittany. Because the film's budget was so small, part of his deal had been an extra first-class air ticket for me. I wasn't going to miss being in France with a newly sober husband. We had only begun to work on our relationship, and I thought two weeks in France would be the break we needed.

I booked my trip for the last week of shooting in August, Monday the seventeenth, an overnight flight to Paris and then a short connecting flight to Brittany. When I scrambled out of the plane, shook hands with the mustachioed pilot, and stepped onto the felt green lawn of the airfield, I felt like Dorothy arriving in Oz. I had never been in the French countryside before, and I was stunned at how perfect it all seemed—the undulating hills, the Constable-like sky, the gray stone village in the distance. Even the dirt road leading away from the airstrip seemed picturesque. It was so charming that when Brad was nowhere to be seen—and the pilot and stationmaster disappeared into the scenery on bicycles—I simply sat down on my luggage to wait it out. I had the number of Brad's hotel, but since I didn't speak French, I was uncertain about using the pay phone. A half hour, I gave myself, then I would wrestle with all that.

I sat there two and a half hours, from ten to twelve-thirty, before I saw a puff of dust chugging up the road and the most minute French car appeared, Brad tumbling out, full of apologies. Or rather, excuses. Yes, he was late, but they'd had an unexpected call that morning, reshooting a scene, and then of course he'd gotten lost because no one even knew there was an airport here let alone where it was. As we bumped over the dirt road, I could feel my chest tightening with anger. Another lovely location visit with Brad.

It was the tag end of the lunch hour when we crunched onto the gravel driveway of the inn, the bougainvillea and morning glories tumbling about the doorway and down on the lawn, the lingering luncheon party, the tablecloth stained with wine and bits of bread crusts, and everyone—Helen and Alan Shallcross and Piers Haggard, the director, and Edna O'Brien, who had the most gorgeous red hair, and a couple of crew members—sprawled around the table, chatting in that desultory summer way. As Brad and I picked our way across the grass, I braced myself for the introductions, feeling like an alien or an interloper, the wife who shows up to spoil the fun.

Maybe it was an unexpected bonus of Brad's sobriety. Or maybe it was just that foreign filmmaking was so much lower key than Hollywood. Whatever it was, I was surprised to find that I liked everyone enormously and, more to the point, that they liked me. Helen was the warmest, funniest woman—not beautiful but striking—who, unlike Brad's previous costars, actually seemed pleased to be meeting his wife. And Edna was in a class by herself, the sauciest, most opinionated woman, but with an Irish wit you fell in love with. It was obvious the two of them were great pals and that they were also fond of Brad. It was one of the few times I could recall being with Brad in the company of women and not feeling any weird, sexually competitive vibes.

I sat there thinking maybe, just maybe, the whole nightmare was over. That is until I glanced over at Brad and saw a glass of white wine on the table in front of him. I hadn't seen Brad for almost two months. But in the three months before he'd left for France, he hadn't slipped once. Not once. "It's not his," I said to myself, closing my eyes, trying to will the glass away. "It doesn't have to be his."

But it was. When I opened my eyes, Brad was sipping from the glass. I kept staring at him, his mouth, his lips on the glass and then curling into laughter, until he finally met my gaze. "Excuse me," I said, getting up from the table, murmuring something about the ladies' room.

It took Brad about a minute to reach me in the lobby, grabbing my elbow. "What are you doing?" he said.

"What am I doing? What the fuck are you doing?"

I couldn't believe he was drinking again, that he was jeopardizing the shoot, my visit, the otherwise perfectness of the whole thing, for a glass of wine. "You're so fucking stupid," I said, shaking with rage. "You're so stupid, you don't even know I'm leaving."

This was met with a flurry of excuses. No, no, no, don't do that because—"Because what?" I said. "You'll what?"—because I would embarrass him in front of the others, in front of Helen. After all the humiliations he had put me through, this is what it came down to? His embarrassment? "Fuck you," I said, and marched out to our room.

That night, Brad got blinding drunk, drinking cognac with Helen in the living room until the decanter was empty. When he finally staggered back to our room, a little two-story cabin behind the inn, he collapsed in a heap at the base of the stairs. I didn't even get up, just let him lie there all night.

He was still there, passed out, the next morning when Helen knocked on our door, to check on Brad.

"See for yourself," I said, nodding at Brad's crumpled shape on the stone floor.

Although she didn't say as much, I thought Helen got the picture. Later it came out that she and Brad had been in a car accident earlier in the shoot, late one night when they had been out to dinner and tried to pilot themselves home after one too many bottles of wine. Helen had been so concerned about their liability that she'd retained a lawyer.

Not that Brad conceded as much when he came to. Typically, he blamed me: "I was fine, doing fine until you showed up. I was never drunk until you got here."

We spent the rest of that Wednesday arguing, me threatening to leave, and Brad, finally, pleading with me in that AA argot. "I'm going to get sobriety," he said. "I can really feel that I'm at the end of my drinking days."

For once in his life, Brad did what he said he'd do. He quit. That Wednesday he got sober. He never had another drink. Not for the entire rest of the trip. Not for the rest of his life. And August 19, 1981, became his AA anniversary day.

And I stayed to watch it—that week, while they finished filming, and the following week when Brad and I, with Helen as our guide, took the first real vacation we'd ever had, a driving tour of Brittany and Normandy: endless inns, beautiful country houses, and gorgeous meals that went on and on, the three of us just laughing in candlelight, because now that he wasn't drinking, Brad was totally into food, meat and desserts and coffee and chocolate. And I began to relax with Brad and I actually thought we might, in fact, have a sex life again, because it was the first time in years that I felt physically comfortable with him.

At the end of the week, Helen invited us to London, to her flat where she was living with Liam Neeson since they'd met on the set of *Excalibur* the year before. So we went on with her, flying from Brittany on a prop plane that Helen had found. It had been chartered by a British rock band, but she talked her way on in that "Oh, darling" tone she used, just charming the pants off these guys in dirty jeans, with skulls dangling from their earlobes.

I knew then that Helen would become one of our closest friends. I didn't envy her, she was too genuine in her affections for that, but I was struck by her sense of self-possession, her lack of self-consciousness, and the freedom, the absence of apology, with which she lived her life. I had never met a woman like that and it opened my eyes.

That first night in London the four of us went out for Indian food and talked for hours about acting and the film business. Liam was this huge, gorgeous Irishmen, at least eight or nine years younger than Helen, but obviously in love with her. And it was clear that she was the famous, successful one in that relationship, something of a Professor Higgins to this striving actor who had been, Helen confided, just a poor kid, a boxer from a small Northern Irish village who was so green he practically ate with his hands. Now Helen was trying to help him break into English films and television, but he wasn't having much luck given the anti-Irish sentiment in Britain at the time. At dinner, Liam really questioned me a lot about Hollywood because he was having such a hard time in London. Years later, when I heard that he was in L.A. filming *Darkman,* I wasn't at all surprised.

It was so easy being with Helen—to her total credit she never said a word about Brad not drinking, just sat and drank her wine, chattering away as if there were nothing untoward—that it was something of a surprise when we finally met up with John Hurt. He was living with his girlfriend, Marie-Lise, out in the country, where they kept horses. It was a magnificent piece of property—Brad went riding, jumping in fact, something I had never seen him do—but John was in shaky shape, even by his wizened standards. We hadn't seen him since Cannes three years before, and it was obvious he'd been sick—trouble with his liver—and that he was trying to stay off booze.

That was John's approach: he drank until he got sick and then he stopped. When he felt better, he started again. Brad, of course, spent hours talking to him, bullying him about AA. "Well, that's one approach," John said in his usual sardonic way, sipping ginger ale from a cut-crystal tumbler. "Let me know if it works." And I realized no matter how much Brad embraced sobriety, on some level he must deeply miss drinking.

After *Mrs. Reinhardt,* I flew back from London feeling as good as I had in a long time. Not only had the trip given me some much needed perspective, but I felt more confident about Brad's sticking with his sobriety. I was still going to Al-Anon and therapy, but it seemed as if the worst might be over and that our relationship was really on the mend. Since our sex life had resumed, I was even giving some thought to trying to have a baby. I was thirty-five, thirty-five and a half, actually, but even I knew the AA guidelines, that you should wait at least a year before initiating any major changes.

It was hard not to feel impatient, however. I had already been pregnant with Brad twice. Once just before that trip I took to Mexico with Marcia when I had just started seeing Brad and, ironically, had thought we should stop seeing each other. The other time had been in the spring of 1979, after he'd filmed *Small Circle,* at the height of his drug and alcohol abuse. Both pregnancies were accidents—the second a failure of my Dalkon shield—and neither seemed the right time to add a baby to the confusion of our relationship. Now that Brad was sober, it was hard not to jump at the first chance to try again. But I put it out of my mind. For the time being.

And I was busy. Though Brad's career was stalled, mine seemed to be taking off. It had taken us about a year, but now Marsha and I were working at capacity, and I could finally stop fretting about whether I'd made the right decision to leave Gersh. That year we had already cast five TV pilots as well as the Jean Harris movie for NBC. We had also done the sitcom version of *Nine to Five,* the hit Dolly Parton movie, and a test version for CBS of *Private Benjamin,* the Goldie Hawn hit comedy. Now that I was back from France, we were busy with another NBC movie, *All the Way Home,* starring Sally Field and William Hurt. Most days we hardly had time to order takeout from Twain's, just down the block from our offices on Sunset Boulevard.

Brad, however, had come back from London feeling restless. While *Mrs. Reinhardt* had been a good experience, a low-profile opportunity to start acting again, it hadn't solved the dilemma of his career. In Hollywood, Brad was still considered cold. That he was now sober made no difference. No one wanted to take a chance with him. Even when *Chariots of Fire* was released in September, with all its attendant fanfare, David Eidenberg couldn't elicit a serious offer for Brad.

So, like any actor frustrated with his career, Brad fired his agent. He quit Clifford and David to sign with William Morris's Eddie Bondy, one of Hollywood's more legendary figures.

In the button-down world of agenting, Eddie was one of its few genuine iconoclasts. By the time Brad met him, at an AA meeting that first winter of his sobriety, Eddie was one of William Morris's most powerful agents—and even more well-known for his foul-mouthed candor. He'd started in New York in the sixties, working for William Morris where he handled such actors as Joan Hackett, Julie Harris, and Lou Gossett on Broadway. He married and became the father of two young children. But in 1972, Eddie left his wife, moved to L.A., and quickly established a reputation for flamboyance.

In a profoundly conservative industry, its liberal image to the contrary, Eddie was one of the great classic bitchy homosexuals. He was rail thin, looked like an accountant, but talked like a street hustler. Even his own clients were appalled at Eddie's mouth. He called his actresses "cunts," and his standard come-on to new actors was singular: "I won't represent you unless you make a half a million dollars, but I will suck your cock."

Whether you found him grotesque or hilarious in his openness about his sexuality—Brad loved it, but I often wondered about Eddie's wife and children—he was just as forthright about his alcoholism. In Hollywood in 1981, it still wasn't done to trumpet your membership in AA. David Eidenberg, for instance, had a difficult time talking to Brad about his being in the program. But Eddie had no such qualms. He'd already been in AA for nearly seven years when he met Brad, marched up to him at one of Brad's first meetings, stuck out his hand, and said, "Hi, I'm Eddie Bondy and we've been waiting for you."

For Brad, it was a relief to be able to talk business and sobriety with equal frankness. Eddie lacked that sense of apology that Brad sensed in Clifford and particularly David, that "Please give Brad Davis a chance" tone they used with producers. That fall, Brad left STE for William Morris, signing his new contract in Eddie's office on November 3, 1981.

Clifford was furious at Brad, but mostly at Eddie for using his AA connections to poach clients, ironically a practice that would become de rigueur in Hollywood. Eddie, however, was the agent who would have the biggest impact on Brad's career. Not only did Brad have a big agent at one of the big three agencies, but he had an agent who was fanatical about him as an actor.

Eddie really believed in Brad; he called him fondly "the little prick," and unlike David, he had no trouble pushing producers. "Yeah, you're right," he'd say. "Brad Davis is an alcoholic—I know that because I'm one, too—but in the last six months, he's really cleaned himself up and you owe it to yourselves to see him." Eddie relaunched Brad in Hollywood, got him back into television in a big way, landing him the two largest TV films he would make, *Chiefs* and *Robert F. Kennedy and His Times*—films Brad said represented the first time "I played men rather than boys."

The desire to stop playing ingenues and pretty boys and play men his own age was a major issue for Brad. He was thirty-two, sober, and wanted roles that addressed his new maturity. But with few exceptions, all his work, including *Mrs. Reinhardt,* had him cast as the oversexed, out-of-control juvenile. It was exactly what he was offered in his next job, taking over the lead role in the off-Broadway production of Joe Orton's *Entertaining Mr. Sloane.*

As with *Mrs. Reinhardt,* Brad was torn about the offer. He recognized that it was a real plum, especially since he hadn't performed in New York in more than five years. And the production was a big deal, the first successful revival in New York of Orton's fifteen-year-old drama—directed by a rising new director, John Tillinger, and starring Max Caulfield, a hot young British actor. It had opened in May at the Westside Arts Theater, then transferred to the Cherry Lane in June. Brad was to take over the lead in November when Max returned to London.

But Brad was wary about the offer. Not only was he intimidated about getting back onstage after so long an absence, but he was terrified of stepping into an established hit. Most of that fear centered on Max, who was eight years younger than Brad, knock-down handsome, and considered a real comer. Some of this was Brad's old insecurities about competing with other actors, as with Richard Gere and *Midnight Express.* But much of it was a new fear, that he was taking a huge step backward playing Sloane, a sexy gay hustler and the love interest of the play's two other protagonists.

The notes Brad took during his weeks of rehearsal, scrawled in a cheap notebook he kept, are revealing, both in his lack of confidence and his frustrations at typecasting:

> Do I have anything to offer besides sex? I guess I've always felt that was my chief attribute and contribution, but next to that kid [Max] I feel old and foolish. . . . No way can I take ten years off and put six inches on. . . . I guess it has nothing to do with acting, but all to do with ego. Who is the bigger stallion? I hate putting my mind in this place, I HATE it!! . . . I'm finally offered a play. A PLAY—A COMEDY and what is my part? The young stud in black leather pants and a white T-shirt that makes people cream at a glance. SHIT! How long, O Lord? When can I just act, free of the "Stud for Hire" tab clipped on me when that tag was as true as anything about me, but not anymore. I want a [role] for a thirty-two-year-old man.

Whatever his fears, however, Brad did well, although Larry Kramer came to Brad's opening on November 3 and always teasingly insisted Max had been better. The production ran all through the holidays, finally closing on January 31. I flew out right before Thanksgiving and stayed on with Brad through the holidays. Ironically, we were renting an apartment on upper Madison that belonged to Rob Cohen, the director of *Small Circle*. It was a great time being back in New York like visiting royalty. I was proud of Brad starring in a hit off-Broadway. Even he gave in to it, scrawling on my Playbill: "November 21, 1981, To Susan from her Husband, doing what this type of Husband does best. Love, The Husband."

It was during *Sloane* that Brad did land his next film, playing the lead in *Querelle,* a film adaptation of the 1941 Jean Genet novel directed by Rainer Werner Fassbinder, the legendary German filmmaker. Fassbinder was one of the great tortured directors of the twentieth century, a drug addict, openly gay, and hugely talented. He was a leading member of West Germany's second-generation alternative filmmakers, the founders of the so-called New German

Cinema. In his thirty-six years, Fassbinder made forty-two films, the most successful being *The Marriage of Maria Braun* in 1978.

Fassbinder worked with few American actors, so his interest in Brad was a huge honor. Eddie Bondy was so over the moon you could hear him hopping up and down over the phone. Brad, of course, had never heard of Fassbinder, let alone read Genet. "Jennett" as he called him. "Jean Jennett." At Eddie's insistence, Brad said he would read the script. Not that it helped, not when he realized he'd be playing another gay hustler, a sailor who screws and then murders his various johns in the French port of Brest. I can still hear Eddie screaming over the phone, "It's a fucking metaphor— about fucking!"

Brad got it that Fassbinder was an artist. Heroin addicted, but an artist. He also knew that the rest of the *Querelle* cast—namely Franco Nero and Jeanne Moreau—was unlike any he'd worked with before. But he was also convinced that he'd be furthering his own typecasting if he took the role. "I wasn't insecure about doing it, I worried that I would be persecuted in my professional life," he wrote in his notes.

In the end, Brad resorted to AA logic to decide, something that is clear in the interview he gave in the *East Village Eye* with Dieter Schidor, the producer of *Querelle*, a few weeks before the film's American release in April 1983: "I believe very much in a power greater than myself, a will greater than my own, which helps all people see things they're supposed to do."

Filming was to begin on February 9, 1982, in Berlin; the entire movie was shot on a soundstage with no attempt at realism. Brad was to be in Germany for twenty-two days starting in March. He would be paid $20,000 a week for a total of $60,000.

In hindsight, Brad was glad to have made the movie—the challenges of working with a German-speaking, heroin-taking director notwithstanding—especially when it turned out to be Fassbinder's last film. He died of heart failure on June 10, 1982, less than three months after filming on *Querelle* had finished.

However, Brad's fears about the film typecasting him were borne out. When the film was released, he became a heartthrob in the gay community, literally a poster boy when the film's ads featured Brad in full sailor regalia posing suggestively under a streetlamp. He hated the ad campaign, as well as the film's final cut. The reviews were scathing, and Brad blamed Fassbinder for caving when Gaumont, the film's financiers, insisted on cutting the three-hour film to an hour and forty-five minutes. "Everything that makes sense has been cut out," Brad said. "Now, it looks like this guy just gets off the boat and starts killing people and getting fucked."

Now that Brad was back from Berlin and had stayed sober through all of Fassbinder's drug-taking on the set of *Querelle*, I began trying to get pregnant in earnest. Brad's official AA anniversary was August 1981, but I dated his sobriety to Thanksgiving 1980, when he attended his first AA meeting. By October 1981, I felt as if I'd waited my year the way Al-Anon recommended. It was during the run of *Entertaining Mr. Sloane*, when I flew out to be with Brad all those weeks in New York, that we had first started to try.

I can only describe Brad's participation as grudging. On the topic of children, he and I were polar opposites. I had never, *ever* wanted a life without children, and he had *always* wanted a life without children. It was one of those things you figure you will work out someday. Well, someday was now. I was thirty-five and had seen my easiest, best childbearing years wasted on Brad's excesses. He was not going to cheat me out of this again. I owed it to myself to have the child I always wanted. Brad owed it to me.

So I just pushed him and I didn't listen to his complaints, his objections. I didn't care about his career. I didn't care about money. I just wanted a child, a family. "Do this," I said. "Just do this for me and I promise you will never, ever regret this."

It took something like a year before I got pregnant. After that second abortion, I'd gotten a bad infection that had left a lot of scar tissue on my tubes, something I only discovered after six months of trying to get pregnant. Eventually, I gave up and went back to my old gynecologist in New York, the same doctor who had helped clear up the infection after that botched abortion. He was the one who started Brad and me on medications, the temperature taking, and the whole nine yards. He wasn't big on explanations or even emotions. He just said, "Do this, do this, do this, and you should get pregnant."

And I did. I got pregnant. Within about another six months. Not that it wasn't tricky doing it all bicoastally. Working with a Manhattan doctor meant I had a lot of flights to New York. Like the time he needed to do a postcoital test within six hours of intercourse. Brad and I had to have sex at a friend's house—that of Neil Bell, a trainer Brad had been working with who lived conveniently near LAX in Venice—right before I got on the red-eye.

But my persistence paid off, as it had when I decided to stick it out with Brad. I'll never forget that morning in July when I took my temperature. "My God, it's up," I said to Brad.

I knew I was pregnant. I just knew.

"You can't know from just that," said Brad, who insisted on going out to get an E.P.T. test, although God knows why we didn't have one in the house. But he got it and I was right, it was positive. Sitting there on the bed, with Brad waving the blue stick around, I couldn't tell if he was excited or terrified. But I thought, it doesn't matter. I'm finally getting something for myself, that finally, we might actually be a family.

Now that I was finally pregnant, I began to look at things with a different perspective. Was our house big enough? Did we have enough money for me to take time off and for how long? Could we hire a nanny and when? I knew I didn't want to work right after the baby, at least not for nine months, so it was hard not to emotionally just check out. Especially when the feature film we were casting that fall was this awful quasi-porno thing, *Private School.* Here I was pregnant, just into being a mother with this sexless body, and I was having to look at all these actors to see if they would get naked for a stupid movie. I was ready to cast anybody who'd take their clothes off.

If I had my hands full with pregnancy and work, Brad seemed to have slipped into slow motion. Day after day, his life was one endless phone game. Even Eddie wasn't able to conjure up any major offers. After *Querelle,* Brad didn't work for a year and a half.

He was convinced the film had sunk him in Hollywood, "another hooker part" he called it. He'd never been one to worry about money, that was always my job. But now that I was getting bigger by the week, even Brad was getting concerned. So he did what all desperate actors do, he did theater.

That winter, Brad did two plays, a version of Franz Kafka's *Metamorphosis,* at L.A.'s Mark Taper Forum, and *Toyer,* a two-hander by Gardner McKay in Washington, D.C., at the Kennedy Center. The Taper job was mostly about local publicity, since it paid all of $450 a week. Brad had never played L.A. before and Eddie made sure that producers and all his big-name clients, such as Julie Harris, trotted out to see it. I didn't make it to the opening in October, but Brad was a nervous wreck at the party afterward, meeting all the actors he considered "stars."

Toyer was supposed to be a bigger deal, a pre-Broadway tryout. It costarred Kathleen Turner and was directed by Tony Richardson, the famous British director who'd done John Osborne's seminal drama *Look Back in Anger* in London in 1956. *Toyer* was set to open in Washington in January, run until March 15, and then, ideally, transfer to New York for an indefinite run. Financially it made sense, but Brad was worried that he'd miss my due date. I didn't care about that as much having some money coming in. I simply wrangled Neil Bell into being my substitute birthing coach. Well, he'd been there at the beginning, why not at the end?

But the play bombed, closing after a week and a half, and Brad was back home by February. And he was there when Alexandra was born at Cedars-Sinai Hospital on April 23, 1983. I had worked right up until ten days before, beginning work on *A Streetcar Named Desire* for ABC. Those last few days I just tried to do everything— attending a shower that Marsha threw for me, painting the guest room, trying to turn Brad's junk room into a nursery—but I felt like doing nothing but sleeping. Then came the mad drive to the hospital. I thought of all those times I had ridden with Brad when he'd been drunk; now he was careening around because of a baby, our baby.

And then it was all over, and the sun was streaming into my room and I felt as if I'd spent fifteen hours breathing helium. Everyone seemed to be piling in to see us, the three of us, our friends, Neil of course, and Stan Jones and Norbert and Tandy and even Marcia Inch, who had been in Texas on business and who flew out to see the wrinkled, blue-eyed baby girl that Brad and I had made, the very best end I could have imagined to everything we'd been through.

9

Now that we had Alexandra, our lives changed radically. Or at least mine did. For one thing, I was home all the time. And exhausted. Like any new mother, I was thrilled with my daughter, but I was also stunned at how time-consuming it all was. The interrupted nights and the long days when I nodded off whenever she fell asleep, waking in a fog to her cries, stumbling into the whole cycle all over again. I was on my own here—Brad made clear he wasn't into baby stuff at all—and I didn't have my mother to help me get started.

I needed someone to help out now, but especially later on, when I planned to go back to work. Brad still wasn't getting any solid offers, and we were dependent on my income. I needed a nanny who could also double as a housekeeper. After a few weeks of looking, I hired Doris, a young Guatemalan woman. Or rather, Doris picked us over several other job offers. I always thought she chose me because I was such a basket case, because I needed her most.

And in truth, it was a challenging time. I was feeling slightly overwhelmed in addition to my usual worries about money, Brad's career, my career, my weight. I had gained something like sixty pounds during my pregnancy, and Brad was really riding me about

Brad in the late 1980s. Although already HIV-positive, this was a favorite picture of himself and one that we used at his memorial service.

Eugene Davis

Brad Davis

Brad's father, Dr. Eugene "Doodle" Davis, at his weekly poker game.

Brad's mother, Anne Davis, as a young woman. Brad thought she resembled the actress Joan Bennett. By the time I met her she was ravaged by mental illness.

Gene Davis

Our wedding picture taken at the courthouse in Cairo, Georgia, on December 29, 1976. We eloped.

Brad in 1974, before he changed his name from Bobby to Brad Davis.

Brad in Brian Friel's *Crystal and Fox*, April 1973, his first off-Broadway production and his first real paycheck as an actor. Rue McClanahan played his mother—before she moved to Los Angeles and became one of the "Golden Girls." Because Equity already listed a "Bobby Davis" among its members, Brad had to change his name for this production.

Bert Andrews

photographer unknown

Brad, Alan Parker, Billy Hayes, John Hurt, and Davit Putnam *(behind)* in the Palais de Festival in Cannes moments after the screening of *Midnight Express*. The crowd went wild, our first indication that Brad was going to be a star.

Brad on location in Malta for *Midnight Express* with Patrick, the little dog he rescued and brought back home as a gift for his mother.

Brad and his agent, David Eidenberg *(far left)*, and producer Neil Bogart *(center)* meeting President Gerald Ford just after the release of *Midnight Express*.

Magazine photos from a series taken of Brad in 1978 working out at Carrieros gym in Los Angeles. Brad's close friend Neil Bell was his trainer.

Peter Sorel

Brad made the cover of Italian *Vogue* after *Midnight Express* became a sensation in Europe. The magazine was on the stands when I went to Italy after leaving him in February 1979 in Boston, where he was filming *A Small Circle of Friends*, his first film after *Midnight Express*.

Peter Sorel

Brad as he looked at the beginning of *A Small Circle of Friends*, shot in Boston in 1979.

Brad and me during the final weeks of filming for *A Small Circle of Friends*. Brad had been doing $2,000 worth of cocaine a week.

Brad and me in San
Francisco in 1979.
Brad was drunk
during most of
the trip.

Tony Inch

Helen Mirren

Brad and me in Brittany after he finished filming *Mrs. Reinhardt*.
This is my favorite picture of us, perhaps because I have such fond
memories of that trip—when Brad first got sober—although it
started out very rocky.

Brad and Helen Mirren during the filming of the television movie *Mrs. Reinhardt,* in France. This was his first job after he got sober. It would be some time before he got a Hollywood job again.

Brad and Helen Mirren in our kitchen cooking eggs just after the filming of *Mrs. Reinhardt.* They were wearing matching sailor shirts we'd gotten during our trip to France.

Brad, actress Jeanne Moreau, and director Rainer Werner Fassbinder during the filming of *Querelle* in Germany in 1982. The cult film, in which Brad played a dissolute sailor, would be the director's last before he died.

Brad and Alexandra during a trip to his parents' house in Florida, shortly after she was born in April 1983.

Susan Bluestein

Joseph Lambie

Alexandra and me when she was four months old.

Brad and Alexandra in 1984, when she was
barely two years old. This is her favorite
picture of her with her dad.

Brad and Alexandra in our backyard. They were off to see the dog Benji at an AIDS benefit in 1987.

Susan Bluestein

Brad Davis

Alexandra at six. This was Brad's favorite picture of her. He carried it with him always.

Brad as Robert Kennedy, Jr.—taken under a portrait of Kennedy during the filming of the TV movie *Robert Kennedy and His Times* in 1983. This would become one of the favorite roles of his career, the first time Brad felt he played a real adult.

Alexandra, age five, during a visit to Australia, where Brad was filming *The Rainbow Warrior*.

Alexandra and me in Australia in 1988—it was her first trip abroad to see what making a movie was all about.

Brad and German actress Marrianne Sagebrecht in a scene from the 1989 film *Rosalie Goes Shopping*, directed by Percy Adlon. Brad was at a career low and was thrilled when Adlon offered him the role of the Midwestern crop duster. Ironically, this was Brad's only comic role.

Brad and Larry Kramer during the 1985 run of *The Normal Heart*, in which Brad originated the role of Ned Weeks.

Original cast of *The Normal Heart* in 1985, including Lawrence Lott and William De Acutis *(first and second from right, last row),* both of whom would die of AIDS.

Brad at the reading of *The Normal Heart* for the AIDS benefit in New York in 1990. Also attending were Rodger McFarlane *(third from left, back row),* Larry Kramer, and Colleen Dewhurst *(seated to the left of Brad),* who would shortly die of cancer.

Joanna Miles

Brad on the set of *Habitation of Dragons* a few weeks before he died. As his face shows, he was very sick when this photo was taken.

Accepting my Emmy Award in 1995 for casting *NYPD Blue*. Three other casting directors were also honored for the show: Donna Ekholdt, my associate; Alexa Fogel; and Junie Lowry-Johnson, the original casting director of the series.

© 1996 Craig T. Mathew/ATAS

Weekend trip to Big Bear in the fall of 1988. This is one of my favorite pictures of the three of us.

that. As if I really needed to hear it just then. But Brad was having his own troubles adjusting. As an out-of-work actor he was unused to having his home, his little refuge, invaded by another being whose needs took precedence over his own. Most days, he simply left, got up in the morning and after checking on Alexandra, headed out on his usual routine of AA meetings, gym, lunch, a stop by Eddie's office in Beverly Hills, and then dinner with Stan Jones or whomever.

It was a relief actually not to have him underfoot. It was even more of a relief when Eddie called one morning about four weeks after Alexandra's birth—his usual cheery greeting on the machine, "Hey, you cocksuckers, get up!"—to tell us Brad was up for a lead role in a CBS miniseries, something about cops in a small Southern town. I couldn't have cared less if it was about mice on the moon. The role paid in excess of $200,000 and meant a month-long location shoot in South Carolina.

Eddie really wanted this for Brad. *Chiefs* was the first big job Eddie had been able shake out for Brad since he'd signed with William Morris more than a year and half earlier—a six-hour miniseries exploring race relations in the American South. It was based on the Stewart Woods novel about three generations of police chiefs in a small rural town. Brad was to play one of the three sheriffs, along with costars Keith Carradine and Charlton Heston.

Brad recognized that this was a good part for him, a real step up from the sexy boy toys he'd been playing. But there was a catch. Although Martin Manulis, the producer, and Jerry London, the director, were intrigued by Brad, they were also wary given all the stories about him still floating around. Eddie had laid the ground-work, but Brad still had to do a little tap dance at the requisite lunch, first with Martin and then with Jerry, his little "I'm sober now, so don't sweat it," spiel over glasses of Perrier with lime. In the end he got the role and even helped them get Keith Carradine on board.

Brad would be gone a month—all July in Chester, South Carolina. I had no intention of joining him, not when it was one hundred degrees and humid and I had an infant. Instead, I flew to New York and spent part of that month on Fire Island with Marcia and Ellen, my oldest friends, in the beach house Ellen rented every summer. That week, there were seven of us, me and Alexandra, Ellen and her two children, and Marcia and her son, Casey, who had been born just the year before. It was exactly what I needed, to be with friends, mothers who understood everything I was feeling, the happiness as well as the fears and insecurity.

That summer was really the beginning of a new chapter in our lives, not just with Alexandra but with Brad's career, years when he finally began to work regularly—thanks in no small measure to Eddie—years when Brad was away more often than he was home. By the time *Chiefs* aired that November 1983, a huge ratings hit for CBS in sweeps month and with Brad on the cover of *TV Guide* again, he had already been approached about starring in what would become his best-known role after *Midnight Express*—playing Robert Kennedy in another CBS miniseries, *Robert F. Kennedy and His Times.*

It was a plum role, one of those rare prestige TV jobs, and, at first blush, an unlikely role for Brad. In fact, Rick Rosenberg, one of the two producers on *RFK* with Robert Christiansen, had originally considered Dennis Quaid for the role. But Rick was familiar with Brad's film work, and he thought Brad, more than Dennis, could be made to physically resemble Bobby Kennedy as well as capture his wiry intensity. "We'd heard all the stories about Brad—drug addict, alcoholic, difficult, impossible," Rick recalled. "But we checked him out on *Chiefs* and heard that it was a thing of the past, so we said, 'Let's meet him.'"

That meeting, on Halloween at the old Iron Horse restaurant on Ventura Boulevard, not only clinched the deal, but launched what would become the last great male friendship of Brad's life. Not only was Rick a smart and proven producer, but unlike most of Brad's other friends, he wasn't intimidated by him or his career. He recognized that Brad was pulling a bit of a star thing by refusing to meet in his office. But he also knew that Brad, more than the producers, desperately needed the film—to relaunch his career in earnest and to retool his image, to "get out of blue jeans and become a man" as Brad put it. "To finally play a character who has a vocabulary of more than one hundred words."

At that meeting, Brad was so wired he plowed through endless cups of coffee, talking almost nonstop. "I wondered about him drinking all that coffee and running to the bathroom," Rick remembered, "but I liked him, we all liked him, so we made the deal."

And it was a great deal for Brad, $450,000, the most he'd ever been paid for a single role. Eddie was over the moon, and Zane was right behind him. Finally, we'd be able to get out of debt, pay the $40,000 that we owed Zane, as well as the God knows how much in back taxes we also owed. All of us breathed a sigh of relief that, maybe, just maybe, we were out of the woods.

For the next year or so, *RFK* was Brad's life. Filming began on December 5 on Warner's back lot with weeks to come on location in Boston, Hyannis, New York, and Washington, D.C., before they wrapped in mid-March.

Much of Brad's involvement had to do with the scope of the film and his enthusiasm for it. For the first time since *Midnight Express,* Brad was in almost every scene. But *RFK* also marked the beginning of a group of friends who became known to one another as the Clique—Brad; Rick; his longtime partner, Tim Thompson; Veronica Cartwright, who played Ethel in *RFK;* and Lynda Gurasich, the hairdresser from *Small Circle,* who had been hired on *RFK.* By Christmas, we were socializing, and an impromptu gathering at our house on Christmas day was the first time I had seen Rick in a nonwork setting. I could tell he was bit taken aback seeing us *en famille,* the relative modesty of our house, our usual chaos with the baby and the pets roaming around, and Brad trying to get everyone to play one of those interminable word games he was hooked on now that drinking wasn't an option. Give up booze and you learn to play Scrabble with real feeling. But I also sensed that within the group would develop one of those Hollywood rarities, a genuine and lasting friendship.

In hindsight, some of that instant camaraderie had to do with Eddie Bondy's death earlier that month. Just two years after Brad had signed with him, Eddie collapsed unexpectedly on December 15, 1983, at the age of fifty-two. Brad was devastated. I think if he was ever tempted to fall off the wagon, this was when. Not only had he lost that rare agent who really cared for his clients instead of merely booking them, but he'd lost one of his closest friends, one of the first people who'd believed in Brad's sobriety as well as his abilities as an actor. It was fitting, in a way, that Brad attended the memorial service, held at the Doolittle Theater in Hollywood a few days later, dressed in his *RFK* costume. He'd taken a limo directly from the set of the last job Eddie would get him. Something like seven hundred people were there, and a lot of outrageous, funny Eddie stories were told, including one from Lee Grant, who said she'd remember how wonderful Eddie was if only she could forget that he called her "a cunt" every day. But for Brad, Eddie's death was a huge loss, one that left a hole I saw Rick able to step in and fill.

That January, Brad left for almost two months of filming *RFK* back east. They started in Boston on January 19, and I flew out with Alexandra two days later. It was meant to be a belated Christmas gift to ourselves, a trip to replace the nightmare of our first visit to Boston during *Small Circle* five years before. And it was a magical week. Boston's Back Bay was beautiful, wintery and glittering with the lights still up on the Common. Brad was in his element and I felt like a queen. I was thin, finally—I'd lost sixty pounds after a six-month fast I'd gone on with some awful powdered stuff Brad had found for me—and I had a gorgeous nine-month-old daughter and a handsome star for a husband. I loved to sit in our hotel suite with Rick and Tim and Veronica as a fire crackled in the fireplace and watch Brad hold Alexandra's tiny hand as he helped her take her first steps across the carpet.

Down in Hyannis on Cape Cod, where we'd decamped for the filming of the Kennedy-compound scenes, that domestic tranquillity came to an end with a phone call from Joel Thrum, the head of casting at NBC. They were looking for a casting director to pull together a new series they had in development—*Punky Brewster,* a pilot dreamed up by the NBC entertainment chief, Brandon Tartikoff, about a little orphan girl he had known as a kid. Nobody at NBC productions wanted to deal with it given all the politics involved, so they were looking outside.

The offer was a bolt from the blue. I hadn't been going to movies or watching TV or even reading the trades, and I felt really out of it. But I recognized that it solved the dilemma of how and when I was going back to work. So I sat in our hotel room in Hyannis and I negotiated my first deal for myself. I couldn't believe it when I heard myself saying, "Tell them to double the offer and I'll take it." To my amazement they did, and the next thing I knew, I had cut our vacation short and was on a plane back to L.A., the head of my own one-woman casting agency.

Brad stayed back east since *RFK* didn't wrap until March 7 in New York. During the rest of the trip his friendship with Rick was really forged, when they began to have dinner together every night, usually with Veronica and Lynda. They became such a tight-knit group that at the end of the shoot in D.C., they all burst into tears in Brad's trailer. Those were also the weeks when Brad and Rick began the kind of screaming fights that characterized most of Brad's close relationships.

Rick's birthday and the wrap party fell in the same week in New York. They'd taken the train up from D.C., arguing the whole way about whether Brad should wear a diamond stud in his ear to the wrap party at the River Cafe, where he would meet, among other Kennedy notables, Arthur Schlesinger, whose book the miniseries was based on. "I'm not going as Kennedy," Brad said. "I'm going as me." By the time they got to Penn Station and Brad got off the train with his boom box blaring Billy Joel's "New York State of Mind," Rick wanted to crawl under the nearest subway car. "Here was this guy who'd been paid something like half a million dollars to play one of the most important public figures in this century, and he's walking around like an asshole," Rick thought. My sentiments exactly, although I wouldn't hear about the incident until later.

But that night at the Ritz Carlton, Brad, Lynda, and Tim ganged up on Rick, lambasting him for not letting people, artists, be who they are. Three days later, they threw him a surprise party, scattered daisies all over the room, on the windowsills, even in the toilet, and invited all of his old friends including Maureen Stapleton, who had such a fear of elevators that they had to get her drunk to get her up to the party. It was the official birth of the Clique, a term coined by Brad, of course, and sealed with Rick's gift to each of them, a silver-framed photograph he had taken of the group in D.C.

My usual reaction to Brad's work-related cliques was to feel like an outsider. Maybe it was his sobriety, or that we had a child now, but just as Helen had been in France, the Clique proved very inclusive. After *RFK* wrapped, our social life became centered on the group—dinners, birthdays, Brad's AA birthday, the Olympics that summer when we all rented a limo to tool around in, parties, most often at our house because Brad was such a control freak about the food, the ice cream he had to have, and his insistence that everyone hit the sauna beforehand and play games afterward. There were temporary additions to the group: Helen Mirren and John Hurt when they were in town, staying either at the Château or bunking in our den, and later, the director John Erman, who'd worked with Brad on *Roots*. It was the most visible sign of all the changes in our life together—we had friends, Alexandra, money, even a future that looked bright—and I took all of it as proof that the worst was finally over, the financial uncertainties, the drinking, but also the furtiveness, the secrecy, the lying that had colored so much of our marriage, had come to an end. I felt connected to Brad again, and by more than just an address and a checking account. I felt as if we were, finally, a family.

The rest of 1984, Brad was still involved with *RFK*, which wasn't scheduled to air until the following January. Editing sessions lasted through the spring and summer, then in September came weeks of screenings and further fine-tuning. During those months, Brad spoke to or saw Rick almost every day. In fact, the two of them came up with the ending of the film after director Marvin Chomsky had left the project—a dissolve out of the funeral-train shot into a long shot of Brad on the beach in Hyannis. Brad had to loop the voice-over, a speech that Schlesinger had pulled out from some-where. It was a great ending, Brad looked amazingly like Kennedy in those final scenes—even if the famous Kennedy hairline was due to Lynda's wizardry with a hairpiece—far more effective, Rick felt, than the earliest shots when Brad and Veronica had to play teenagers.

That winter, there was a major press tour—Brad, Rick, and Veronica traveled to New York, Philadelphia, Chicago, Detroit. By the time *RFK* finally aired, on January 27–29, 1985, Brad was on the cover of *TV Guide* again. *Los Angeles Times* TV critic Howard Rosenberg, who'd covered Kennedy in 1968 presidential primary, wrote in his review: "Davis captures the same melancholy and ambivalence, a mix of ambition and vulnerability, that I detected in [Kennedy] in 1968. . . . Davis brings that all back for me."

Brad was ecstatic, less about the miniseries in general because he was quick to find flaws in his performance, but he felt he'd finally driven a stake through the heart of *Midnight Express.* "Now, they can quit asking me what I've done," he said. And to a certain extent he was right. *RFK* was a new calling card, one that was pivotal in getting him his next role, playing Ned Weeks in the premiere of Larry Kramer's *The Normal Heart.*

Brad didn't realize that, when the script arrived at our house that last week in January, it was due to Michael Lindsay-Hogg, the director of *The Normal Heart,* rather than Larry. Michael had seen an early screening of *RFK* and thought if Brad could convincingly play Kennedy, a Harvard grad and U.S. attorney general, he could certainly play Ned Weeks, the political-activist protagonist of *The Normal Heart,* which chronicled the birth of anti-AIDS movement in New York.

It was Larry's first play in eight years, the first since *Sissies Scrapbook* and its reincarnation, *Four Friends,* which Brad had done off-Broadway. In the years since we'd left New York, Larry had become a major political figure, a lightning rod for the city's gay community and an outspoken critic of Mayor Koch's administration. It was a far cry from what I remembered of him, a tortured, failed playwright, a former film producer and screenwriter who'd won an Oscar nomination for the film version of D. H. Lawrence's *Women in Love.*

Now Larry was better known for his politics than his artistry.

After the failure of *Four Friends,* he'd taken a break from playwriting and written *Faggots,* a darkly satirical novel about being a gay man in New York in the late 1970s. The book managed to ridicule both homophobic heterosexuals as well as the homosexual community, which he criticized for mistaking mere promiscuity for politics. The book was reviled within the gay community, and it turned Larry into an activist and a figure of controversy.

Now he had written *The Normal Heart,* another highly autobiographical narrative, this one about the founding of the Gay Men's Health Crisis, GMHC, the most powerful grassroots organization to come out of the growing AIDS epidemic. Ever since the first cases of the "gay cancer" had appeared in New York and San Francisco in 1981—the story first appeared in the back pages of the *New York Times* on July 3, 1981, "rare cancer seen in 41 homosexuals"—Larry had been among the first to sound the alarm.

For the next four years, Larry's life was one political battle, for funding, for recognition that AIDS, acquired immune deficiency syndrome, as the Centers for Disease Control would soon come to call it, was a nationwide health issue. Out of his efforts, GMHC was created with Larry as its cofounder, along with five other gay men, including Rodger McFarlane, Larry's lover and, at the time, executive director of the GMHC. It was that struggle that Larry chronicled in *The Normal Heart,* and it was the character of Larry—Ned Weeks in the play—that Brad was to play.

"Larry sent me his new play," Brad told me that evening in January when I got home. "Great," I said halfheartedly, because in truth I had never been crazy about Larry's work and I was far more focused on the airing of *RFK* that week than any upcoming off-Broadway production.

But Brad was excited. He'd kept in far better contact with Larry since we'd left New York. It had also been a year since he'd worked, and he was flattered that Larry had sent him his new play. That night, he stayed up late reading and rereading the script. I woke the next morning hearing exactly what I didn't want to hear—that he wanted to do *The Normal Heart,* that he wanted to play Ned Weeks. I couldn't see it, not from a casting standpoint, not from a career standpoint. It made no sense to me for Brad to squander his hard-won momentum from *RFK* by disappearing off-Broadway for six months. William Morris, I thought, I'll let them talk him out of it.

But within a matter of weeks, Brad had the part and was in New York rehearsing for the opening in April at Joe Papp's Public Theater. He'd landed the role, he'd discovered, against Larry's initial instincts. It was Michael Lindsay-Hogg, the director of the BBC hit *Brideshead Revisted,* he realized, who had first suggested him after seeing a cut of *RFK*. They wanted him to audition—Papp always insisted on personally seeing every actor—something he loathed doing. But Brad was so keen on it, he'd flown out, hauling his old navy overcoat on the plane. The reading was scheduled for February 9, a Saturday afternoon in the dead of winter down at the Public in Astor Place. By that night, the role was his, a unanimous decision by Larry, Joe, and Michael.

That Sunday before he caught his flight for L.A., Brad had brunch with Larry at the Pink Teacup in the Village. There, Larry filled him in on the problems confronting the production. It had taken a year to find a home for the play, six months longer than it had taken Larry to write it. Papp, he said, had been the only producer willing to stage a potentially controversial drama about AIDS. But then Papp, who liked to think of himself as the city's cultural maverick, was not shy when it came to the uses of controversy.

Once Papp was on board, the production acquired a certain buzz. But it had been insufficient, Larry added, to overcome casting problems. None of the actors they'd given the script to had been willing to play a gay role, at least not in a production that was perceived as agitprop for the gay community. Among gay and straight actors alike, it was still considered career suicide to play an openly gay character in 1985. *Kiss of the Spider Woman* was coming out that year, and already there was speculation about the impact of that on William Hurt's career. It would take another eight years, or until Tom Hanks won an Oscar playing a gay AIDS victim in *Philadelphia* in 1993, for the stigma to begin to fade.

Certainly Brad had felt its effects. Despite the large number of gay roles on his résumé, starting with *Song of Myself* in 1975, he'd had major doubts about doing *Entertaining Mr. Sloane* and *Querelle,* fears of being typecast as promiscuous. "This is different," Brad told me. "This isn't about sex, it's about politics."

Yes, well, as far as I was concerned, it was about money. Working at the Public paid less than the Taper did, a few hundred dollars a week. Brad had gotten his final *RFK* payment more than a year ago. Our debts, our back taxes, and buying Brad's parents' house for them the summer before—acquiring the $120,000 mortgage on their Skipper Lane home in Tallahassee when they couldn't make the payments—had pretty much taken care of that $450,000. What Brad needed was another fat TV role. If he did *The Normal Heart,* even for a limited six-month contract, he'd be out of circulation for a year.

But I was on the losing end of that stick. Wanting Brad, Papp stepped in and offered to pay Brad's rent and expenses—so our out-of-pocket costs were nominal. Papp also agreed to a three-month contract, from the opening on April 21 through July 14. Even I could see this was a done deal. Brad left for New York on February 20 for two months of rehearsals.

From the beginning it was an emotionally fraught production. At the first read-through, practically the entire cast, which was equally divided among gay and straight actors, had burst into tears. But if they were all moved by the play, others saw it in a far different light.

A few weeks into rehearsal, Joe got a call from Ed Koch accusing him of staging a play that defamed him. And in truth, Larry was sharply critical of the mayor in *The Normal Heart,* portraying him not only as a political hypocrite but a closet homosexual. Papp asked Larry to tone down some of the anti-Koch rhetoric. As a recipient of public funding, Papp felt he had an obligation not to deliberately antagonize the mayor. Larry, of course, went ballistic. He hung up on Joe and told Michael and the cast he would shut the whole thing down rather than censor himself. Brad called that night to say he might be home early. Michael, however, kept on rehearsing and eventually it blew over.

Shortly after that, Brad called to say that as part of his research, he'd begun to spend time with a gay couple, one of whom was dying of AIDS. Rodger McFarlane, the head of the GMHC, who'd been brought in by Larry as a consultant on the production, had found them. It was Brad's first introduction to someone with AIDS, and the beginning of his friendship with Rodger.

In *The Normal Heart*, Rodger was portrayed as Tommy Boatwright, a flamboyant, wisecracking Southerner who was as hell-bent on bedding Ned Weeks as on founding a political action group. Although Rodger was twenty years younger than Larry, he had in fact become more important to the day-to-day operations at GMHC. As a former hospital administrator in Mobile, Alabama, Rodger had started the group's hot line, using his home phone those first few weeks, answering more than a hundred calls a day and spending hours ferrying AIDS patients to city hospitals.

Now, he was GMHC's executive director, heading up the day-to-day operations from their offices in Chelsea. Larry, meanwhile, was no longer even a board member after an acrimonious vote removed him the year before. But Larry wanted Rodger's help, his medical expertise, on the production. So he'd been brought on board to educate the cast about AIDS—giving tours of the GMHC offices, conducting field trips to hospital wards, locating the gay couple for Brad to interview.

Rodger and Brad became close, sharing dinner almost every night, joined by Michael, Larry, and Joe. At six foot six, and with a shaved head, Rodger towered over Brad by almost a foot. But as two Southerners, "white trash" as Rodger liked to put it, they had a lot in common. Both of them had a long history with drugs, a shadowy sexual past, as well as a mean wit. They also shared a feeling of being permanent émigrés. Each of them had come north to New York to escape the parochialness of their upbringing. "I'd recognize Brad anywhere," Rodger would drawl. "Honey, we're cut from the same fucking cloth."

With Brad in the middle of rehearsals, phoning me nightly to talk to Alexandra—she would have her second birthday two days after *The Normal Heart* was to open on April 21, 1985—as well as to fill me in on the production, I started to pay more attention to the whole AIDS issue. The AIDS virus had been identified two years before, but no antiviral drug was available for treatment. This was pre-AZT, and the CDC had yet to issue a definitive statement about the transmission of the disease through ordinary human contact.

The Reagan administration hadn't even addressed it. There was mounting hysteria. Firemen were refusing to give mouth-to-mouth resuscitation to anyone they suspected of having AIDS. Shockingly, similar concerns were being raised by doctors, nurses, and hospital workers. Saliva, sweat, tears, even simple touching, were the occasion for panic. People began to wonder apprehensively about toilet seats, doorknobs, dishes, even telephones.

I always hated that phrase *consciousness raising,* but that's what Brad's involvement in *The Normal Heart* did for me. By the time I flew to New York the second week in May—I missed the opening because of a job I'd had, casting a movie of the week called *Wild Horses* out in Montana and Wyoming—I felt like an informed insider. The play had exploded like a bomb across the city. It was a sellout. Joe had to move it out of the tiny LuEsther Hall up on the third floor down into the three-hundred-seat Newman Theater, where *A Chorus Line* had opened a decade before. As Frank Rich had hailed it in the *Times:* "There can be little doubt that it's the most outspoken play around."

Certainly its politics was evident even before the curtain went up. The set was a rough-hewn billboard, with a tally of the numbers of AIDS victims, the CDC's weekly counts, as well as figures comparing the number of stories the *Times* had done on the Tylenol scare of 1982 versus its AIDS coverage. There were also government funding statistics—$20 million spent on investigating the seven deaths from Tylenol but only $5 million on AIDS research. I remember that on May 12, 1985, the night I attended, the total was five thousand AIDS-related deaths.

The play itself was equally unstinting in its finger-pointing, taking swipes at everyone from Koch to the medical community to the gay movement itself. I remember thinking, "This will either make Larry's career or ruin it."

Yet as strident as its political message was, I felt a more personal link. An element of risk struck me as I sat there in the dark watching Brad hold and kiss another man onstage—a man who was meant to be dying of AIDS. Brad's career, I thought, and yet there was more, as my mind raced back to Brad's early days in New York, before we had met, when he'd hustled, men, women, whomever, and I wondered, for the first time, if I was seeing Brad's past here in the present.

Brad left the production on July 14. "Dear Brad," wrote Joe in a good-bye note. "God! What in the world would we have done without your noble fire, your feisty, dynamic eloquence!!! Thank you, dear Lord, for giving us one of your finest beings—! My love to you Brad, and thanks for a stunning performance!"

Brad was replaced initially by Stephen Rowe, then in September by Joel Grey, who'd won an Oscar for *Cabaret* in 1973. He remained with the production until it closed on January 5, 1986. *The Normal Heart* never moved to Broadway. And in many ways, its fire was replaced by the another powerful AIDS drama, Tony Kushner's 1993 Tony Award–winning epic, *Angels in America*. However, Larry's play stands as an important historical document. It still holds the record as the longest-running play at the Public. It has spawned more than six hundred other productions. While it has yet to be made into a film—Barbra Streisand's involvement eventually came to naught—Larry continues to search for a producer. Brad was always proud to have originated the role.

And in hindsight, it was a far more significant job than anything he got back in L.A. that year. Now that Eddie was no longer alive to serve as his champion, Brad was working with several William Morris agents, including Beth Cannon and Pam Prince. Pam got Brad his next two jobs—an episode of *Alfred Hitchock Presents,* "Gigolo," costarring Sandy Dennis, that August, and another TV miniseries, *American Cousin/Blood Ties,* to be shot in Italy starting in September. Although *American Cousin* wasn't in a league with *RFK* or *Chiefs,* Brad's fee was high. His contract called for $237,500.

Life seemed to be getting back to normal, but that summer a lightning bolt flashed across Hollywood. Less than two weeks after Brad had left *The Normal Heart,* Rock Hudson held a press conference announcing he was ill. Flanked by his old costar Doris Day, Rock appeared shockingly frail and far thinner than even his rumor-spawning performances in *Dynasty* had suggested. Eight days later, *Variety* reported that Rock had AIDS. The usual denials were issued, but within forty-eight hours, Rock himself confirmed it through a publicist in Paris, where he had gone for a second treatment of HPA-23, a then promising experimental French drug. He'd collapsed on the flight over and had been taken to the American Hospital, where he received a much-publicized phone call from his old Hollywood friend President Reagan. It was Reagan's first acknowledged contact with AIDS.

That disclosure changed the whole AIDS battle, in Hollywood and the country as a whole. In the dog days of summer, Rock Hudson became *the* story, on the front pages of newspapers and magazines for weeks. Even though Rock was gay, an ill-kept secret for years, AIDS had finally captured the attention of straight America. *Life* magazine's cover seemed to sum up both the compassion and the fear: "Now, no one is safe from AIDS."

The tabloid stories, the cadaverous photographs, were like watching a car wreck. A national death watch. You could feel the paranoia settling like dust across town, a hush. By the time of Rock's death at home in Los Angeles on October 2, 1985, everything that had come before it in Hollywood was over— cocaine, drugs, John Belushi's death, the AA-coffeehouse recovery phase. Gone. AIDS was now the issue.

"He died," I said to Brad on the phone to Rome, where he'd arrived ten days earlier. "You heard? He's dead."

He'd heard. How could he not? Rock Hudson's death was international news. "I know," Brad said. "I know, but it's not us. It's not us."

I hung up the phone as if I were turning off the nightly news. There were horrors out there, and God knows, I had known my share living with Brad, but this was not one of them. No, this was not one of them.

CHAPTER

10

What hit me first was the question *why*. I would get to *how* soon enough. But as I sat there in the post office parking lot holding the letter from Cedars-Sinai, I thought, Why in the cosmic scheme of things has this been visited on us? After all Brad had been through—the drinking and drugs, the infidelities, the career ups and downs—now that he was sober and working again and we had Alexandra, why did this happen?

I didn't know then that, with AIDS, the whole question was unanswerable. Cause and effect, beginning and ending, are largely a mystery. Even now, when the distinction between being HIV-positive and having AIDS is more definable, the disease remains cruelly elusive. Like Job, I would find no answer for my question. Brad was HIV-positive. Why it had happened, I did not and would never know.

All I knew was that in the time it took to slit open an envelope, it seemed as if Brad—as if we—had been singled out. For all the bad things he had done, all the mistakes he'd made and thought he could undo with apologies and restitution and by being a good husband and father, he'd been caught. In the end, he was guilty. We were guilty.

I sat in the car holding the letter very very still and feeling physically light. I was so certain of our guilt that I was startled to look up and see not policemen approaching the car, but ordinary people: mothers wheeling babies, young girls with their hair in ponytails, old men leaning on canes, oblivious to me and the horrible verdict I held in my hand.

And what about me? If Brad was HIV-positive, surely I would also be infected. We had spent months, almost a year, having unprotected sex while I tried to get pregnant. It seemed absurd that I would somehow not be infected. And if I was, then what about Alexandra? She was only two, but already I was concerned about her health. She'd had a lot of colds, and many strep throats. Was it too many? Maybe she, maybe we were all already sick and didn't know it.

My fears were not assuaged when I spoke later that day to Dr. Goldfinger. After I'd reached Brad in Rome, and his subsequent flurry of calls to the doctor at Cedars, Goldfinger called me and said I needed to be tested immediately. Although I guessed he'd been more candid with Brad—and in fact he'd told him that it would take "a miracle" for me not to be infected—I sensed what the doctor suspected, that there was only the slightest possibility I was not infected. And if I was infected, it was almost certain that Alexandra was.

"We will only test you initially," the doctor told me over the phone, scheduling me for a blood test the following Monday. "Because if you're negative, then there will be no reason to test your daughter. Both of you will be in the clear."

In the clear? And how would that be? In the sense that only Brad would sicken and die instead of all of us? That weekend before my test was one of the longest I ever faced. Even if I wasn't infected— and I was certain I was, given my parents' history with cancer and their early deaths, I already felt marked for death—Brad still was. There was no changing that even if we didn't know exactly what being HIV-positive meant in 1985. Maybe Brad was just a carrier and would never get ill himself. That was one theory making the rounds. Maybe I was a carrier, too? Maybe being HIV-positive wasn't a death sentence, Rock Hudson's death notwithstanding? Maybe we could both live long enough to keep Alexandra as a child from seeing her parents die?

Those were the questions, the scenarios, I ran over and over in my mind that weekend. Besides Brad and the doctor, there was no one I could talk to, no one I could confide in. Instead, I wandered the house aimlessly, opening and closing kitchen cabinets, staring out the window, studying my face in the bathroom mirror. Should I try to put it out of my mind, as if that were possible? Or should I just give my vent to my fears? Maybe an anal burst of housecleaning, a sense, however fleeting, of being in control?

I found myself instead sitting in the den, pulling out old photographs, ancient family snapshots—my parents and me in Queens, baby pictures of Brad, his horse, and later, shots of the two of us in New York, L.A., and then press clippings, such as the *People* magazine spread on Brad after the release of *Midnight Express*. The awful black-and-white shot of Brad picking me up and trying to twirl me around our backyard. The dizzy new star and his darling wife. I was struck by the picture. We looked ridiculous, me especially. I looked fat and my hair was a mess, but more to the point, I looked absurdly happy. How had I managed to be happy? In the length of time it took to take that picture, what force had permitted me to let down my guard and actually feel happy? And for the first time in days, I laughed out loud. On the floor of the den amid the sea of photographs, I laughed at my ignorance and naïveté.

I had no idea how Brad was dealing with the weekend. He was working, I knew, shooting both Saturday and Sunday, a love scene in *American Cousin*. That was a dilemma in itself as it required a fairly passionate kiss, a potentially lethal act for someone who was HIV-positive. Ever since Rock's death after his on-screen love scenes with Linda Evans in *Dynasty,* the whole idea of kissing had become a hot-button issue in Hollywood. Already the Screen Actors Guild (SAG) had issued a warning to members about "openmouthed kissing" and threatened to invoke the "danger clause" in actors' contracts. There was even talk of "stunt kissers." "Until we know more, I think it's a good idea," Ed Asner, SAG president, had said in a *Newsweek* cover story in August.

But when I had spoken to Brad on Friday, he wasn't sure what he was going to do. Maybe he could fudge it, or maybe he would drum up some reason to refuse to do the scene. "I'm praying for a sign," he told me. "For God to show me what to do."

God. If there was anything I had less confidence in, it was God. I felt cursed in my life, but I didn't think it had anything to do with a god. It was simply fate, my rotten luck to keep drawing the short straws in life. It was why I was so focused, so specific in my goals. Getting Brad sober. Getting pregnant. Getting work. Getting thin. That was what I had wanted, what I had thought I could reasonably hope to get. If I could just have those few tangible things, I would be happy and secure. Or at least, I thought I would stop feeling so vulnerable, so frightened.

But Brad was completely the opposite. As long as I had known him, he'd had a fascination with metaphysics, with the possibilities of a spiritual life. He thought I was almost venal in my desires, as if he had never coveted a gorgeous leather coat or a new car. But in his mind, life was a mystery controlled by a power you could appeal to, even bargain with. It was a position, I assumed, that you adopt when you already feel guilty. Certainly, he'd been that way ever since I'd met him, an angry, abused kid who didn't know whether to lash out or suck you in. It was, I guessed, what was at the root of Brad's desire to act, that constant dance in front of an audience that is judging you, but that is also capable of being seduced.

But it wasn't until Brad joined AA and their insistence on relying on a power greater than your own will that he became more open about his spirituality. Now that he was sober, Brad wanted a passion, a principle for life that was as deep and as inflaming as drinking and drugs had been. He wanted a sense of ecstasy, a sober high. He wanted a god. To me, it was still about giving in, if not to a bottle, then to this other thing you thought had power over you. But I guess I could see it, especially since Brad had tried, unsuccessfully, to get sober on his own. I mean, if it worked, who could argue?

Except it didn't stop with AA. In the four years that he'd been sober, Brad had begun to sample various churches and denominations. He even went to a few Christian Science services, the

Wednesday-evening testimony meetings where people stood up and testified to the healing power of God in their lives. But Brad was also fascinated by Eastern mysticism, and he'd taken to haunting the Bodhi Tree bookstore over on Melrose, stocking up on crystals and incense and books on meditation and transcendence. There he also found a self-described spiritualist and metaphysician, whom he started studying with in February 1985.

They began meeting weekly, meetings supplemented with numerous, lengthy phone calls. At her insistence, Brad began keeping a journal, a record, he called it, of his struggle to know God. "She's helping me discover God's plan for me," Brad told me. Our checking account was more like it. I thought she was a charlatan, another New Age huckster that Los Angeles seems to breed, especially when I learned from Zane how much she was charging. I was furious. At least AA was free. "She's not a licensed therapist," I told Brad. "And it's not like she's practicing an established theology. She can tell you whatever comes into her mind and you'd believe her."

But my objections only made Brad more dogged about seeing the spiritualist—sometimes their candlelit "sessions" lasted until 5 A.M.—and about keeping his diary. He kept it for about a year and a half, and I only saw it once while Brad was alive. I was stunned at the blind fervor of the entries, the references to seeing his own "aura," the bargaining with Jesus. "I release my life to the loving will of God," went a typical entry, "in perfect right action, harmony and order, for the good of all. I release to the light, the light, light."

It was so opposite to the funny, cynical Brad that I knew, the Brad who made me and all our friends laugh with his pointed, even mean observations. I tried to reconcile these entreaties to God with the screaming, profane fights I remember him having with Eddie Bondy. At those moments, I could only think of that old Cheech and Chong routine, where the guy says, "I used to be all fucked up on drugs, now I'm all fucked up on the Lord."

Or maybe I was just jealous, jealous of Brad's faith, his unwavering belief in some divine justice so that he could write in his journal: "The news that I had been exposed to this virus took all the wind out of me, but the thought that Susan could be exposed through me was practically unbearable. That Alexandra would be exposed was unbearable to the point of suicide. . . . I went through my own Gethsemene [*sic*] for 3 days of prayer. . . . I asked only for this, giving my word in faith that if Alexandra and Susan were spared . . . if this cup would pass from Susan and Alexandra and give it all to me, I will do whatever is required of me in humble gratitude and joy."

Certainly I could have used something to hang on to that weekend, and then on Monday, December 9, 1985, when after another sleepless night, I dressed, left Alexandra with Doris, and drove across the Hollywood hills to meet my destiny. My test was to be done in a lab somewhere in the bowels of the Cedars-Sinai complex, just down the road from the Beverly Center shopping mall. Not a hospital room or Dr. Goldfinger's office, but the blood bank hidden away on one of the numerous floors of the hospital.

Even though I had spent almost four days at the hospital when Alexandra was born, I felt as if I had entered an alien universe where everyone averted his gaze. When I finally found the office, bursting in with my heart pounding because I was terrified I was going to die and also terrified that I was late, it seemed as if I'd blundered into a church. It was so still, so quiet, one heard only the hum of machines. Even the technician, an Oriental man, was quiet, still.

"I want you to know that we will never discuss the finding of this test with anyone except you and your husband," he told me as I sat there perched on the metal table, with that tissuey paper underneath me. "We'll make this as quick and as painless for you as we can." At that moment, I wanted so much to believe him, to believe anyone who could reassure me that my life wasn't about to end, that I never even felt the needle as it sank into my arm.

Lying there, I ran the odds in my mind. The University of California study that Brad had read as part of *The Normal Heart* research had said the risk of transmitting the AIDS virus through heterosexual sex was one in five hundred if the partner was infected and no condom was used. Another study said that of all heterosexual HIV-positive men, only 20 percent passed the virus on. Good, good odds, I thought, lying there, staring at the ceiling. There was no way for anyone to know that by 1992, AIDS would become the leading cause of death among people aged twenty-five to forty-four and that heterosexual transmission would be one of the primary causes. Besides, I felt good, healthy. I was sure I'd feel different if I were infected. I mean, I knew within a matter of hours that I was pregnant. I felt that and I was right, so why not now?

But the thought of being pregnant made me think of other, less hopeful studies, statistics about pregnant women who are or become HIV-positive while carrying a fetus to term. One-third of all babies born to HIV-positive mothers will also have the virus. And I thought of Alexandra, her little blond head, and how many times she had been sick, all those nights I had rocked her feverish body into a fitful sleep. If Alexandra was sick, then I was surely sick because I was the cause.

But it didn't turn out that way. The news that I was not infected, that my tests results were negative—a call from Brad two days later—elicited in me a relief, yes, but also a certain primal selfishness at the news that I wasn't going to die and that Alexandra wasn't going to die. At least not right away. But I also felt a door close behind me, leaving Brad on the other side. I knew that our lives were about to change irrevocably. This wasn't about the ups and downs of stardom, the ongoing struggle with alcoholism, or even about raising a child. This wasn't about the possibility of change. This was about loss. I had spent so much of my life living with a mother who thought every day she was dying—and who did die, as my father had, too soon—and now I was living with someone who was, however imperceptibly, really dying.

As I hung up the phone, I felt the first chill of what that meant: the loss of my physical relationship with Brad, the loss of any chance of having a second baby, the loss of normal life where a drinking glass, a shaving cut, a tube of toothpaste, don't loom as issues of life or death. "How many summers left?" I thought, standing there in the kitchen. "How many of Alexandra's birthdays left? How many years before I am left alone again?"

We had planned to spend that Christmas in Italy, meeting up with Brad in Rome after filming had wrapped. But even before we knew about his HIV status, we had canceled our reservations in October shortly after Brad arrived in Italy. He'd gotten a phone call from Annie, his mother. Doodle needed a biopsy on his throat, the result of all those years of a two-to-three-pack-a-day habit. So instead of Italy, we decided to meet in New York, spend ten days at the Mayflower Hotel seeing old friends and my family, and then head for Tallahassee on December 24. Alexandra and I would stay until January 2 while Brad would remain a few more days, or longer depending on the results of the biopsy.

A few days after Brad learned my test results he got a call from his mother. Doodle had tested positive. The operation was scheduled for the first week of January. It was depressing news. Smoking had killed my father and now it seemed as if Brad's father was to be another victim.

Brad tried to put on a good front. "I seem to be going through a major initiation," he wrote in his journal. "But I suppose when one asks for self-mastery, one must have experiences to master. Thank you, Father, for the opportunity to grow."

I, however, took the short view. "Christ," I thought, "Brad's 'positive,' too, but we don't get to tell anyone. We have to go around acting like everything's fine."

Telling. That was the key issue now that we knew Brad was HIV-positive. Whom do we tell? No one? Close friends? Zane? Who would have to know? Probably a doctor, but when? When Brad had symptoms? Or would Brad simply get sick and die like Rock within a matter of weeks?

We didn't have much to help us make an informed, responsible decision. In 1985, little AIDS research and few AIDS specialists were available. Dr. Goldfinger wasn't one. Brad seemed to know as much as anyone after *The Normal Heart*, all those weeks spent hanging round Rodger at the GMHC and the hospitals. Brad knew the official estimates—that the number of HIV-positive people who would develop full-blown AIDS was considered to be only 5 to 10 percent; that people could just be "carriers" and never get sick. Within two years, those estimates would be totally revised: 100 percent of those with the HIV virus were thought to develop AIDS—an estimate that would be revised again and again so that by

1993, it was thought that perhaps 5 percent of HIV-positive individuals might never develop AIDS. That's how shifting and inconclusive medical opinion was—and has remained—in regard to AIDS.

"I'm just HIV-positive," Brad said to me when we finally met in New York. "I don't have any symptoms and we don't know what—if anything—will happen."

It was awkward talking about this in the hotel, whispering in our room, trying to act as if nothing were wrong in front of Alexandra, not to mention our friends, Marcia Inch and her husband, Tony, and my brother, Alan, and his wife, as well as Larry and Rodger. I suppose if there was anyone we could have told, it would have been them. They would have understood the horror and the uncertainty.

What they would not have understood was our need for silence, for secrecy. Unlike New York and San Francisco, with their highly politicized AIDS activists, Hollywood in 1985 was no place for heroes. If Brad and I were uncertain about our knowledge of the disease, we had no such doubts about the discrimination it engendered. Hollywood, like most of the country, was highly intolerant of the growing epidemic. Although outwardly the industry seemed to be taking the high road in response to Rock Hudson's death, with public hand-wringing, and the rush to create benefits and boards, privately discrimination was running at full throttle.

The signs were everywhere. California's governor George Deukmejian had already vetoed antidiscrimination legislation for people with AIDS not once but twice that year, and SAG, while denying it believed kissing could spread AIDS, was threatening to invoke new clauses, new guidelines. Even Rock, one of the industry's most beloved actors, knew he would be ruined if it was known that he had AIDS. In fact, Esther Shapiro, one of the producers of *Dynasty,* Rock's last acting job, conceded that she wasn't sure they would have hired him if they had known he was ill.

Or look at Burt Reynolds, generally considered to be the worst victim of the AIDS-scare paranoia. He didn't have AIDS, but rumors sprang up after he dislocated his jaw. When coupled with the persistent gossip that Burt was gay, he couldn't get a job for years. "Poor Burt," went the whispered refrains. "But don't hire him." It wasn't until he finally landed *Evening Shade* on CBS and showed up healthy on network television week after week that rumors died. But God knows, that was a cautionary tale. That was the unspoken assumption about AIDS: not only were you labeled a modern Typhoid Mary, but it was assumed that you were gay or at the least bisexual—rumors that would come to plague Tony Perkins, director Tony Richardson, and even the NBA's Magic Johnson, when they were later discovered to be HIV-positive.

Brad and I were too aware of what a stigma, any stigma, could do to a Hollywood career. It had been hard enough getting him back on track after he got sober. Add to that all the gay roles he'd played—which rightly or wrongly Brad had come to feel had also hurt his career—and without even stating it, we knew there was no way we could risk the kind of ostracism that AIDS guaranteed. Our decision to hide wasn't about embarrassment or shame. It came down to hard-nosed realities. Self-preservation. Brad needed to keep on working. If not for himself, then for Alexandra and her future. Because who knew where the discrimination would stop. Consider Ryan White, an innocent little kid in Indiana forced to run for his life. What if disclosing Brad's HIV status meant that I also couldn't get work? What if it meant that Alexandra would be shunned?

Such a future was unthinkable to us. "I'll be a hero later," Brad said simply, closing the door on the issue as if he were throwing an old sweater in the back of the closet. Because in truth, he, we, didn't want to talk about it. Not to anyone. Not even to each other. And we didn't. Not for four years. We never said the words *AIDS* or *HIV*. "What's to talk about?" I said to myself, silently adding HIV-positive to our never-ending list of secrets.

I can say now that my resolve about AIDS, like so many of the secrets I kept in my life, was based largely on ignorance and fear. Because in all honesty, we didn't know what our decision would mean. Not really. We're buying ourselves time, we told ourselves, buying ourselves our private life and Alexandra's future.

But at what cost? Our decision to hide meant enormous loneliness and isolation when we could have been comforted by friends and by each other. It meant that Brad would reach out late—too late?—for medical help. It meant that we would pay for his hospitalization and his doctor bills out of our own pocket because we were too afraid to use our insurance, too afraid that we would lose it. Our decision to hide would even define the terms of Brad's death, turn the most personal and traumatic event in my adult life into a public controversy. It meant having to lie once again.

Our decision to conceal Brad's HIV status had come easily, and I had wrestled, Job-like, with the question of why this had come into our lives. But the question I was reluctant to confront was *how*. How had Brad gotten the virus? I knew the choices were limited but also maddeningly infinite. Sex, needles, or blood. Take your pick. With Brad I could easily have chosen all three and been right—as if there were ever a "right" answer to how one contracted AIDS. Many victims never know how they became infected. Many sex partners? One sex partner? A contaminated blood transfusion? A dental exam? An innocent cut?

In theory, that kind of mystery can lead to its own serenity. HIV? It happened. As we would collectively come to realize, ultimately there were no innocent and guilty victims of HIV, no good and bad AIDS sufferers. As a country, we would be forced to see that what began as the "gay plague" had erupted into a full-fledged national health crisis that knew no boundaries. Gay, straight. Married, single. Young, old. Black, white, Latino. No one was exempt. So the question of how one contracted the virus was ultimately unimportant. If there was any silver lining to be found in the nationwide spread of AIDS, it was this redefinition of prejudices. Even the *New York Times* would write about the popularity of androgyny as a personal style and the rise of bisexuality. Gay or straight would become a moot question. You either were HIV-positive or you weren't. You were either going to die or you weren't.

But in the first few months after learning that Brad was HIV-positive, those shifts in the country's collective consciousness had not yet begun. So in my wrestlings with the idea of HIV, I couldn't leave it there. I needed an answer, even if it was only conjectural, about how Brad had contracted the virus. If his being HIV-positive seemed the ultimate price to pay for my life with Brad, then I felt compelled to know exactly what sins I was paying for.

During those first torturous weeks after my blood test, I added to the torture by trying to run down the list of possibilities in my mind. After fifteen years of involvement with Brad, I knew several ways he could have gotten it, given his compulsions: the drinking, the drugs, the manic behavior, the indiscriminate sex. It wasn't pretty, but as far as I was concerned, knowing what I did about Brad and his parents and their lives in Florida, it was all a learned response to his sexually abusive childhood.

But I also knew it was behavior, especially in the hothouse environment of Hollywood, that had led to the rumors and stories and innuendo, both about Brad and his sexual preferences, as well as speculation about our relationship. I knew what people were thinking—and within certain circles what people are still thinking—about the two of us. How could he do what he did if he wasn't gay or fucked-up or both? And what kind of woman would put up with it?

Those questions had dogged us, silently and not so silently, ever since *Midnight Express*. To a certain extent they continue to this day, something that makes me wonder what Alexandra faces as she begins to go out into the world. It angered me, it still angers me— anger at Brad for doing what he did and opening that Pandora's box, anger at myself for not confronting our problems sooner, and anger at this industry that continued to suspect the worst of us even after Brad got sober and we had become parents.

But far less troubled people than Brad have seen their careers buffeted by rumor, specifically questions about their sexual orientation. John Travolta, Tom Cruise, Richard Gere, and Hugh Grant are only a few of the Hollywood stars, married or not, fathers or not, who have had to deal with that kind of speculation. Brad was small potatoes compared to those multimillion-dollar stars. No studio, no producer, no high-profile public relations agency was rushing to our defense. We were just trying to have as normal a life as possible—something that seemed increasingly unlikely—one that would allow Brad to work as long as he was able.

Given all that, I didn't need to guess the effect of a public confession of HIV in that rumor mill. Hollywood hands out its rewards with a grudging hand, but the toughest by far is not stardom but redemption. Brad was one of the damned. The only true way out of that purgatory was another box-office hit. The money was the least of it. A far more Darwinian principle was at work: if you're a star, they don't fuck with you. After all the years of gossip, that is what I longed for more than anything. But public knowledge of Brad's HIV status would put that forever beyond our reach.

That is the scenario I replayed in my mind those first days and weeks after I got the Cedars-Sinai letter, a tape loop of potential disaster. Whatever doubts I may have had about keeping his HIV status a secret were erased. But I still had my questions about how Brad had contracted the virus. I knew that ultimately it didn't matter. Brad was infected. We would make changes, we would adapt. We would do what we needed to do to survive. But it spoke to my needs as the spouse of an HIV-positive individual—needs that I was barely aware that I had—to determine, just for me, not for anyone else, which of Brad's actions, which behavior had brought him in closest contact with the AIDS virus.

So I began the painful reexamining of our life together, and under the harshest light possible. I began with the hustling I knew Brad had done during his early days in New York. Sex for money. With women. With men. I had known about this for some time. I didn't like it—who wouldn't feel hurt learning someone they loved had sold themselves that way—but I understood it, especially after I'd met Brad's parents and learned the stories of his sexually exploitative upbringing. But I also knew, and I mean I *knew* that the hustling, the sex with men, had stopped when Brad and I became involved. As far as I was concerned, that was no longer an issue.

I was less sanguine when dealing with all the affairs Brad had had since our marriage. Like many Hollywood wives, I could take some of these in stride. An actor on location . . . was usually how it began. The end result was usually the leading lady, an extra, or sometimes, call girls. As surprising as it sounds, even stars pay for sex—witness the Hugh Grant scandal with a streetwalker on Sunset Boulevard in the summer of 1995 or the Heidi Fleiss scandal in 1994, when many of the industry's biggest names were purportedly logged in the Yuppie Madam's little black book.

But some of Brad's affairs were more personal, and the knowledge of them cut me deeply. Many of them I didn't learn about until years after they had occurred, and some of them, I would not discover until after his death. But in thinking about Brad's sexual past, I went over some of his relationships in my mind, the women he had been close to at various times and with whom I suspected he may have had affairs—Rue McClanahan, his old off-Broadway costar and our first landlady in Los Angeles; Jeanne Moreau, his *Querelle* costar, in the same year I had been trying to get pregnant; among others. I didn't think any of them had anything to do with Brad's becoming HIV-positive. They were simply a sign of a deeply troubled marriage. But I had passed the point of analyzing the whys and wherefores of my relationship with Brad. It just was, for better or worse. This was about trying to understand the extent of a disease and possibly determining who else might be at risk.

And my thinking hardly stopped with Brad's sexual excesses, not with all the drugs he'd taken. I had never thought of him as a junkie, he didn't have the temperment for it, but I knew Brad had used needles. I never saw him put a needle in his arm. I never even saw needle marks. But I knew that he had, knew that he had shot cocaine—and God knows, whatever else—with Joey Tubens in 1979 during the shooting of *Small Circle of Friends*. He had used drugs for more than five years. He didn't get sober until 1981. Who really knew what he took, and how, during those years?

So those were my choices. Not great ones—I could literally pick my poison—but then they seldom are when it comes to AIDS. How could I be sure which one had given him the virus? For that I had to look at some of the AIDS research, the pathetic amount that existed in 1985. But even then it was known that the earliest documented cases in the United States occurred around 1978. That would seem to rule out Brad's hustling days in the late 1960s. What remained was heterosexual sex, most likely with prostitutes, and drug use.

But whichever was the cause, by 1979, Brad was almost certainly infected.

That year he came down with two attacks of herpes zoster, better known as shingles. Technically, it is an outbreak of the chicken pox virus that lives in almost all adults, but flares up only in those whose immune systems have become weakened. Brad had his first outbreak of shingles during the filming of *Small Circle*—a rash and a swelling so severe that filming was halted until he'd seen a doctor.

The second attack occurred about a month later, in late June after Brad had returned home from Boston. He'd complained of feeling run-down, and on the spur of the moment he decided to take an impromptu vacation and visit John Hurt on location in Montana where he was filming *Heaven's Gate.* Instead of a restful few days in Kalispell, however, Brad became ill. Another rash and swelling, this one distorting the whole left side of his face. Instead of returning home, Brad decided to fly to New York, to see a specialist there, Dr. Ron Grossman. It was one of the worst cases of shingles the doctor had ever seen. He told Brad he should be prepared to lose the sight in his left eye.

Brad was frightened. He spent the rest of the week in bed, holed up at the Park Sheraton on West Fifty-fifth Street. The only people he allowed to see him, besides the doctor and a terrified bellman who brought Brad his daily bottle of room-service vodka, were Larry and Kathleen. Kathleen Letterie said later that she thought Brad looked "like a monster."

Those two incidents, plus some swelling in his lymph nodes that he experienced during the run of *The Normal Heart,* were the only possible AIDS-related health issues Brad had experienced prior to his discovering he was HIV-positive. Depending on medical opinion, shingles, or some other illness, can signal the onset of HIV infection as recently as two to six weeks earlier. Or it may mean that infection has occurred years before, as in the case of Magic Johnson. He experienced an attack of shingles in the mid-1980s, years after it was thought that he had contracted HIV. As one doctor later told Brad, "Shingles isn't usually a primary viral symptom."

And where did that leave me? After all my inventorying, could I say with any certainty how Brad had contracted the virus? Or when?

It was not until later that year, when I learned that Joey Tubens had died of AIDS in May 1986, seven years after he'd shared needles with Brad, that I felt as if a curtain had been brought down on that question. I could say with a certain finality, "How did Brad become HIV-positive? I don't think we will ever really know."

CHAPTER

11

It seemed ironic, given all our bad news, but in January, just a month after I picked up the letter from Cedars, I found myself negotiating a deal for my first feature film—*Crimes of the Heart,* directed by Bruce Beresford from the Pulitzer Prize-winning play by Beth Henley. Amid a future now defined by HIV, I had somehow landed the biggest job of my career.

It felt almost obscene to be excited about a job, but given our decision not to go public with Brad's HIV infection, we felt we had a mandate to live our lives as normally as we could. And maybe it was for the best. If neither of us was prepared to actually look at our lives in terms of HIV—what it meant and would in all likelihood mean—then it was simply easier to be busy, to be consumed with our careers. In fact, that was how we would spend most of the next four years, until 1989 when Brad finally began to exhibit symptoms of AIDS.

And by any measure, *Crimes* was a plum job, not only my first feature, but a quality project and a chance to work with one of the hottest directors around. I had landed it through Toni Howard, Brad's agent at William Morris, who recommended me to the film's producer, Freddie Fields, her old boss and the founding partner with David Begelman of CMA, where I had worked for Stark. I had memories of Freddie from the weekly staff meetings at the agency, when he would sit there cold as ice while all the agents nervously blurted out their status reports. Now he was a fairly big producer in Hollywood. *Crimes* was his first film since leaving MGM in 1984 where he'd been head of production. He was looking for a TV casting director, he told Toni, who was desperate to break into features and would work for nothing.

By the time I finally met with Freddie over at his offices at MGM, he was his usual all-business self. "Should I hire this girl or what?" he barked into the phone at Toni while I sat there twiddling my thumbs in the hallway. It was like being a kid at the agency again. I knew he was screwing me on the money, but I didn't care. I was crazy for the job. I'd seen the original Broadway production in 1981 and had loved it. And Freddie was right—getting this would mean finally breaking into features casting. So I swallowed my pride and accepted his offer.

Even if *Crimes* hadn't been my first feature, it would still have been a great gig—a chance to work with the director of *Tender Mercies*. Bruce Beresford was Australian and something of a gentleman and an artist by Hollywood's usual standards. His first international hit had been *Breaker Morant* in 1981. Two years later, he'd landed his first Hollywood film, *Tender Mercies,* starring Robert Duvall. It was a big hit, well received and nominated for Best Picture. Suddenly, Bruce was a director everyone wanted to meet. By 1989, his direction of *Driving Miss Daisy* would win the Oscar for Best Picture.

But *Crimes* was only his second Hollywood production, which partly explained why Freddie and not Bruce hired me. In TV, the producer does most of the hiring, but in features, it's the director who calls the shots. But that January, Bruce was still in Australia— filming wasn't set to begin until April—and Freddie decided they needed a casting director. He and his partner, Burt Sugarman, had already lined up the three female stars Bruce wanted to play the Southern sisters: Diane Keaton, Jessica Lange, and Sissy Spacek. I was brought on to do the L.A. and New York casting, filling in the other principals, namely the role of Barnett, a good ole boy Southern lawyer, which is how Brad wound up auditioning for a film I was casting.

That February, I spent weeks looking for potential Barnetts. Bruce was coming into town that month and wanted to see several actors read. But after my first choices were rejected, I decided to suggest Brad.

I had never before mentioned him for any project I'd worked on. It seemed unethical to me. As if I were shilling for my husband. Certainly Brad had never looked to me for that. If anything, he'd gone the other way, virtually ignoring the films I cast. But now, this seemed different. Maybe it was the part. "Barnett's supposed to be Southern, short, and edgy, and Brad is all that, so why not?" I thought. Or maybe it was, unconsciously, a way of overcoming my fear that with HIV, Brad might not get work so easily now. Certainly, *Crimes* would have been his first feature job in six years, since his cameo in *Chariots of Fire*. Whatever my reasoning was, I broke my own rule and mentioned him to Bruce.

"But I hear he's an addict, a junkie, and an alcoholic," Bruce said. "I heard that in Australia."

"Well, I happen to be married to him and I know for a fact that he's been sober five years."

Bruce was enough of a gentleman to be embarrassed. "Well, in that case, we'd better see him."

To my surprise, Brad was actually up for it. I had thought he might pull some attitude, but he knew Bruce's reputation. Besides, he badly needed a diversion, not only from the HIV news, but also from some minor surgery, 120 hair transplants, he'd had done in January. I had urged him to cancel the procedure given everything else we were dealing with, HIV as well as his father's cancer surgery. "Why put yourself through all that agony now?" I told him. But Brad was dogmatic. He'd planned this months ago and had no intention of changing his plans. I suspected it was actually part of his resolve to act as if life were unchanged by an HIV infection. It was also, it turned out, the first opportunity Brad had since learning he was infected to lie to a doctor. He kept his HIV-positive status a secret from the surgeon, a decision that seems irresponsible given today's information about AIDS transmission, but which was not so clear-cut back then.

By the end of January, Brad was resting at home, taking Percodan for the pain, and wrestling with the guilt of violating, even under medical supervision, four years of sobriety. *Crimes* was the ideal diversion, I thought. But there was a catch. Brad would have to read. "They're reading everybody," I told him, "it has nothing to do with you."

Reluctantly he agreed. But then Freddie insisted that I read with Brad. "Don't make me do this," I pleaded with Freddie. "He's not good at auditions under the best of circumstances, and this will only make him worse."

But Freddie seemed to have some kind of agenda about my recommending Brad for the role, and this was his way of getting even. Brad was, of course, hysterical that I was going to be there, that I would be one of the ones judging his performance. I knew Brad hated casting directors the way he hated auditions. He thought we were an uncreative bureaucracy that kept actors from getting parts. "You're not an acting teacher, you have no education in this," he would say to me. "What gives you the license to say whether someone is right or wrong for a part?" It was another one of the little dances we did with our careers, the competitiveness that can come from working in the same business, one that is exacerbated by an actor's almost constant insecurity.

I really hoped for the best, but as I feared, Brad gave a horrible reading, one of the worst he'd ever had. I felt awful sitting there watching him, so stiff and so scared. Afterward, Brad was totally depressed about it, angry that he'd been humiliated again and that I had been there to see it. Bruce, however was wonderful. "Look, we could do another audition, do it another way, because I can see that he's a wonderful actor," he told me. "But, Susan, he's just too sexy for the part, too dangerous. You've got to tell him it isn't because of the audition."

In the end, Bruce wound up going with David Carpenter, a completely unknown actor whom I had seen on tape and showed to Bruce. *Crimes* at least was on its feet and I had my first screen credit.

But Brad was not rebounding well. It didn't help matters that that same month he lost out on another feature role, in Roger Donaldson's political thriller, *No Way Out,* starring Kevin Costner, Gene Hackman, and Sean Young. Brad was filming an episode of *Twilight Zone*—four days work for a paltry $3,808 after commission—when Toni called and said they wanted to see him for the role of the gay, psychotic aide to the secretary of defense, played by Hackman. Brad was intrigued but also ambivalent about the role. "As I said, 'no more gays,'" Brad wrote in his diary entry for February 13, 1986. "The more I look at my deepest feelings, the more I am committed to not playing another homosexual."

So he turned Roger down, something that annoyed me and Toni. Especially Toni Howard, who knew Brad's agency contract was up for renewal that month and wanted to go into the negotiations with something in her pocket. I just thought Brad was being stupid. It was one thing to try to reorient your career toward more mainstream roles, it was another thing to willfully turn down an audition on a major studio feature. "Get the job first," I told Brad, "then you can fine-tune the role."

Luckily, that also seemed to be Roger's thinking. If Brad would read for him and subsequently get the role, Roger would write out the homosexual aspect. It was enough of a concession to convince Brad to agree, albeit reluctantly, to another reading—a screen test actually since it was coming down to Brad and Will Patton. His diary entry for February 28 captured his mixed emotions:

"I woke up filled with joy, a miracle in itself, waking with joy on the day I am going to run the gauntlet. But the truth is, I knew it was going to be a success. . . . I wasn't able to get a perspective on my performance because I sweated and my mouth got very dry, but I knew the meeting—this lesson—was a perfect success because this is what God wanted me to do."

But the outcome was all too obvious in Brad's subsequent entry.

"Well, it appears that it is not God's will for me to do that part because they offered it to the other person," he wrote on March 6. "I'm tending to feel a bit lost in limbo now—not fully understanding what all this was about, what it means. As for the part, I truly felt that it was more mine, which baffles me a little. But I won't try and explain what I don't understand for I know that the truth will be revealed."

Truth, in this case, turned out to be a rather dismal little feature called *Heart*. It was a remake of some forties film noir about a prizefighter, written and directed by Jimmy Lemmo, an unknown filmmaker, and costarring the also then unknown Steve Buscemi. I thought the script was weak and that Brad's role as the down-and-out boxer was nothing special. But Brad was up for it, especially since, as in *Chariots of Fire*, he had to physically train for the role. I tried to take the long view. At least he was working again—$100,000 and two months on location in New York. Another diary entry, April 11, was written from the first-class cabin of his TWA flight to Kennedy: "I'm on my way to another job that I'm 100 percent excited about . . . and all it took was a 100 percent surrender to the will of God."

That year there would be many references to God, most of them recorded in his diary, some of them spoken aloud. Since any reference to God outside a profanity was a marked departure for Brad, I could trace this change to Brad's involvement in AA. But what began with simple sobriety, and the program's emphasis on reliance on a higher power, had become a full-blown metaphysical search. Ever since he'd started seeing his spiritualist—his weekly Monday-night appointments—in February 1985, ten months before he learned he was HIV-positive, Brad had gotten completely into crediting God with guiding his life.

On one level, I was glad he'd found something that provided him a measure of equanimity. But I was less crazy about all this "thy will be done" business, especially when it was coming from his spiritualist, a charlatan in my mind, who seemed to practice a concoction of religion, therapy, and philosophy of her own design. I was hard-pressed to share Brad's enthusiasm for willfully passive responses to bad news whether it was an HIV infection or a job loss.

I had never been a big believer in God. Even if I had been, I'm not sure his power would have extended as far as Hollywood. In my eyes, the town was a brutally self-interested business where impressions, reputation, and buzz can matter far more than actual talent and ability. I thought Brad's career—both the hype he had experienced after *Midnight Express* and the pariah he'd become with his drinking and drug taking—was proof of that, and it disturbed me that he seemed to be taking this hands-off-the-wheel-let-God-provide attitude.

But there wasn't much I could do about it. I had learned long ago that I, at least, couldn't tell Brad anything. Not about his career anyway, especially not after the debacle of his *Crimes* audition, which he still blamed me for. So I just let it go. At least he was busy. If the projects weren't that great, well, it was Toni's problem now and, I suppose, his spiritualist's. They could deal with Brad's career.

Besides, it was getting awkward for me to weigh in with advice and questions about his various film possibilities when I was so busy and obviously having the best year of my career. In all my years as an agent, I had never achieved any real distinction. But now, after six years as a casting director, working first with Marsha and then on my own, I was finally getting some recognition—consistent work and some fairly prestigious projects.

That spring, I was casting not only my first feature film, but I was also juggling a number of projects for CBS. I had started work on *Foley Square*, the Diane English comedy, for the network earlier in November. Because Jean Guest, the head of casting at CBS, liked my work, the network offered me a big project, *I'll Take Manhattan*, an eight-hour miniseries based on the Judith Krantz novel. Although the lead was already in place when I signed on in April—Valerie Bertinelli—literally dozens of roles, English and American, needed to be filled, with location casting to be done in Canada. It was a huge job and my first exclusive, which meant that I couldn't take another job until July.

For the next several months, and really for the rest of the year, my life seemed to be defined by an endless round of scouting trips, mostly to New York but frequently on location. That year, I felt I was gone more than I was home. With Brad also away for weeks at a time, it seemed as if we were connected only by Alexandra, our nightly phone calls to her from our respective cities.

To cast *I'll Take Manhattan*, I spent a week in New York—one of the rare times when my trip coincided with Brad's shooting schedule—just making the rounds. I was out at the theater at night—*Hamlet* starring Kevin Kline, *House of Blue Leaves* with John Mahoney, *Loot* with Alec Baldwin—and then interviewing dozens of actors during the day, including Alec, Kathy Baker, Phoebe Cates, Kate Mulgrew, Ken Olin, Kelly Lynch, Patricia Wettig, Laura Dern, Andy Garcia, Keanu Reeves.

It's hilarious, looking at the list now, remembering the reaction I got from the producer, Steve Krantz, and director Richard Michaels. Kathy Baker was "too unattractive." Alec Baldwin "was a bit of a stiff," and on and on. It was a Judith Krantz movie, for God's sake. But I was finding that so typical. As the casting director, I'd recommend people and the producers would pass, and two years later, you couldn't get the actors they were so big. For example, I thought Andy Garcia would be perfect for the miniseries, but no, Steve wanted to go with Jack Scalia, who was, yes, very pretty, but who could not act anywhere near as well.

The pressure only got worse when in July I was asked to help launch *A Different World,* the *Cosby* spin-off that was to star Lisa Bonet. I was working on another CBS miniseries, *At Mother's Request,* which required me to be on location in Utah a fair amount, but when I got the call from Tom Werner and Marcy Carsey, the producers of *Cosby,* well, when Carsey-Werner called, you answered.

Tom and Marcy had been two garden-variety network executives before they joined forces as producers. The phenomenal success of *Cosby,* which served as NBC's flagship show for eons, had put them on the map. In 1987, Carsey-Werner had become one of TV's hottest shops, the producers of *Roseanne,* and the soon-to-come *Grace Under Fire, Cybill,* and *Third Rock From the Sun.*

It was my first experience of working with real heavyweights in television. Little did I realize the nightmare I was in for.

Despite my frustrations with Carsey-Werner, I knew I was working at a much higher level than I ever had. By December 1986, I would have had my most successful year ever. I would have broken into feature films, cast seven major television projects, and made over $200,000, far more than I had ever made as an agent—a figure that pushed our income, for the first time since we'd moved to Los Angeles, over $1 million. In our first year of living with HIV, we had made $1 million, and I had to ask myself, Which fact mattered more?

On the face of it, it would seem that I had accomplished one of my long-sought goals—a comfortable, if not entirely steady, income. And given where I had started, earning $225 a week answering phones for Stark, it seemed an amazing figure and something of a milestone for Brad and me. But another one of Hollywood's little secrets is how irrelevant ordinary standards of wealth are. If Brad and I had still been in New York, $1 million would have seemed like a fortune, even with agents' commissions, and we could have lived on it for years. But in L.A., $1 million was a few poker chips. We weren't players in the true sense of the word. And we knew it. In reality, we were simply two of the legions of people who make up the bottom of the Hollywood iceberg. While the Tom Hankses and Sylvester Stallones and the Demi Moores of the world fight for their few minutes on top, the rest of us struggle on below.

I'm not being snobby when I say it is difficult for someone not working in Hollywood—a "non-pro" as *Variety* likes to put—to grasp that discrepancy. It took me years to learn it. Despite the growing public awareness of weekend box-office grosses and the salaries commanded by top stars, few people outside the business really understand the line that separates the haves and the have-nots as Hollywood defines them.

Very infrequently does that distinction become public—as with Art Buchwald's lawsuit filed against Paramount for a percentage of the profits of *Coming to America,* the Eddie Murphy film that he helped write, or Winston Groom's similar suit against the studio for a share of the hundreds of millions generated by the film adaptation of his book *Forrest Gump.* Only in these few instances does the curtain sufficiently part for the public to see that, in Oz, the really big money goes into a very few hands. Despite the mythic perception that Hollywood is paved with gold—that famous Herman Mankiewicz telegram, "Millions are to be made here. Your only competition is idiots"—the reality is that with the exception of those elite stars and directors commanding a hefty percentage of a film's gross profits, everyone else fights for his or her every dollar.

Ironically, even the studios cry poorhouse, since far more cash is regularly generated by their television and music divisions than films.

So we'd made $1 million, but like so many people in the business, we had shockingly little to show for our record-breaking year. Although we treated ourselves to two new cars that we needed—a Mercedes for me and a Jaguar for Brad, to replace the battered Jeep that he'd bought in 1979—that was the extent of our indulgence. Most of our income was still going to pay off debt, back taxes, Zane's fees, credit cards, veterinary bills—all those things that add up when you don't have a regular cash flow.

We also had Brad's parents' mortgage to pay every month. It wasn't much, but the principle of the thing angered me—paying their mortgage when we were still renters ourselves. After ten years in Los Angeles, we had never managed to come up with a down payment. Maybe it was my New York sensibilities, that perpetual lease syndrome. Or maybe it was Brad's fear of becoming totally bourgeois, a middle-class homeowner with a lawn to mow. Or maybe it was simply our chronic inability to manage our money. Whatever it was, it wasn't until our future seemed suddenly hemmed in by HIV that we decided we needed our own home.

I had actually started looking for a house a year earlier. Brad was in New York doing *The Normal Heart,* while I was at home trying to raise a two-year-old in a run-down rental. Suddenly, I was just fed up. I wanted a house I could fix up the way we needed now that we had a baby. I was also sick of dealing with our landlady, actress E. J. Peaker. After five years living on Teesdale, every plumbing problem, every broken appliance, had become grounds for a classic landlord-tenant battle. It was as if she were a part of the family. I just wanted out.

So I scoured the Valley. I knew it was hot and smoggy and living there was the antithesis of chic. But Brad and I liked it, especially now that we had a child. Its tacky normalcy, its unvarnished middle-classness appealed to us more than the shrill, striving Westside. Within a few weeks of looking, I found a good-sized house with a pool, a huge backyard, and a tiered lawn on a cul-de-sac a couple miles away in North Hollywood. It was $400,000, which doesn't seem so much now, but at the time it was the upper limit of our price range. Somehow I managed to convince Brad that this was it. We scraped together the earnest money and went into escrow.

But then Brad's father called. Not for the first time, Brad's parents needed money. I couldn't believe the timing. But then again, I had never been able to believe how Brad remained such a soft touch for them. Instead of buying our house, we bought his parents' house in Tallahassee. It was something I would resent for years, even after we eventually bought our house on Rhodes.

We stayed at Teesdale for another year. This time, Brad got the bug to move out. Now that he knew he was HIV-positive, he was anxious to get out of E.J.'s house and into our own place where we could batten down the hatches if things got rough. Brad was even more concerned about our privacy than I was. That spring, before he left to do *Heart* in New York, he began roaming the neighborhood. It took him all of a weekend to find it, a three-bedroom fixer-upper just a few blocks from where we lived in Studio City.

"This is it," he said, calling me at the office that afternoon. "We've got to see it tonight, before they put it on the market."

I was dubious. The house didn't have any of the things that I thought we'd agreed on, amenities such as extra bedrooms and a new kitchen. But it was cheap, less than the $275,000 we had to spend, and I let Brad drag me over to see it. Of course, I loathed it. It was everything I was hoping to escape—a cramped, pool-less, non-air-conditioned box—with no more room or style than what we were living in.

"Look, let's rent another year and maybe we can save enough to get a house we really want," I pleaded with him.

But that ship had sailed in his mind. Like his proposal of marriage, it was this or nothing. Two days before he left for New York on April 11, we passed the initial set of papers. The down payment was carved from the last of Brad's *American Cousin* money, and we would use his $100,000 fee from *Heart* to redo the house that summer.

We did not move in until August 30. What was supposed to give us a sense of security had resulted in months of chaos. First it was the nightmare of dealing with Zane and the banks—he had a horrible time getting us a mortgage because our credit was so bad— and then months of renovation work, new paint, carpet, bathrooms, and a kitchen, which was total hit-or-miss given how much Brad and I were away that year. At one point we didn't have a bathroom in the house, just one of those portable, plastic outhouses parked in our backyard. As Brad noted in his diary as late as November 4, the work was still not finished.

"It always seems to take me time to adjust to the bumps of being back home in L.A.," he wrote after his return home that fall from shooting *Hitchhiker,* an HBO movie, in Vancouver. "Everything bugged me, the sloppy work on the house, the sloppy painters, this not finished, that not finished, and my career."

That was the irony: in the midst of all our busyness, our relentlessly life-is-normal-even-with-HIV front, Brad was slowly realizing that his career wasn't happening. At least not in the way he wanted. After the optimism he'd felt working on *Chiefs* and *RFK,* Brad had drifted into doing kitsch just to keep the money coming in. Although that September, *American Cousin* would win first prize at the Venice Film Festival for Best Television Movie, tied for first place with an Ingmar Bergman made-for-TV film, it was the only bright spot in a year otherwise filled with forgettable projects—*Heart,* which he filmed in New York that spring, *Vengeance,* a CBS movie he shot in Jacksonville in July, and *Hitchhiker* for HBO, which he filmed in Vancouver in October. Like many actors, Brad also devoted a lot of time to two films that would never make it into production, *Intercept,* an Italian film that had Brad spending a month in Rome in September, and *September Song,* written by Stan Jones, Brad's screenwriting friend from AA, an aborted project that would ultimately break up their friendship.

That year, Brad's career was the crisis, not HIV. I saw it, Toni saw it, even Brad sensed it. Despite the various contracts and start dates and first-class air tickets, he was becoming increasingly marginal as an actor. It's a tough point in an actor's career, one that is usually fixed in one of two ways—swinging for the fences and hoping for a box-office hit, or the slow but steady climb back with small but acclaimed supporting roles.

Brad was clearly angling for the big hit. He wanted out of TV and low-budget features, so he was constantly on Toni Howard at William Morris to push the agency's feature division to put him up for big-budget projects. If they wouldn't do it, he said, then he would have to think about leaving the agency.

But Toni knew the score. She knew the features division was uninterested in Brad, that his name had no box-office appeal. He hadn't done a mainstream feature since *Chariots*, and that had been just a cameo. She knew that if Brad had any hope of coming back, she had to convince him that the slow-but-steady route was the only option. And that would mean big, painful changes—acting classes, auditioning, small parts.

It was everything Brad had hated, and now that he knew he was HIV-positive, he was even less interested in the slow-but-steady route. Literally, there wasn't the time. Not now. His meeting with Toni on November 4, after his return from *Hitchhiker*, was predictably fractious. "No more big movies, great parts," he wrote in his diary that day. "My agent basically telling me that I was going to have to settle for so-so parts to get back into movies—and then Susan agreeing with her. I felt like I was being slapped every way I turned."

It's no wonder that Brad had earlier recorded in his journal his dream that Eddie Bondy had come back. "Tuesday night when I was so depressed, I dreamed Eddie B came to me," he wrote in September during his trip to Rome for *Intercept*. "I sobbed and sobbed on his shoulder, crying and saying how much I missed him. He was the most loving he'd ever been, divinely so, and telling me everything was going to be fine and not to worry."

But Brad was worried. Despite his meditation, his meetings with his spiritualist, all his efforts to reconcile his life with God's plan, he was already feeling the strains of coping with HIV. The rest of that day's journal entry addressed, for the first time, the deeper unease that both of us were feeling: "To all outward appearances there seemed to be nothing really wrong. Everything was really ok, but inside I felt tortured."

Reluctant as I was to admit it, that sense of torture was the reality of both our lives. On the surface, everything appeared to be fine.

We were healthy—Brad even quit smoking that month, on November 6, 1986, his thirty-seventh birthday—we were working, we had money, we had our house. But underneath it all we were as unhappy, even frightened, as we had ever been. Despite a lack of overt symptoms, HIV was already taking its toll. As the final paragraph of his diary entry read:

"Last night I got into bed, lay there a little while, and all I could get out was 'Okay, Father, show me what to do with this.' Practically no sooner than I had said it Susan turned over and started feeling for me to see if I was there. When she felt my arm, she said, 'Would you hold me?' And we held each other in bed for the first time in at least a year and a half, probably longer."

You never know how much time you will be given, but you think that in times of challenge, you will take the high road, that you will respond with compassion and love and a maturity that perhaps you didn't even know you had. In your mind, you will be like Job. You will ponder, question the fates, but you will never curse, never accuse, never fall weeping onto the ash heap.

I had hoped I would be like that. After all, hadn't I lived through the horror of Brad's early days—the alcohol, the drugs, the womanizing, the running out in the middle of the night to score, the hideous scenes in public, the drunk driving, the jail cells—with a measure of dignity? Despite the awfulness, the fights, hadn't I stayed? And more than that, hadn't I thrived? Look at my marriage, my career, my child. HIV could hardly be more of a challenge than what I had already lived through. I would succeed and triumph again. My only struggles would be private ones, hidden even from Brad.

But what I was not prepared to see was how different this time was. In its most abstract form, disease is faceless, irrational. Cancer, diabetes, multiple sclerosis. It happens. Who's to blame? The victim? Could they have done something different, done something to stay fate's hand? Part of our makeup as human beings is our need to rationalize, to assign cause and effect to our existence, and when necessary to affix blame. When Brad had been drinking, it was so obvious. He was doing this. He was at fault. But now that he was HIV-positive, it was far less clear.

Or was it? I had no way of knowing, but already the seeds were being sown. More than any other disease of the twentieth century, AIDS would test the limits of the public's ability to remain compassionate toward its victims. It would become the modern equivalent of the bubonic plague. And in my own house, I had already succumbed to that attitude. No, I was not succeeding in my efforts to cope with the disease. I was failing, and in the most unforgivable of ways. I was trying to punish Brad.

I could rationalize it, tell you that picking up that letter from Cedars was what triggered my delayed-stress syndrome, my return to all the rage that I'd had toward Brad, the rage that I thought I'd put aside when he got sober and when I had become pregnant. Now, instead of a happy, normal household, my life was an endless series of losses—the loss of any more children, the loss of family, loss of intimacy, and on the deepest level, loss of sexuality. I felt all that, and instead of blaming HIV, I chose to blame Brad. And in that regard, I was far more guilty than he had ever been.

Later, I would deeply regret my behavior. I would look back and wish that I had been a better wife, more in love with Brad, or simply more kind, because what I did not yet know was that those days, those weeks, when I gave free reign to my anger and my self-pity would be the only time that HIV would not physically rule our days. But at the time, I felt as if I had no choice but to turn away.

I knew where Brad was most vulnerable, where any human being is most vulnerable. But I chose to withdraw. I was busy, I was unavailable, physically and emotionally, to the man who needed me more now than he had ever needed me. We still shared the same bed. We didn't have another room. But literally, for months and months, for almost two years after we learned he was infected, I could not bear to be touched by him or anyone else. I was simply not there.

Instead, I threw myself into my work. No wonder my career flourished. That year it was my life. I also got very involved in my therapy. I'd been seeing Gaylan on and off since December 1984, but now I had a standing appointment on Saturdays. In fact, the whole day was now my day. I had a sitter until four-thirty, and I spent the day on my own, my Overeaters Anonymous meeting in the morning, then my appointment with Gaylan—she was the only one I told about Brad's HIV status—and then I would go to a movie.

Not only did I now have a day that was mine, but I also took over a room at home for my exclusive use. Brad had always been the one who got to co-opt the extra bedroom. Now it was my turn to commandeer the den. Officially it was my office, but in reality it was like a private living room where I could make phone calls, read my trades, just do what I wanted to do, alone.

Brad would try to break that rule. "I like your office," he said when I came home and found him sprawled all over the room. "I don't want to sit out in the cold alone." But this was my space. This was mine. And I threw him out. But none of this, not the therapy, not my day alone, not my office, was the battleground that our bedroom was.

No one was more surprised than I was that I had become completely cold to the man with whom I had had the best sex of my life. When we were younger, we had sex three and four times a day. For days and days. When you're a kid, this seems like freedom. An endless opportunity to fuck.

But after we had been married for a few years, I realized I was angry about the constant pressure to have sex. Brad had an insatiable need: if he couldn't have sex four times a day, he masturbated. Or he found someone else to fuck. I realized sex wasn't about romance or love or even intimacy. It was about control, about Brad using me to satisfy a compulsion. I had become a drug. In the crudest of terms, I felt like my vagina was Brad's drug.

Even before I knew he was HIV infected, my physical withdrawal from Brad had begun. As he noted in his journal, our sex life had pretty much come to a halt more than a year before. I told myself it was the unfortunate result of Alexandra's birth, and our conflicting schedules. But in reality, it was all the unresolved physical revulsion I felt toward Brad left over from his drinking days, all his sexual excesses. But now that I had done so much therapy, I was at the point of rationally telling Brad, "I'm not going to have sex now because this is about control, not love, so don't talk to me about it, don't bug me about it. I need to go to bed at night without fearing that I will be awakened in my sleep, pounced on, literally."

I was at that point when I found out he was HIV-positive. From that moment, our sex life was never, ever the same.

I honestly don't remember if we had sex in New York and Florida that first Christmas that we were together after we had heard from Cedars. I only remember the conversation we had, over the phone, I think, when Brad was still in Rome. We spoke about condoms, told each other that that's what we would use. It was something we had never done, since I had always used an IUD or a diaphragm. But that was our decision. No more unprotected sex. That was that. It was easy to see why HIV didn't come up much in conversation those first few years. We weren't having sex. What was there to discuss?

There were times, in the beginning of his diagnosis, when we tried to have sex with a condom. I remember one time when we came close, when I thought we could actually do this. But I also remember thinking that it was the most frightening experience of my life. The condom could come off, it could break, and then what? Another AIDS test. Months of waiting and then another test and another until I felt certain I wasn't infected. But what if I was? I couldn't do it. I tried but I couldn't.

So we just didn't. Not again, not ever. I learned that that's the way you make a momentous, inexorable decision, one day at a time. I know Brad wanted to, that he wanted to be close—not in a careless or casual way because he was concerned about my staying healthy and about Alexandra's staying healthy. But he would have continued to have sex. I was the one who was too afraid. Or maybe, I was using my fear as a way to justify my anger, all the anger that I now had toward sex. On this one issue especially, I wish I'd had someone to talk to, someone to ask, How do you love someone who has HIV?

But I didn't have anyone, no one who could tell me what I would soon learn, that loving an HIV-infected person involved so much more than a forced separation of bodily fluids.

That was, in fact, proving to be the easy part, changing the house around, living in a house with two separate sides, separate everything—separate sinks, separate toothpaste and brush, separate sides of the medicine cabinet. We got to the point when we didn't even use the same shampoo. With Alexandra we simply said, "That's Daddy's, don't touch. That's Daddy's glass, get another one." With friends, Brad was careful to simply get another glass, another fork, without calling attention to it.

Later, we would get a box of plastic gloves and keep them in a drawer in the house in case Brad was severely cut. We didn't pay particular attention to the Centers for Disease Control recommendations, but we did think about that. Like the time that fall when Brad cut himself shaving and he picked up Alexandra to kiss her and I motioned him to put her down. Brad didn't like that, didn't like being reminded to take care of other people.

"It's on the other side of my face," he said.

"But you have to take care of that," I said to him, quietly because I didn't want Alexandra to notice. I didn't want anyone to notice that we now lived in a house that was, however subtly, divided.

It would take me almost two years before I learned how to cross that divide. It moves me beyond measure to remember that Brad was waiting for me, the way he had waited for me so long ago, that day in Stark's office when I had told him I didn't want to see him anymore, but he just sat there, smiling at me, with that stuffed squirrel peeking out of his pocket. As he wrote in his diary on January 27, 1987:

"I just want to make a note here of appreciation for my wife and the power working through her so lovingly for her highest good and for mine. I have been lamenting the fact that of late we haven't been, or aren't, physically affectionate with each other and wondering how to go about telling her I think we should just touch and hold each other more. We were in the den the other night when I heard, 'Brad, would you hold me?' and there was Susan sitting on the couch holding out her arms to me. We sat there hugging and all I could think was, 'Thank you, God.'"

CHAPTER

12

On January 6, 1987, the first month of our second year of HIV, Brad wrote in his diary:

"Well, volumes have passed since my last entry . . . But let's pause a moment and take a broader look. In the past year, I have made more money than in any other year of my life, some art, some good TV. It meant a Mercedes for Susan and a Jaguar for me. And a big lesson in what? Transformation? Transcending? In getting out there and just doing it? Whatever the truth is, I know it will be revealed. Susan, Alexandra, and I have radiant health and an abundance of everything that we need. My lessons have been gentle and the results perfect."

Despite Brad's optimism, however, 1987 would prove to be our loss of innocence. This was the year we started to get the picture—when the whole country started to get the picture—that we were not going to get out of this. There wasn't going to be any escape. This wasn't like Brad's alcohol and drug problems. There wasn't going to be any recovery from HIV.

Little by little that year our world began to close in. Like that morning in September when you realize, suddenly, summer has gone. In a single night, the planets have slipped. The shadows are longer, the sun is now cold, and you feel time tightening its grip. That's how 1987 was for us.

That year, across the county, the shadow cast by HIV grew slowly but inexorably larger. In 1987, those people who had become infected in 1979 began to develop full-blown AIDS. It was no longer possible to consider HIV as a static or resting state. It was a disease, slow death, the gradual but certain failure of the body's immune system.

It was a huge change in the country's attitude. Only the year before, in 1986, the Centers for Disease Control (CDC) had estimated that approximately 20–30 percent of those who tested positive for HIV might develop AIDS. By 1988, the CDC would revise its estimates—99 percent of HIV-infected persons would develop AIDS, with a mean incubation period of less than eight years. And they would report an even more ominous statistic: no reported cases of recovery from HIV.

Even if I had wanted to hide myself from news of HIV, I couldn't. That was no longer possible. Literally every day, in magazines, newspapers, on TV, the flood of stories about AIDS was relentless. And not only statistics, but graphic stories about the diseases now directly attributable to AIDS, diseases such as pneumonia, heart failure, and worse, which were killing people by the thousands.

This would be the year that Larry Kramer started ACT-UP, his New York–based activist organization. This would be the year when President Reagan would make his first speech about AIDS, when he publicly mentioned for the first time the ninety thousand AIDS-related deaths the CDC had tallied so far.

And this would be the year when the fear and paranoia about AIDS began to explode. Even at work, which had been my haven from anything outside the neurotic, insular world of Hollywood, I was hearing now AIDS was starting to cut a swath among friends and colleagues. It was simply a part of every conversation now, part of the Hollywood gossip, the way cocaine had been in the seventies. Howard, my old pal from Gersh, would call with stories of friends who were "sick" as he put it, people we both knew who were dying.

Yes, it was gossip. It was also terrifying. People were dying. But I also knew that one day, despite our best efforts, one of those "sick" friends that everyone talked about was going to be Brad.

I knew it now because this was the year when the first signs of the disease began to show up at home, in the bathroom and in the kitchen. Not symptoms exactly, but little things. His skin began to bother him, and his weight. It wasn't that he was thinner, but it was the way he ate now, all the time, eating huge amounts and two and three desserts a night, three helpings of peach cobbler with coffee Häagen-Dazs. Eating like that but never gaining any weight.

It felt as if I were living with an alcoholic again. You couldn't say anything, not yet, but you watched everything, you saw everything when you wanted to see nothing at all.

By the end of that year, I would have given up any hope. It would no longer be a question of if, but of when. I knew Brad would get very, very sick. And I realized, for the first time, that we would have to get a doctor. But not yet. It would be months, in fact three more years, before we reached out for medical help, before we could admit, even to a doctor, that Brad had HIV. That was what our secrecy would cost us. Years of help. By the time we reached out, it would already be too late.

But that was months, years away, and for most of 1987, life seemed much as it had been. That January, while Brad was expressing gratitude for our health and well-being, I was starting my first executive job, heading the casting department of TriStar's new television division. I'd never held a corporate casting job. My whole career was freelance. This was a real job, senior management with a staff and an office in the studio's headquarters over in Century City, and a million other candidates were better qualified than me.

But Scott Siegler, president of the studio's new TV division, and Phyllis Glick, head of creative affairs, really wanted me. She convinced me that this was the job for me. It wasn't that corporate, she told me. It was only for pilot season and I didn't even need to be exclusive. During the summer hiatus, I would be free to take other jobs, including working with the studio's feature division. All of that was hugely attractive. That and the salary they were willing to pay me. Tom Hoberman, the lawyer I got to negotiate my contract, told them, "You're looking at a woman who made two hundred thousand dollars as an independent casting agent. You're going to have to match that." By January, I had officially joined corporate Hollywood.

For the next twelve months, I experienced life on the inside, life as a "suit." I had no idea how different it would be. Not only was it completely different from freelance casting, but it was completely different from agenting. As a casting director on a project, you are still an employee. As an agent, your whole motive is to get someone else to write a check. Working at a studio meant having the checkbook. For the first time in my career, I was the one with power, I was the one doling it out—jobs, money, the chance to work on a pilot, a series. It wasn't about asking, it was about being in charge. And I was shocked, really surprised, that I didn't love it more than I did.

On the face of it, it should have been a perfect year. I was making good money, great money in fact, and it came in regular paydays, so for the first time Brad and I had a steady income. I was busy, but it wasn't crazy, not like some previous years. I had nine pilots to cast in four months, but I had help, a staff. And the shows were fun. I hadn't done that many sitcoms, and it was great to work with people like Paul Reiser, a young stand-up comic making his first series, *My Two Dads,* the forerunner to his hit series, *Mad About You,* costarring Helen Hunt. I was also working on several films that year.

So what was my problem? Some of it was just the whole idea of being part of a company rather than working for myself. Working out of the studio's offices on Century Park East brought back my days in New York working for Stark at CMA. The weekly staff meetings, the whole idea of being obligated, responsible to a company, to a boss. It was so different from what I had grown used to as a freelancer.

But mostly it had to do with Brad. Maybe if he hadn't been infected, it would have been different. But entering the corporate side of Hollywood turned out to be too hard on Brad and

Alexandra. I didn't know it yet, but the job would become a threat to the fragile balance we maintained at home.

Like any working mother with a four-year-old, I was torn with guilt. Most days, I left early in the morning, before Brad was even up. And most days, I didn't get home until early in the evening, long after Alexandra had eaten her dinner. It became clear to all of us that Doris, our housekeeper, was raising our daughter. She spent the day with Alexandra, she gave her her meals. "Mommy, you're never here," Alexandra would tell me at night when I dragged myself in the door, loaded down with scripts and the trades, an evening's worth of reading and then some. "Mommy," she'd say in her little voice, "when are you staying home?"

I know every working mother experiences that guilt. But it didn't stop with my child. It was Brad, too. It was obvious to both of us that my career had real momentum now while he was still struggling. My working at TriStar meant in the midst of all his struggles with HIV, Brad had to add jealousy to his list. All those mornings when I rushed out the door, dressed in a suit, earrings, and carrying a briefcase, I left Brad sprawled in bed with rumpled sheets, clothes strewn everywhere, trades in a heap on the floor. That was the start to his days and it only added to my guilt.

It was almost a relief at the end of the year when the studio sold the division to Columbia, a precursor to the de facto merger between the two studios when Sony bought them out and moved them to the old MGM lot in Culver City. Because Columbia's TV division was larger than TriStar's, I was redundant. But I went out in a blaze of glory, released from my contract with a second full year of salary as a consultant.

There was never any question of looking for another studio job. Within a few weeks, I had set up shop on Radford across from CBS in Studio City, not far from where Brad had first gone to his AA meetings. I would keep that office for five years. I would still have it even after Brad was no longer alive.

That year, while I buried myself at TriStar, Brad was struggling with his career. It was the long slog that any actor faces when he is no longer hot. Hanging in there, hoping something will pop. Brad was trying to get back some of the cautious optimism he'd had when he'd done *Chiefs* and *RFK* three years before. But his diaries that year are filled with that inevitable rhythm—the buildup over a job possibility, the subsequent fear about the audition, and then the inevitable disappointment. "I need to understand more," he wrote again and again as he sought to come to terms with the ebbing tide of his career. "I need to understand God's plan for me."

And I know he didn't get it. He'd become a star by flouting all the rules, a nobody in a nothing film. Now, he was trying desperately to play the game. He was sober, a father, willing to start over—TV, character roles, all of it after having been a leading man. For a while, in the first flush of sobriety and Alexandra's birth and Eddie's involvement and the whole "Hey, Brad Davis is back" buzz, it seemed as if he might just make it. But after Eddie died, before Brad had really clinched a comeback with a box-office or ratings smash, he'd started to sink again. Without Eddie, it was as if he'd lost his direction, his faith in himself. He still had Toni at William Morris, and for one disastrous year he would have Todd Smith over at CAA—a desperate move on Brad's part, as if attaching himself to that fabled acronym would change everything. But the light had really gone out of him; HIV or no HIV, stardom was receding faster and faster. That year, our world closed in on us in more than one way.

Of course, I had my own ideas about how to fix Brad's career. As a casting director, I had seen too many actors—actors on their way up, on their way down, actors struggling to make a comeback—not to have an opinion. To me it was no different from his alcoholism. If Brad wanted to get back on track, he had to participate in his recovery just as he'd done with AA. As far as I was concerned, that meant virtually starting over: acting classes, workshops, auditioning for anything and everything. Forget the size of the part, Brad just needed to get working again.

But I also knew he needed a strategy. Like Eddie, Toni and I realized that TV was Brad's best chance, the market where his name still had some marquee value. Later, he could try features again, with small, carefully chosen roles.

But illusions die hard in Hollywood. Particularly self-illusions. It was easier for Brad to dream about hitting one out of the park than to face the reality of having to slowly work his way back into Hollywood's good graces. As Brad wrote in his journal that January 1987:

"I got a sign tonight that a seed I had planted two months ago has taken root. In late November, I sent out a strong thought to David Putnam [sic] to call me with the perfect movie—that the movie that would bring me back would come from David. Tonight, Susan said someone had told her that Ed Lamata [sic] had a meeting with David in which he told Ed that he owed me a favor for Chariots of Fire and was looking for a script at Columbia for me. I desire, demand, the right part in the right film—abundant in every way from my highest good—presented to me through David Putnam, Now!"

While he waited for David to move mountains for him, Brad also did what every other actor desperate about his career does. He started developing scripts. If no one was coming to him with great roles, then he would come up with them himself. He could have gone to any number of people. But Brad did what he always did. He went to someone who was halfway in love with him, Stan Jones, his old AA friend.

Like Brad, Stan was trying to revive his career now that he was sober. Although I had my suspicions about Stan, I had to admit he had talent as a writer, the lack of produced scripts notwithstanding. Stan thought, as many screenwriters do, that if he could attach Brad to one of his scripts, it would help get it optioned. I thought it was a long shot, but I kept my opinions to myself. All during the fall of 1986, Brad and Stan had worked on September Song. As Brad noted in his diary that November: "I read [Stan's] new script tonight. I love it without reservation. I wanted some kind of career sign (of freedom) before my birthday. Freedom within my career. A sign of re-entry into movies, marking me as a highly valuable, much desired contribution to movies. After I finished reading the script, it occurred to me that this could be it."

Not only was it not it, but it led to a fractious falling out between them when *September Song* nearly derailed Brad's next job, *When the Time Comes,* an ABC movie about assisted suicide directed by John Erman.

Although John had been one of the original directors on *Roots,* he and Brad had not worked on the same segment, and they didn't actually meet until several years later, when John was directing a television version of *Streetcar Named Desire* with Ann-Margret. Marsha, my old partner, was the casting director, and she suggested they call in Brad. He went into the reading with Helen Mirren, and for once in his life he'd done all right. Although he was clearly not right to play Stanley to Ann-Margret's Blanche, John was impressed with Brad's acting. He cast Treat Williams in *Streetcar,* but John later told Brad that it had been that audition that got him the role in *When the Time Comes.*

Although it wasn't a theatrical feature, Brad was keen to do the film. Part of that had to do with John, and how he made it clear that Brad was his first choice to play the difficult role of the man who helps his terminally ill friend to die. There was no audition, no reading. Just the offer and then lunch to talk over the film. It was in December, while I was negotiating my deal at Tristar, that Brad met with John, a gray day, but as John remembered it, Brad looked wonderful, driving up in his bottle-green Jaguar and looking like a million bucks in his black Italian overcoat, tweed jacket, and his scarf. Brad always wore a scarf in those days, the successor to his omnipresent suspenders. In Hollywood, clothes sometimes do make the man. John and Brad spent two hours huddled at the Hamburger Hamlet in Beverly Hills, talking about the script and the whole subject of death and euthanasia.

John knew it was going to be a difficult film, not only to make but to sell. In 1986, the whole idea of assisted suicide was not the pressing social issue it is today with Dr. Jack Kevorkian and the various state ballot initiatives. Who knew that within ten years it would become a viable option for many terminally ill people, especially AIDS patients. Back then, euthanasia was seen in Hollywood as one of the more depressing diseases-of-the-week. And even though *When the Time Comes* had been written by Bill Hanley, who had won an Emmy for writing *Something About*

Amelia, the ABC movie about incest that starred Glenn Close and Ted Danson, John and Sherry Lansing, his coproducer, had had a tough time getting the network to green-light *When the Time Comes.* Nobody at ABC was thrilled about the potential ratings for a movie about suicide, and clearly the aftermarket sales were weak. The budget for it was minuscule.

But John was passionate. He was a close friend of Betty Rollin's and had watched her go through an assisted suicide with her mother, who had been suffering from terminal cancer. He was also earning a reputation as a director of films on controversial social issues. He had directed *An Early Frost* with Aidan Quinn, one of the first films to deal with AIDS, in 1985. In 1988, he would direct *David,* a television movie based on the true story of a man who tried to burn his son to death, a role he also offered to Brad—with a $250,000 fee—but which he turned down. In 1991, John would direct *Our Sons,* starring Julie Andrews, a TV film about a mother who learns her son is dying of AIDS.

Brad really responded to John's commitment. Just as he had with Larry Kramer's *Normal Heart,* he threw himself into the film, reading and rereading the few books on the subject: *Last Wish,* Betty Rollin's chronicle of her mother's death, and Elisabeth Kubler-Ross's classic, *On Death and Dying.* But there was a problem, a possible scheduling conflict with Stan's movie. *When the Time Comes* was supposed to start shooting in Dallas, right after Christmas. But Stan kept telling Brad that he had to stay available, that *September Song* was about to get the go-ahead.

If Brad hadn't been so deluded about landing that one big feature film, he would never have done what he did. But he was convinced Stan's movie would be the one to relaunch him. As he noted in his diary that fall, "I thank you, Father, for the right starring role in the most outstanding and abundantly successful movie in the world resulting in my winning my Academy Award as Best Actor."

So Brad did the unthinkable for an actor not considered an A-list star; he asked John to delay the start date a month, push it back from January to February. He even offered to compensate John for the delay, something that no actor normally does. Most directors would not have been as indulgent as John. But he wanted Brad badly enough. He took Brad's $50,000, a quarter of his $200,000 fee, to buy everyone's time for that month.

Stan's movie never did get made. By January 17, things were tense between Brad and Stan. As he noted in his diary, "[Stan's] production company now owes me $50,000. . . . I am searching for understanding."

By February 5, it was all over. Brad had left for Dallas to join costars Bonnie Bedelia and Terry O'Quinn in *When the Time Comes*. Rehearsals started on the ninth, shooting began on the seventeenth.

When Brad left for Dallas that month, he had known he was HIV-positive for slightly more than a year. If he was not yet dealing with any of his health issues, he was aware of one change in his body: his weight. He simply couldn't keep it on. He flew to Dallas with suitcases full of Italian clothes and one big priority, getting enough to eat. Brad knew that unless he ate like a stevedore, he would just shed pounds and, within a matter of weeks, would start looking sick.

Brad hadn't had much trouble hiding his cocaine use when he chose to, but his eating habits were a different matter. Even John noticed that Brad had an appetite "that made Orson Welles look like a piker," as he referred to it after watching Brad plow through plates of food at Parigi's, the local pasta place where the cast liked to hang out. John had reason to notice. He had once worked with an actress whose weight had ballooned thirty pounds during a shoot. It was a nightmare he didn't care to repeat.

"You know, if you keep eating like this, you're going to look like Peter Lorre," John told him one night when Brad was working his way through the last of the three peach cobblers he'd ordered. John recognized that like many actors, Brad could be incredibly vain. "Peter was a pretty good-looking guy," John added, "until he got his hand in the cookie jar."

Brad couldn't believe it. His vanity had been wounded, but he was also worried that John and the others might suspect something. "I can't believe you said that," Brad said, trying to turn it into a joke. "I can't believe you really said that."

But it wasn't a joke. Like his drug use, Brad was consumed by his need for food, where his next fix was coming from. If the rest of the cast treated his appetite as a running gag, so be it. The shoot one day at the El Paso airport dragged into the lunch hour, and between takes Brad bolted for the cafeteria. John knew there was no use in arguing but simply sent the makeup artist in after him. While Brad sat there devouring his ice cream, the guy kneeled on the counter sponging makeup on him.

John never suspected anything. He accepted Brad, eccentricities and all. During the filming of *When the Time Comes,* they became close, the start of a friendship that lasted for years. John saw a side of Brad that few directors had seen, his ability to be serene. His eating habits aside, Brad had been on his best behavior during the film, the darling of the crew, who showered him with cream pies on the last day of the shoot as a show of their affection. It was a marked change from Brad's usual reputation. But as far as he was concerned, it was all part of his pact with God, how he was dealing with the HIV. During a break in a particularly tense day on the set, John and Brad walked to the coffee table together. "What's your secret?" John asked. "How do you stay so calm in the middle of all this chaos?"

"Well, I have the same secret a lot of the other people you know have," Brad said. "I'm in the program and I have a sense of where I am with God."

Whatever serenity Brad exhibited during the making of *When the Time Comes* did not translate into the rest of his life. That year, as in his first year of sobriety, Brad's mood ricocheted between elation, depression, volatile anger, and denial. They were, I realized, his first symptoms of living with HIV. And not just the disease, but the daily struggle of living with so much secrecy and fear, the fear of being sick, the fear of being found out, the fear of the loss of intimacy in our relationship, and, ultimately, a fear of dying.

Although we never openly discussed our feelings, it was a horrible strain, one made even more difficult by Brad's ongoing recovery from alcoholism, his attempts to come to terms with his past while moving his life to a more spiritual plane. Initially in AA, and then in his work with his spiritualist, Brad had begun dipping into his past, specifically the sexual abuse he had experienced as a child. That year, as we struggled with the growing presence of HIV in our lives, Brad was also wrestling with even more painful realizations about his childhood.

After a year and a half working with his spiritualist, Brad realized he needed help from someone more qualified than her. That April, while I was in New York for TriStar, looking for new faces at what was then an annual ritual—the yearly auditions for the new drama-school graduates from such places as Yale, Juilliard, and NYU—Brad began looking for a new therapist. With Stan Jones's recommendation, he found one.

I suppose it was inevitable that Brad would wind up with the kind of self-appointed therapist who thrives in Los Angeles. I knew Brad needed some real help, what with all his problems now complicated by HIV. We both needed help, if for no other reason than we hadn't had sex in more than two years. It's why I continued seeing Gaylan every week, a place where I could let down my guard in secret. So while I was glad Brad was reaching out, I was angry that he had chosen someone like this therapist. Although she billed herself as a "therapist" rather than a "spiritualist," in my mind, she was no different from the spiritualist and was another New Age healer who preyed on the edges of Hollywood, living off the wealthy, self-obsessed, and insecure. They were less interested in being your therapist than in becoming part of the clique that included your agent, manager, business manager, hairdresser, you name it. Paid friends.

"Is she a licensed psychologist?" I asked Brad. "Is she a psychiatrist?" No. Her credentials consisted of Stan's recommendation "plus a lot of other people in Hollywood see her and say she's wonderful."

In Brad's eyes, his therapist was his soul mate, a recovering alcoholic who had grown up in a dysfunctional family. Hardly unique circumstances in Hollywood, and hardly the qualifications I had hoped for in Brad's therapist. Even Zane was apoplectic. She was "a crackpot," as far as he was concerned, and he fumed about paying someone who had conversations with Brad but who also began to socialize with us, showing up at screenings with Brad and me, including that of *When the Time Comes* at the Directors Guild that May, and that of the long-delayed *Heart,* screened in June. Because she wasn't a licensed therapist, Zane couldn't write her off on our insurance. And unlike Gaylan, whose $50 fee I paid out of my weekly discretionary funds, Zane wrote Brad's therapist a check every month, sometimes as high as $600.

But my real concern about her was not financial but psychological. I knew what lay ahead for Brad, the issues he needed to address: how his parents had used him as a weapon in their battles; how his mother had forced Brad to sleep in her bed for years as a way to strike back at her alcoholic, philandering husband; how she used Brad as her surrogate sexual partner. I knew, too, how his father had retaliated, how he would punish Brad for being his mother's favorite by dragging him into his office and whipping him, naked, with a belt. And I knew how it had ended, when Brad had refused, finally, to sleep in his parents' bed, how his mother had a nervous breakdown and was committed to a hospital where she underwent shock treatments.

I knew all the guilt and rage Brad carried around with him. I had lived with effects of it my entire married life, watching Brad's chronic insomnia, his sexual compulsiveness, his self-mutilation, the scars on his forearms from all the razor cuts. And I had experienced the rest of it, the other less obvious but no less damaging effects of sexual abuse, such as Brad's need to control others by seducing or berating them. He had an inability to see boundaries between himself and other people. He needed to possess and control everyone, not just me, but our friends, his various lovers, even Alexandra, treating her like an extension of himself, refusing to let her cut her hair, refusing to let her eat meat, denying her wishes the way his wishes had been denied him as a child. "Daddy," she would write him in her little notes when he was away on location, "I want to go to McDonald's and eat a hamburger! Why won't you let me?!"

I knew all this, and I knew Brad had a long way to go in confronting it, let alone undoing it. I also knew that if our relationship was to have any chance of really healing, he had to confront these issues. But as much as I supported him, I feared his weekly Wednesday meetings at 11:30 A.M. at his therapist's house were taking Brad down a dark road with someone incapable of lighting the way.

And I was right. When I got back from New York that month, Brad had already scheduled his first appointment with his therapist for April 22. For the rest of that year, and really for the next three years that he continued to see her, Brad became very traumatized. His visits with her completely unsettled him. He would arrive at her house fresh from the gym, his hair still damp, carrying a large cup of take-out herbal tea. Hours later, he would emerge, a total wreck. I had never seen Brad cry before in my life, but now I would come home to find him sitting in the dark crying. It was unnerving, and not at all what I expected from therapy. Although I didn't see much healing going on, seeing him this vulnerable, this frightened, drew me to him.

That schizophrenia between Brad's fraught emotional state and my growing tenderness toward him was obvious during the trip we took that fall to Big Bear. The weekend of October 3, 1987, the Jewish New Year, Brad and I had taken Alexandra, and, with Rick Rosenberg and Tim Thompson, rented a cabin on Big Bear Lake. It was just a stupid little trip, a chance to do silly, tourist things: rent boats, horses, go to tacky restaurants in town. But it was our first trip anywhere as a family since we'd learned Brad was HIV-positive.

I had really wanted to get away, not just to be with Brad and Alexandra, but to unwind. Brad and I had just come off a frantic month. He was trying to negotiate his deal to play Captain Queeg in Robert Altman's TV-movie version of *The Caine Mutiny,* and I had just finished a big project that had gone nowhere, *Total Recall* with Bruce Beresford. Now, literally the day after the 5.9 Whittier Narrows quake rocked L.A. at 7:42 A.M. on October 1, we headed out to the lake that Friday for the long weekend. We had a beautiful two-story cabin right on the water with its own dock and little sand beach. Although a big 5.5 aftershock jolted us awake Sunday morning, I remember that trip as being one of the first times Brad and I had felt romantic toward each other in a long time. It seemed as if his demons were put to rest for those few days, and I really loved being with him again. That Rick and Tim would later recall that trip as being one of the most uncomfortable times the four of us had ever spent together, that they thought Brad had been in a terrible, even abusive mood all weekend, only highlighted the behind-the-scenes trauma that Brad's therapy was causing.

The one benefit of his visits to his therapist, in my mind, was that she was pushing Brad to see a doctor. In their meetings, she had been urging him to directly confront his HIV status and get beyond his denial, his spiritual stupor. Because of her, Brad first reached out for medical help that fall.

Jeffrey Hawkins was a licensed M.D. who also practiced a kind of holistic healing, a real L.A. mix of herbs, diet, and psychic handholding. Stan had been seeing him for years; although he didn't know Brad was HIV-positive, he recommended him to Brad. I was torn about Brad's seeing him as I was about his therapist. In the end, I decided some help, even from someone I considered flaky, was better than none. "Go see him," I told Brad. "At least he's a licensed doctor, how much harm can he do?"

That he saw Hawkins exactly once shows just how far Brad still had to go in acknowledging his HIV status. To Hawkins's credit, when he realized Brad was HIV-positive, he refused to take him on as a patient but instead urged Brad to go to a clinic and begin drug therapy. It was, in hindsight, exactly what Brad—and I—needed to hear. But neither of us was willing to listen. Brad remained so enraged that months later he wrote Hawkins a scathing letter:

Monday, November 16th

Dr. Hawkins–

I came to see you some time ago because I wanted to find a doctor for myself and for my family who was in tune with truths higher than just those of the AMA.

. . . After much insistence from [Stan] (for months) about how evolved you were, how high your level of understanding was, and finally, being encouraged by [my therapist] that you were the genuine article, I came to see you and for those reasons felt totally comfortable in telling you everything about myself . . . I expected nothing more from you than any other guy [Stan] has sent to you for your diets, herbs, and general body purification, etc., etc.

. . . [But] telling me to go to a clinic for treatment when in actuality there was NO condition to treat was probably the single most insensitive, ignorant, and fear-ridden thing I've ever heard.

Jeffrey, for God's sake, if you're going to talk the talk, then walk the walk or shut up. Otherwise, you're dangerous . . .

I wish you light,

Brad

P.S. I trust there are enough ethics to keep this confidential. If I met with this much ignorance from within your office, you might try and imagine how much lurks outside of it.

Brad's anger toward Hawkins was enough to keep him from contacting another doctor for almost three years. "This is it," he said, "this is how it is out there."

But something else was behind his anger and that letter: a self-righteous, self-destructive attitude that I saw Brad adopting at his therapist's urging. At a time when he needed to be reaching out to friends, when both of us should have been building a support network, his therapist had Brad begin to write a series of letters, long, accusatory letters, to those people—friends, relatives, colleagues—who he felt had hurt him. It was, as Brad tried to explain it to me, an empowering way to right the wrongs that had been done to him.

I had never been one for confrontation, and I was wary of this whole idea, especially when it became obvious that instead of confronting his parents, the root of all Brad's problems, he sublimated his anger and lashed out at others. The letters he wrote that year and continued to write up until his death cost Brad not only medical help, but many friendships, including his relationship with his brother, Gene, and his wife, Penny, and our friend Kathleen.

It was the beginning of the circle's growing smaller. Not only was

Brad dropping people from his life, but that year we began to hear about those friends, colleagues, and simply the famous who were leaving us. That summer, Michael Bennett, the celebrated Broadway director, died of AIDS in July. Two months later, Dieter Schidor, who had worked with Brad as the producer of Fassbinder's *Querelle,* died of AIDS. Brad and I learned about his death just a month after we had learned that Stark was dying·of AIDS in New York.

That August, I got a call from our mutual friend Stanley Sobel. "I think you should know this," he told me in a voice that could only be bad news. "Stark has AIDS. He's had it for a while, and actually, Susan, it's pretty close to the end. If you want to get in contact with him, you should probably do it now."

To say I was stunned doesn't capture my reaction. Yes, I had known Stark was gay, we all knew that, but somehow it had never occurred to me that he could get AIDS. Stark had always seemed a throwback to another, earlier era when being a homosexual was not about politics or even sex, but a simple flamboyance, a scarf-around-the-neck disregard for convention. It had never occurred to me that Stark might get AIDS.

"Stanley, why didn't you call me a month ago?" I said, sounding scared even to myself. I couldn't imagine why he had waited that long to tell me.

"Because he didn't want anyone to know," Stanley said. And that I understood.

I could only imagine what Brad was going to think. That night, after I broke the news to him, Brad and I talked about it in bed. It seemed the only way we could deal with AIDS was in connection with someone else. We spent a long time talking about Stark, rehashing all the years we had spent with him, our first meeting outside his office at CMA. It was an incredible conversation, recalling our past, but then we had to confront it. What to do? Should we call him? Maybe he was already too sick. As bad as I felt, I also felt awkward given how acrimoniously our relationship with him had ended. I thought I might break down on the phone, let it slip about Brad. I decided to write Stark a brave, cheerful letter full of news about Brad and me and our careers and Alexandra, thanking Stark for all he had done for us and expressing my deep sadness about his illness. Brad thought that was cowardly. "I have to call him," he said. "I want to have that last contact with him."

But it was what Brad said next that really stopped me in my tracks. "I want to have that contact, because when this happens to me, I want to have made all my amends."

It was that one word, *when,* not *if* this happens to me. It was, I realized, a milestone for Brad to have finally addressed the reality of his own death, the reality that it was coming for him as surely as it was coming for Stark. And I wish, now, that I had been able to support him in that.

But I couldn't. Everything that I blamed Brad for—his silences, his denial about his disease—I was also guilty of. And more than guilty. I refused to validate his fears. Just as my mother had spent her life belittling and disregarding my feelings and my father's feelings, I was now guilty of the same thing.

"How do you know this is going to happen to you?" I said. "Just because this is happening to Stark doesn't mean it will happen to you. Why would you even say something like that?"

Even as I said it, I knew I was wrong, but I couldn't face AIDS. Not with him. Not that night. And not for many many nights, until years later, when it would be too late.

My decision cost me. Brad didn't say anything, but he saw how I reacted. It would be the last conversation he and I had about AIDS for a long time.

I don't know if Brad told Stark he was HIV-positive when he called him the next day at his country house in East Hampton; they hadn't spoken in eleven years. I never asked him and he never mentioned it, just told me that Stark had been grateful for the call.

On August 20, I got Stark's letter.

"Dearest Susan, your beautiful letter and Brad's thoughtful call have meant so much to me," he wrote. The brief letter was full of gossip and praise. "I see your billing credits all the time and am very proud. Your child looks beautiful. I guess she takes after her parents!!!"

I sat there in the kitchen reading it over and over the way I had read Brad's letter from Cedars-Sinai. Stark's lack of bitterness or rancor over the past, his total support of us, his cheeriness in the face of death—his excessive use of exclamation points—touched me. The pages blurred as my eyes filled. I felt sad, afraid for Stark and for us. But mostly I felt ashamed, ashamed that Brad and I had behaved badly toward Stark, that we hadn't remained close and that, even now, in his time of need, I hadn't been able to reach out. It all mixed together in my mind: my relationship with Stark, with Brad, with everyone, my talent for simply shutting people out when it got too painful. I sat there stupidly, crying over the letter, not just for him, but for me and for all of us. Without even his even knowing it, my old boss had taught me one final lesson.

Stark didn't die until almost three months later, on November 4, 1987. I immediately called Brad, who was in Port Townsend, Washington, working on *Caine Mutiny*.

I don't remember what we said or even if I reached Brad right away. I just remember that we both cried. Stark was the first person we knew personally to die of AIDS, and we both recognized what that meant.

That night in his hotel room, Brad wrote one of the more somber entries in his journal: "I no longer have the dubious luxury of ignorance or even denial by affirmation—my only road is to hang in the center of truth."

But I didn't feel any center. If anything, I felt nothing was holding us together, no rules, no laws, nothing except death coming closer and closer, picking us off one at a time. I hung up the phone and sat there in my office looking out at the dusk falling over Century City. I stared out for a long time, until the only light I could see was the bloodred taillights of the cars receding faster and faster into the night.

CHAPTER

13

As 1988 rolled around, and with it, our third year of living with HIV, I had no inkling of the health problems we would face that year—problems that would ironically have more to do with me than with Brad.

That January, I was consumed with work. The merger between the Tristar and Columbia television divisions looked like a go-ahead, and I knew, without even talking to Scott Siegler in our meeting on February 2, that it would almost certainly cost me my job. Tim Flack was my counterpart at Columbia; I knew there was no way they would bring me in over Tim. For one thing, he had seniority, and for another, Columbia cranked out twenty shows to Tristar's eight.

To Scott's credit, he never pushed me to take the demotion and move to Columbia under Tim. "Look, I know there is no way you're going to work for anybody," he told me. "So, I think this should be the end of your contract."

I totally agreed. I liked the job well enough, especially the opportunity to work for TriStar's feature division, but after a year, I was still ambivalent about the corporate world. Hollywood is divided into two halves, the suits and the talent, and I really wanted to stay as part of the talent. Besides, with Brad's health and career in flux and the problems I was starting to see in Alexandra—her anger about Brad's and my absences—I needed to have more flexibility in my life, not less. At the very least, if I stayed at TriStar, we would have to sell the house and move into the Westside.

So it was a total relief when Scott offered me a graceful way out: salary as a consultant for the remainder of my two-year contract, the use of my office until July, and a two-month job casting the TriStar feature *Who's Harry Crumb?* for an additional $25,000.

It was a great deal and I leapt at it. Although I still went down to Century City every day, the return to freelance casting was so liberating that when Warner Bros. called me a couple weeks later about a casting job in their television division, I didn't even give it a second thought.

That winter, for the first time since we learned about Brad's HIV, I felt as if I had my ducks in order. We were both healthy, I was back freelancing so I could, ideally, spend more time at home, money was okay—and I was also as thin as I had been since dropping sixty pounds on my fast after Alexandra's birth five years ago. After years of fits and starts in Overeaters Anonymous, I was suddenly doing well. I had my weight and my eating habits under control, and I was going to my meetings every Tuesday and Saturday like clockwork. I was even beginning to sponsor people. Maybe it was the result of my therapy with Gaylan. Or maybe it was a reaction to knowing Brad was HIV-positive. Whatever it was, for the first time in my life I felt able to focus on my health, my well-being.

Out of that resolve, I also felt able to confront my other health issue, my ongoing difficulties with my thyroid. For as long as I can remember, or, rather, as long as I had been seeing a diet doctor, I'd suspected I had thyroid problems. Not just because of my tendency to gain weight, but also because of my throat. It wasn't as if I were in pain: my throat was just slightly, but chronically, swollen. But no doctor ever mentioned it to me, and as my parents had ignored their health problems, I ignored mine.

But after Alexandra's birth, I noticed a change. I felt moodier and my throat seemed enlarged. For a while, I wrote it off to the birth, to stress, to anything. But by August 1985, literally the week before

Brad gave blood at Cedars, I had decided to see a specialist, Dr. Boris Catz. One look at my throat and he knew I had thyroid disease, hypothyroidism. One-half of my thyroid was dead, and the other half had become enlarged to compensate. It had been aggravated by the hormonal shifts in my pregnancy. Now, I had a condition like diabetes that I would have to manage the rest of my life.

For the next two years, the same two years we were struggling to adjust to Brad's being HIV-positive, I had monthly appointments with Catz as we tried to get my medication right. But by 1987, I knew it wasn't working. I didn't have a cough or any hoarseness, but my neck was swollen, I virtually had a goiter. Finally I couldn't take it anymore, not the medication, the ultrasounds, and the yo-yoing of my moods.

That fall, Catz and I discussed a biopsy. "Just to eliminate the possibility of cancer," he said. Given my family's medical history, I agreed. I was scheduled for November 20, three days after Brad wrapped *Caine Mutiny*. I hadn't known whether he would be back in time, so my friend Judith Weiner agreed to go with me. And thank God. Even though it is an outpatient procedure done in a doctor's office, it is still nasty, a needle being stuck in your neck to aspirate a piece of tissue. The test isn't foolproof, mostly because the sample is so small. But when my test came back negative, I decided for all our sakes—as Brad noted his gratitude over the results in his diary—to put my health issues behind me.

A lot of my resolve had to do with Alexandra. Even before we learned Brad was HIV-positive, Alexandra had showed signs of stress. What baby wouldn't with our lifestyle: Brad's months-long absences, my late hours, the lack of a routine, not to mention the tension we always seemed to be living with. All of this had taken its toll. Although Brad and I never liked to admit it—what parent does?—even when she was a toddler, just two and three years old, Alexandra had been a difficult child, refusing to eat and given to frequent tantrums.

Like Brad, Alexandra could be tremendously willful. Like me, eating seemed to be her main avenue of expressing her anger. She would refuse to eat, and then, as she got older, she went the other way and overate. This particularly annoyed Brad. Although he was devoted to her, he also seemed intent on controlling her, the way he tried to control everyone. Food became yet another battleground. In the past, he would put little notes to me on the Haägen-Dazs in the freezer, little notes with the skull and crossbones drawn on them. Now, he refused to let Alexandra eat any sugar or meat— anathema to a child who might be expected to go to McDonald's more than once in her life.

Like many parents, I had, foolishly, hoped she would outgrow her problems. But now that she was turning five in April and would start kindergarten in September, I realized this was not to be. Already others—family friends such as Rick Rosenberg and Tim Thompson, and even her teachers—were noticing how aggressive and sullen Alexandra could be. That winter, I got calls from the Maggie Haves School, a progressive nursery school in the Valley in which we had enrolled Alexandra.

I knew what was at the root of all this, that it was Alexandra's way of trying to establish some control over a life that seemed out of control. It wasn't just the HIV, it was all of it, the insanity of our lives, that was making Alexandra frightened and angry. The thing we most feared from Brad's infection, that our daughter would be left alone, she was already feeling.

I knew this because she told me, told me she was afraid we were "getting a divorce." I remember the first time she asked me if this was what divorce was, were we divorced? Is that why Brad went away?

I tried to reassure her that this was the way that Daddy has to work. But how could I expect her to understand? How can you explain away a two-month-long absence? It's why Brad had always made it a priority to call home every night, no matter where he was, no matter what time zone he was in, just to have that daily connection. When she was a baby, this had seemed to work— Brad's getting on the phone to sing lullabys. But now Alexandra was refusing to speak to Brad when he was away. Every night she'd be up crying that her daddy was gone and never coming back. But when Brad would call, she refused to come to the phone. Or she would get on and just yell at him. "I'm really angry at you," she would say with amazing self-possession. "Why are you away? Why are you doing this to me?"

It bothered me but it really cut Brad to the heart. Whatever difficulties he and I had, he wanted to be there for Alexandra. This was why I had been happy to leave TriStar. I knew one of us needed to spend more time with her, that one of us needed to change our life to accommodate her much more than we had. It's why I spent most of that winter and early spring taking her out on that L.A. ritual, the private-school applications. Part of me hated to do it—to drag a four-year-old in for interviews. But with all her problems, Brad and I were not going to put her in public school. So I dutifully made the rounds—the Curtis School up on Mulholland, Campbell Hall, Oakwood, and Children's Community School, a progressive school out in Van Nuys where we eventually wound up. It's also why that spring, when Brad got a role in an Australian film, *The Rainbow Warrior,* that meant he would be in Australia and New Zealand for nine weeks, I decided to take Alexandra, to show her, finally, what it meant when we said, "Daddy has to work."

In hindsight, it probably wasn't the best trip I could have picked, but that spring I didn't feel as if I had much choice. I wanted to do this before Alexandra was in school, and I knew I needed to do this while Brad could still travel outside the country.

That was the real issue on that trip, the first time Brad realized traveling as an HIV-positive person might be a problem. He wasn't taking any drugs yet, he wasn't even seeing a doctor, but he knew at some point he would be. How would he get his drugs, how could he see his doctor, in a foreign country? And more importantly, how could he do it without anyone finding out? This wasn't like cocaine, easily scored by any actor with a hefty per diem.

That was one concern. What Brad was more worried about was a blood test. He knew some countries required one for a visa. He knew some insurance companies required them for certain productions, for certain actors. He was terrified that he was going to be confronted with a blood test on some shoot and that he would have to pull out or risk exposure. That March when he left for Sydney, he knew that it was quite probably the last foreign trip he would make.

Ironically, that Brad was going at all was because for the first and only time in my career I had cast him in a movie. Bob Loder, an Australian producer, was looking for an American to star in an Australian film he was producing about an environmentalist group whose ship, the *Rainbow Warrior,* had been blown up off the coast of New Zealand. I barely remembered this story from the news, but Brad was on the line—that was one of his cuter tricks, listening in on my work calls—and he knew all about it.

"Is that the Greenpeace *Rainbow Warrior*?" he asked.

"Bob," I said, "meet my husband, Brad Davis."

After the call, Brad said he had to do the movie. "You haven't even read the script yet," I said, but it didn't matter. This was a moral issue, the way *The Normal Heart* had been.

So I got him the script. And it was lousy. His role was a composite and had clearly been shoved in there just to have an American star in the film. But he didn't care, and by this time Bob loved the idea. To him, Brad was Hollywood, he had a name and a reputation in Australia. It also helped when Bob went to sell the film to Showtime since Brad had done *American Cousin* for them two years earlier. So for the first and only time in my life, I got paid for delivering my husband. The fact that Brad had practically begged for the job didn't help my negotiating any. For a nine-week shoot, I could only get him $100,000.

Whatever fears Brad had about leaving the country had vanished by the time he flew out of LAX on March 22, 1988. He had a job again in a movie that was about something, and Alexandra and I were scheduled to join him for the last three weeks of the shoot in May. But his mood didn't stay up for long. By the time we arrived in Sydney on May 7—after a twenty-hour plane flight most of which I had spent fighting food poisoning—I realized Brad was in a total funk.

It was hardly the greatest of beginnings for Alexandra, who was supposed to be the point of the whole trip. We were all exhausted, I felt sick, and even before we got out of the airport, Brad started in on me about my hair, which I'd had cut short—something he never let me do—right before I left. But he was also angry about the movie, hated the whole thing, the script, his part, even Australia. But mostly he hated Bob, whom he considered a sexist, a real throwback male chauvinist. Most of this reflected that Brad had become big pals with the female lead, Mary Reagan, an actress from New Zealand.

We spent a lot of time with Mary those two weeks: more than once I wondered if she and Brad had had an affair. But that became a minor point as the whole trip quickly became difficult. Although Mary was giving us the insider's view of Sydney, dinners and parties with her friends, and Bob had us up to his beach house for a weekend, between Brad's mood and the Australian ambience, it was hard. I just didn't like the country. Most of the people we met were incredibly conservative by normal American standards, and the men all seemed to be boozers, big drinkers, sexist—and this was supposedly the artistic crowd. Also, I was having a hard time keeping to my abstinence in OA, which for me meant no eating between meals and no sugar. Adding to the stress of the trip was Brad's perpetual bad mood. But I was really trying to keep it together, mostly for Alexandra.

That was actually the only fun part, going around with her and doing the silly touristy things you're supposed to do: the boat ride in the harbor, and the trip to the zoo to see the kangaroos and the koala bears. That was nice, but I felt bad when too often the day ended in another restaurant with another group of actors and Alexandra falling asleep in a little jerry-rigged bed, two chairs shoved together with Brad's jacket over her as a blanket, while we chattered on in the candlelight determined to be the life of the party.

By the time we got back to L.A. on May 25, I was relieved to be out of Australia. But Brad's anger persisted for the next several weeks. He was still doing a slow burn about what a waste *Rainbow Warrior* had been when he began to realize that *The Caine Mutiny* wasn't going to set the phone lines ablaze either. It had aired on CBS on May 8 while we had been in Sydney, and now the resulting silence was all too deafening. Neither Brad nor I thought it had been his best work, and of course he was defensive about it. Although he'd liked working with Altman, he hadn't responded to the director's hands-off approach toward actors' performances. Midway through filming, Brad had made the mistake of getting the original book and studying it too closely. It completely froze him, and Altman could do nothing to loosen him up.

As usual, when Brad felt he had done badly, he looked for some place to vent his fury. Coupled with his frustration over Australia, and the pressure he felt about working now, knowing his infection was like a ticking time bomb, he chose to take it out on Toni Howard and the agency. To me it was just another person he was blowing out of his life, the way he had written off the spiritualist and Stan Jones that year with his vengeful, therapist-inspired letters. But for most of that summer, Brad was obsessed with Toni and William Morris and how they had screwed him over. In his mind, his career problems had nothing to do with his stalled talent or unwillingness to make changes. Brad thought he was still being punished for his drinking and his drug-taking, and he blamed his agents for not doing enough to publicly rehabilitate him.

I stayed out of it. In any case, that summer I had my hands full casting three TV movies, *Senior Prom, The Comeback* with Robert Urich, and *The O'Connors* with Hal Linden and Robert Loggia. Despite my resolve to be home more, it seemed as if every other week I was on a plane to New York. I knew Brad was making noises about talking to Clifford and STE, but even I was surprised when on August 2, Brad actually went in for a meeting with David Eidenberg and Jeri Scott at the agency's offices in Beverly Hills.

I had always liked Clifford, but I was dubious about this move. This wasn't like a top-grossing actor getting into a bidding war between CAA and ICM. This seemed like a step backward—going back to your old agency out of desperation—especially given how fractious Brad's relationship with David Eidenberg had been. I had my doubts about David, feeling that his interest in Brad had always been more personal than professional. But Brad saw it as capitalizing on what little movement his career seemed to have, something that he attributed to Jeri more than David or Clifford.

Jeri had, in fact, been the one to get Brad *The Caine Mutiny*. Her sister, Scotty Bushnell, was Altman's longtime producer. When Jeri heard they were looking for a Captain Queeg for the TV-movie version of Wouk's classic—and given Altman's taste for iconoclastic casting—she had offhandedly suggested Brad. So it wasn't that much of a surprise when Brad first approached Jeri that July about a return to the agency. As he put it to me, it wasn't just *The Caine Mutiny*, it was all of it, the fact that Clifford and David and Jeri were like family, a family that now happened to handle people like Andy Garcia, Geena Davis, and Alfre Woodard.

To her credit, Jeri liked the idea. She knew the drawbacks, that Brad wasn't a big earner and that there was still a lot of PR to do. She understood that Hollywood had a fairly muddled view of Brad as both an actor and a man, that his career had taken more than one turn since *Midnight Express,* and that the drug-taking was the least of it. Brad was no longer a drunk, that much was known, but beyond that directors and producers were far less certain about what kind of roles he could play. In some circles, Brad was simply considered far less interesting a performer now that he was sober.

But Jeri also saw possibilities in that, unlike Richard Gere, Brad had not gone from being a young pretty boy into an all-American leading man. Brad was a character actor, which made Brad more rather than less employable on his way back up. But Jeri also knew that given Brad's post–*Midnight Express* résumé—a hodgepodge that ran from small foreign films to TV movies, from *Querelle* to *RFK*—it was no wonder Hollywood was unclear about him. Unlike Toni, Jeri thought Brad could still have a film career. Or rather, she was convinced that television was not his best option. She knew that at a certain point TV becomes about an actor's Q-rating—the all-important audience-recognition factor. The rule that says Jerry Seinfeld will sell far more tickets on television than, say, Anthony Hopkins. She felt that even with his TV-movie work, Brad still didn't have the strongest Q-rating. "There's just no way to put a reel together," she told him.

This was music to Brad's ears. For the first time since Eddie, someone was telling him he could have a film career. He told Jeri to broach the idea of his return to the agency with Clifford and David.

Although David never voiced any reservations to Brad, his first reaction to Jeri's suggestion was lukewarm. In his eyes, Brad had been difficult, professionally and personally. And given the fractious end to their working relationship, he wasn't anxious to open that can of worms again. Besides, it wasn't as if they needed him. The agency was growing, it had good clients and a solid reputation. But David knew it ultimately had to be Clifford's call. By the time David and Jeri and Brad had their first meeting in August, everyone was publicly on board. The agency, David told Brad, could do a good job for him.

Brad had another reason for wanting to go back to STE. Although he never directly told me, I knew he was seriously thinking of telling David and Clifford he was HIV-positive. Keeping it so secret from everyone was a strain. Brad also knew that sooner or later he would have to confide in someone, especially if he started getting sick. He was hoping that by going back to Clifford and David he might rekindle some of the closeness he'd felt with Eddie Bondy.

Even David seemed to think that Brad had something other than his career on his mind during those first meetings. At least, that was David's recollection when two years later Brad finally told Clifford he had AIDS. "He seemed very much on his guard," David remembered. "In retrospect, if I had been more receptive, or if our friendship had proceeded in a different way, I think he would have told me he was infected."

In the end, David's hesitancy about Brad would be right. Despite their initial enthusiasm, Jeri and David would not make much headway with Brad. As much as Brad loved Jeri's idea about features rather than television, he balked at her game plan—to send him out on tons of auditions. Yes, they were film roles, but they were long shots—such as Walter Hill's silly western, *Johnny Handsome*—and Brad would have to read. But Jeri wanted Brad out there, circulating, showing up. It was almost de rigueur, she said, given how the recession was hitting Hollywood and everyone was having to eat humble pie.

But Brad balked. He refused to read for Walter the way he refused to read for almost everyone. Some of it was his old fear,

fear of rejection, fear of competition, fear of failure. But it was also Brad's new fear that he simply didn't have enough time, or energy, to take the slow-but-steady approach. He needed to work now. He needed big jobs now. He needed to make as much money as he could in the time he had left. Brad wanted to swing for the fences. Over three years, by the time David retired from agenting and Brad bolted for Gersh for an abortive six months, the agency had no record of Brad's going out for a single audition.

But that August, none of that seemed likely and Brad saw only blue skies ahead. Especially when two days after his initial meeting with David, Jeri sent Brad out to meet Percy Adlon at the Château Marmont in Hollywood.

It wasn't an audition or a reading, just a lunch with a hot new director who was in town meeting actors. But Jeri knew what was at stake, that the German director's career had exploded that year when his second film, *Bagdad Cafe,* had become an international hit. Now Percy was in town with his wife and producer, Eleanor, scouting actors for his next film, *Rosalie Goes Shopping.* By Hollywood standards it was a nothing film, a black little comedy about a Midwestern crop-duster pilot and his German-born wife. Percy had already lined up Marianne Sägebrecht, the German actress who had starred in his two earlier films, to play the wife, an overweight compulsive shopper. Percy had gone to Jeri hoping to get Fred Ward to play Ray, the dreamy crop duster. Unbeknownst to Brad, when Fred wasn't available, Jeri had suggested Brad.

It tells you something about Brad's state of mind that Percy's first impressions were of a man "who expected to be hurt and who carried all sorts of weaponry for his defense."

"Actually I came here," Brad said, "because my daughter sings 'Calling You' all the time in the shower." The song was from the *Bagdad* soundtrack, but the genuineness of Brad's observation won Percy over. He never even asked Brad if he wanted the role. The two of them just started talking about the film, about the character, his shoes, his hair, his accent. "What do you think of my teeth?" Brad asked at one point.

"Why, what's wrong with them?" said Percy.

"They're too perfect. My dad's a dentist and he always said teeth are important. I think this pilot needs to have a gap between his front teeth."

It was an auspicious beginning for him at the agency, despite the meager $60,000 fee. By the end of August, he had a signed contract, and by September 17, 1988, he had left for Arkansas, three days after Alexandra started kindergarten and the day before I left for a week in Chicago. And in many ways *Rosalie* was the ideal film job for Brad. It was big supporting role in a small but prestigious film, and he didn't have to leave the country. It also turned out to be one of Brad's best performances. It was a departure for him, his first flat-out comedy. Friends would refer to it for years, citing his performance as Ray, the sweetly ditzy dreamer, as the only one that captured Brad's puckish humor.

That September, Brad spent three weeks filming in Stuttgart, a little German-named town Percy had found outside Little Rock. Although Brad loved Percy and his role, he quickly became far less comfortable with Eleanor Adlon and the rest of the German-speaking crew. He had a hard time literally communicating with them. He also wasn't too crazy about Arkansas, which he found racist. During the filming he spent most of his time either on the set or in his room, a huge departure from his usual high profile in a production. This was another HIV-induced change, his growing introvertedness and self-sufficiency. Brad had his room all hooked up with a hot plate and his stereo system, and he would stay in for hours at a time, cooking his food, writing letters, talking on the phone. He did make one close friend, Sarah Markowitz, the costume designer, whose sense of humor mirrored Brad's—an ability to appreciate that their eating dinner every night in a local steak house called Sizzlin' was both deeply ironic and necessary.

By the time Brad wrapped on October 13 and flew out of Little Rock, I had already seen my surgeon. It was my thyroid again. Despite all our efforts with the medication, things had not improved. Catz agreed, although he was lobbying for another biopsy. Easy for him to say. Even the knife (and the requisite anesthesia) was preferable to that needle. If I was going to be on medication for the rest of my days, I wanted to cut the damned thing out.

I was determined to the point of casual when I marched into Mitchell Karlan's Beverly Hills office on September 29. He'd done the biopsy the year before, so I knew him. But when I hit Karlan's office, it all came flooding back—all the women in the waiting room with their mastectomies and magazines and brave smiles. It was a cancer ward and I was among them. Like my father and his lung cancer, and my mother and her breast and stomach cancer, here I came with my bumpy little thyroid and perpetual bad moods.

I was hardly buoyed by Karlan's show-and-tell routine, his books of photos, pages and pages of thyroids, normal ones, swollen ones, cancerous ones, and postoperative shots of vocal chords. None of them severed. That was the point. Minimal scarring and I would talk again. It might take a few weeks to get there, but "I've never severed a chord," Karlan said. "I take the pictures to prove it."

I didn't need to talk it over with Brad. What was there to say? I think I have cancer so I'm going to have my throat slit to make sure? I didn't even go to the second surgeon Catz recommended, just signed up with Karlan for a date late in October. I had to have a second diagnosis for insurance purposes so I saw a throat specialist in Van Nuys the following week. He told me I should have had my thyroid out years ago, saved me a lot of trouble. That's when I broached it with Brad. "Another doctor recommended it," I told him on the phone that night. "So this is what I'm doing."

I will say this, there's nothing like major surgery to take the starch out of your sails. Why hadn't Catz told me? Why hadn't Karlan told me? Told me that getting your throat cut was like getting hit by a car. You wake up in intensive care—had I forgotten this part?— with a mask over your nose and mouth as if somebody's trying to smother you. Only there's steam coming out of it, out of you, as if you're breathing fire. Where is the doctor or even a nurse and why isn't anyone talking to me? When I move my head, my steam wags in the air like dragon's breath. I reach up, try to pry off the hot wire that's searing my throat, and I feel only damp lumps of cloth. My throat. Oh, yeah, my throat. My eyes start to sting, tears, and now I really can't see, except then I do see. Brad. He's here. His hair is wet, combed back as if he's just come from the gym or the shower. "Don't try and talk," he's saying, holding his face close. "They're going to give you something to sleep. I'll make sure they give you something to sleep."

But I don't want to sleep, I don't even want to shut my eyes. If I do, I know he will leave, slip out again. "Don't talk," he says, shaking off my muted gurgles, my steamy protests. He doesn't understand that under this halo of light, I am telling him he looks like an angel.

It was cancer all right. "What did I tell you," I said to Catz, perched there on my bed with his clipboard and waxy, patient face. Two days later and my fate has been sealed, unlike my throat. I haven't seen the scar yet, but I picture it sawed open with a bread knife with jagged little teeth. Like a shark bite. "Yes, but we've been through all this," Catz says, adding that thyroid cancer is slow growing and almost 100 percent curable. "This isn't fatal," he says. "There's still the iodine to come and then that's it."

Did I know about the iodine? This "radioactive cocktail" as Catz puts it? I must look even more scared than I feel. "But that's much later, after you've healed, after you've come back from your trip. The important thing is to rest now."

I guess I told him we were going to Hawaii for the holidays. Our first family trip now that our days as a family might be numbered. "You're just depressed," Brad tells me. Everyone tells me. Well, who wouldn't be? I feel like shit, can't talk above a whisper, and I know Alexandra is at home freaking out. We tried to tell her I was just away on another trip, but she hasn't bought it, not with everyone tiptoeing around as if they're on a death watch. Wait till she sees me. I look like the mummy, all swollen and wrapped in gauze up to my chin.

Brad tries to make light of it when he comes every day, like a churchgoer, sitting here in the plastic chair, his jacket still on, his hands twisting in his lap. Oh, who are we fooling? We're both like scared kids, terrified the other is going to die, terrified we're each going to die. Even Gaylan can't cheer me up when she comes with flowers and fresh trades to ply the convalescent back to health. I'll never have the strength to read *Variety* again, I say, then drift off as if to prove my point.

Five days later, I'm going home, fifty years older than when I went in, an old lady coming lumpily up the walk, past the yellowed newspapers no one has picked off the porch. Alexandra is both hysterical and frightened, the dogs bark endlessly, and Brad shouts at them. Welcome home. I'll deal with all this tomorrow. Then I remember, tomorrow is Brad's birthday. Number thirty-nine. "Well, I'll have to have a million more," he says brightly, and I wonder, stupidly, if that's even possible.

This is our nightmare and it's here for a while, the fatigue, the pain, the compresses on my neck every night and morning, my voice that sounds as if I've inhaled a million packs of cigarettes. I can't even sing to Alexandra at night, not lullabys, not "Amazing Grace," which I've sung to her since she was a baby. I can't carry a tune, and when I try, Alexandra laughs up at me from her bed. "Don't laugh at Mommy," Brad says sharply from the door.

Two weeks and I'm back in meetings, Tylenol in my bag, scarf tied up around my neck. I used to wear them before, no one should notice. No one must notice because no one must know. Not my family, not anyone in the business. Cancer, it's like a death stamp. As if you were tainted goods. Brad knows, it's why he broke down in Catz's office that day he talked to us about the iodine, my "treatment."

"Why?" said Brad, his eyes bright with tears. "Why does she have to have this?"

Oh, it's our life, my love, I said to myself sitting there, clenching his hand. It's just our life.

Whose idea was Hawaii? Certainly not Zane's, this was costing us a fortune. First class all the way, limo to the airport, three first-class tickets to Honolulu, a convertible, and a condo on the beach. We should travel like this every year. It must have been Rick Rosenberg's idea to get us all out of the house. At least he planned the whole thing. He's such a producer, and for once I didn't have to.

Besides, I was already back at work. I'd taken on *The Final Days* in November 1988, a three-hour ABC movie from the book about Nixon's last days in the White House.

Didn't they get it by now? Work was the answer. Work had

always been the answer. On December 19, I was at ABC running over my master list of all my principals, the actors I thought at least resembled Nixon, Haldeman, Ehrlichman—that whole group of crooks. On the twentieth, I was reading for Nixon. Lane Smith would finally get the nod. On the twenty-first, it was time for the girls, Tricia and Julie. On the twenty-second, we flew out of LAX. Casting interruptus. At least that's what the director, Richard Pearce, implies when he calls, panicked, reaching me in Kapalua two days after Christmas. I skip our day trip to the volcano to spend the afternoon dealing with Dick.

I still have the video of that trip. Actually it's Brad's video. He's hardly ever in it, you just know he's there by our pained expressions and our perpetual mewling, "Come on, Brad, put it away." I look at it now sometimes, slip it into the VCR after Alexandra has gone to bed—on the days I can stand to do this—and it all comes back. Our condos were right on the beach, and Rick threw a fit because their unit was too close to a construction site. "All this way to live next to a building site!" I can still hear him screaming into the phone. There we are, crammed into the car for our awful drive to Hana, where we all got carsick and couldn't remember whose bright idea this was. The afternoon at the beach. It was freezing so only Brad went in. There I am, standing, holding his towel and wearing my stupid scarf as if I'm on Madison Avenue, not Maui. There's Brad making Alexandra laugh and me crazy letting that bullfrog loose in the condo one night, the night, I remember, when the mosquitoes got in and the rat ran out from under the sofa, right where I had been sitting. "Come on, let's scare Mommy," Brad says, trying to get Alexandra to hold up the frog.

Sometimes I stop the tape there. You scared Mommy all right. Those nights I came so close to having sex again with you. I could almost pretend nothing had happened, that nothing had changed. That this was our life, you, me, and Alexandra and our friends, that this would always be our life. You looked so damn handsome the day you came back from the volcano, all windblown and full of yourself, I think we were all in love with you. Did I need to tell you? I should have told you. I should have told you all of it, that it was you, it's always been you, even when they all wondered why the hell I put up with you, why the hell I stayed. I stayed because you stayed. And that was as close to love as I had ever known.

So, no, I don't finish the tape, because if I don't finish it, I don't see that day at the volcano. The only day I'm not there with you and Rick grabs the camera. "Come on, Brad, fair's fair," he says, and you grimace and pout while the wind whips your hair, but you love it, I can tell. I could tell the first time I saw you. It's my biggest fear to see you that way and know that at that moment I am a million miles away.

14

After Hawaii, I threw myself into *The Final Days*. I knew with Dick Pearce's call over Christmas that this would be all day every day for quite some time. I also still didn't feel 100 percent. It would take until February, four full months after my operation, before my voice and my energy completely came back.

At least, I didn't have to schlepp over to Century City anymore, now that I was working out of production offices on Radford in Studio City. My commute was five minutes, three if I didn't catch the lights on Ventura. Some days I even came home for lunch, which I sometimes liked to do given how sick Brad was. He'd picked up Alexandra's cold in Hawaii and had come down with the flu. For almost four weeks he stayed in bed, feverish and with chills. Forget about a doctor, he said, reaching for the cup of tea I handed him every morning before I left. "I'll ride it out." At least Doris was there during the day to keep an eye on him and force chicken soup down his throat.

By the beginning of February, Brad was feeling better. Or at least well enough to get out of bed, although he still looked thin and drawn. He insisted on going with me to see Catz on my second appointment about the iodine treatment. I hated the idea of getting back into all that, but Catz said it was do-or-die time. Sounded like die, given that I would be radioactive for a weekend. Catz gave me my choice, quarantine in a hospital, "where they will treat you like a leper," or isolate myself at home. What choice? Jeri Scott said she'd take Brad and Alexandra for the weekend, and so it was settled.

The whole forty-eight hours was like something out of *Outer Limits*. On the drive home from the clinic, Brad began laughing hysterically, holding out his hand, to see if I was hot yet. I wasn't amused. Not after drinking the vial they took out of a lead tank with tongs and oven mitts. I expected steam to be rising from it, but it looked and tasted like water, although it did cost $2,000. Of course, Brad couldn't resist the jokes about my glowing in the dark. "You won't need a light to read by," he said as we pulled into the driveway.

At least I wouldn't lack for things to read. Since I had to spend the entire weekend alone in our bedroom, Brad had stocked it with what seemed like every magazine and newspaper from the newsstand—a generous surrender after all our fights about his never letting me read in bed. "This is your moment," he said on his way out. "You can read until your heart's fucking content."

So that's what I did on my forty-eight-hour exile: read, slept, ate cheese and crackers, and gradually felt worse and worse. The iodine may have tasted like water, but it made me feel like shit, nauseated and swollen. Saturday night the clinic sent over a technician carrying a Geiger counter and dressed in what looked like a space suit. Thank God it was dark and no one saw him. I felt like Meryl Streep in *Silkwood* with all that ominous clicking. But when the weekend was over—another technician came Sunday to pick up my clothes and the sheets—I came up clear in my scans that week. A last little biopsy on some of my scar tissue a couple weeks later was also clear. By March 7, 1989, when the lab report came back, I was officially a cancer survivor. That Saturday, Rick and Tim took us to dinner at Morton's to celebrate.

But our relief was short-lived; less than a week later, Brad came down with the flu again. "More bed rest, just what I need," he joked that first morning when he couldn't get up. But this time, it was bad. For several days, it was the usual routine, days in bed, fever, chills, his refusals to see a doctor. Then one night something happened that made me think we had been incredibly blind, incredibly stupid. Shortly after midnight, I woke up with Brad shaking uncontrollably next to me. He was completely soaked—the bed was soaked—as if someone had poured a pail of water over him.

It was Brad's first attack of night sweats, one of the surer signs of advanced HIV infection, but that night neither of us had any idea what was happening. "I don't know what to do to make it stop," Brad said, his teeth literally chattering.

I was terrified. I had never seen Brad go through anything like this, not during the worst of his drug-taking. I jumped up, grabbing for towels and extra blankets. "What do I do? Call a doctor, take you to the emergency room?"

"No, no," he said, clutching at the soaked bedclothes. "Let's see how long we can wait, if we can wait it out."

I now know how dangerous a situation that was, how close to delirium Brad came that night. Later, when he was seeing a doctor and this began happening regularly, Brad would be given morphine. But that night, we were ignorant, even foolish. I sat there with him for hours, the two of us huddled on the bed, my arms around him, bundled in towels and blankets. I think we went through four sets of sheets before it finally stopped. I don't know when we fell asleep, but in the morning, I woke to find Brad sipping tea in the kitchen.

"Are you kidding?" I said. "Brad, we have to talk about this, we have to make a decision about seeing a doctor. Whatever is going on in your body is taking hold of you."

But Brad wanted to wait a day. "Let's just see," he kept saying. "Let's just see what happens."

That night, he slept through the night. And the night after that, and the night after that. At the end of the week, he was triumphant. "See," he said, "it was nothing but the flu."

I wasn't convinced. "I want you to call a doctor," I said every morning on my way out. But my Chinese-water-torture approach backfired. "Don't ask me about this anymore," he said finally. "Don't you get it? If I go to a doctor, that's it, my career is blown."

If Brad had any idea that he already had AIDS, he chose to bury his fears in his next job, *Unspeakable Acts,* a TV movie about a husband-and-wife legal team costarring Jill Clayburgh. David Eidenberg made no bones about this being strictly a money job, but it was a huge letdown for Brad to go back to television after *Rosalie.* Even the money hadn't been that easy given the discrepancy between Brad's $250,000 quote and producer Alan Landsburg's purse. They were offering only $100,000, so Jeri and David jumped through hoops to cut Brad's workweeks in half, from four to slightly more than two, to preserve the all-important quote. In the end, Brad would be in Charleston from April 7 to April 26.

I was less than thrilled with the production, given the anemic budget and the fact that Alan Landsburg's wife, Linda Otto, a casting director, was trying to turn herself into a director with the movie. I'd heard that one before. But I was too swamped with my own projects to give it much more thought, and as usual we needed the money. Now that I had left TriStar, I was back on the freelance treadmill, the proverbial hamster on an exercise wheel chasing one project after another. *Final Days* had finished in February and now I was working on *Riviera,* a TV movie directed by David Hemmings, and *Tripwire,* a low-budget feature starring Meg Foster. I was having to go out of town a lot, Utah of all places. With Brad on location once again, Alexandra would be left alone with Doris. Before he left for Charleston, Alexandra wrote Brad a furious note. "Don't GO!" she scrawled in black pencil. "Don't you know I hate IT when you leave me!"

Brad was of a similar mind. His phone calls from Charleston were cranky. "I'm bored," he told me, and Jeri and David at the agency. "Jill and I are bored." Boredom was one thing, but when Alan and Linda started tinkering with and then trimming his scenes, Brad got angry. After a few scenes on the set, one day Brad didn't show up for his call.

David Eidenberg was apoplectic when he got Alan's phone call. As far as David was concerned, this was the past all over again—Brad misbehaving on a set, just like Boston, just like Mexico, just like every movie David had gotten him. Brad might as well be drinking again, David thought, given all the signs. David suspected that Brad may have been involved with Jill Clayburgh, his costar. Whether or not David's belief was true, Brad and Jill were spending a lot of time together on and off the set. Even without knowing that Brad was HIV-positive, this angered David, but for those who did know—namely Rodger McFarlane and Brad's therapist—it troubled them deeply.

But for David the immediate issue was Brad's refusal to show up on the set. "Look, you don't have script approval," David told him when he reached Brad at the hotel. "This isn't part of the game here, this was supposed to be about money. Now can you just go to work?"

What David didn't realize, what none of us realized, was that Brad was in a crisis, he had reached a turning point. He knew he was sick. He also knew he needed help. He just didn't know where to get it. If he had any thoughts of turning to Clifford or the agency, David's anger, his willingness to side with the producers rather than his own client, only furthered Brad's resolve to look for help outside Hollywood. By the time filming had wrapped, he had decided to talk to Rodger McFarlane and Larry Kramer in New York.

Brad left Charleston on April 26 and flew to Tallahassee. He spent a week with his parents, then left for New York on May 2. It was a quick trip, three nights at the Mayflower, just long enough to see Larry and Rodger. They would not be the first to know Brad was HIV-positive. Brad's therapist and, by now, Zane knew. But it would be the first time Brad had asked for help.

On the one hand, his dinners with Rodger and Larry at Elaine's were simply Brad's reaching out to some of his oldest and dearest friends. On the other hand, his decision to turn to New York's artistic community can be seen as a judgment on Hollywood. In New York, AIDS was becoming a top priority in the theater, fashion, and art worlds. In Hollywood, AIDS was a reason for shame and hiding. True, in the years following Rock Hudson's death, tens of millions of dollars had been raised for research and care. While that may have been enough to ease the guilt, it had not begun to erase the stigma.

Brad didn't see that he had any real choice. Larry was an obvious answer, an outspoken advocate who had a personal stake in the country's AIDS crisis; six months earlier, in November 1988, he had learned he, too, was HIV-positive. Even more useful was Rodger and his vast network of contacts from his years at the GMHC. This is how Brad slipped into the AIDS underground.

But it was not to be a free ride. Rodger and Larry were distraught but not overly surprised at Brad's news; AIDS was too much a fact of life for shock to be a viable response. Rodger especially saw in Brad a unique opportunity to help a friend and the cause. He proposed cutting Brad a deal: Rodger would find him a doctor, a lawyer, whatever he needed, but in exchange he wanted Brad's promise to go public, to be one of first in Hollywood to speak openly about AIDS.

Going public with AIDS was—is—an enormous political issue, one that has created as much dissension within as without the AIDS community. Rodger and Larry believed that this was the surest way to erase the AIDS stigma. Brad did not in theory disagree. Certainly he had never shied away from controversial work even when it seemed to hurt his career. But Brad was, at heart, an actor, not an activist, and he saw this as a far more wide-reaching decision, one that impacted more than just himself. His decision not to go public with his HIV status, at least not immediately, was his way of protecting his family and his ability to provide for them. Many regarded this decision as wrong and even cowardly.

But Rodger struck a compromise: "When you're too sick to work, or when you've lost your looks too much to work, you'll pay me back by going public."

It was a compromise Brad could live with. "I'll be a hero later," he told Rodger. "I've got Alexandra to worry about now."

Five days after he got back from New York, on May 11, Brad had his first appointment with a doctor. Rodger had given him the name, Alan Weber (name and details have been changed), one of the leading AIDS specialists in the country and a pioneer in the Los Angeles AIDS community. Rodger made the initial call. Weber would treat Brad anonymously, but he wanted to meet with him first. Rodger had also given Brad the name of a lawyer, Mark Senak, the director of client services for AIDS Project LA (APLA). "You're going to need this guy," Rodger told Brad. "Trust me, you're going to need this guy."

The morning of Weber and Brad's first appointment, the doorbell rang while I was still getting ready for work. Brad was already in his office, so I let Weber in.

"Hi, how are you?" he said quietly, quickly, when I opened the door. "I'm here to see Brad."

The man standing on my front porch looked about ten years older than Brad, with dark hair and a slim, somber face. Perfect doctor material. He might have been Doogie Howser, M.D., for all it mattered. After four years of living in secrecy and fear, we had a doctor in our lives.

I don't know how long Weber stayed that morning, because Alexandra and I left shortly after he arrived. "Just someone to see Daddy," I told her when I dropped her at school. "A new friend of Daddy's."

After that I tried to put it out of my mind. We were leaving for Cannes at the end of the week; *Rosalie* was the German entry, and my day was packed, interviews at HBO for a new series, a haircut appointment. It would be hours before I'd have a chance to talk to Brad. By some weird quirk of timing, I even had theater tickets that night, an Irish drama, *Ourselves Alone,* down at the Tiffany.

It was almost midnight before I got home. After all our carrying on about his seeing a doctor, Brad was almost cool about Weber. "There really wasn't much to it," he said. "He examined me, took blood—I won't even know the results for a couple days—and that was about it."

But that was hardly it. What Brad didn't tell me was that their meeting was not only a turning point for him, but completely out of the ordinary for Weber. As an AIDS specialist, he was used to discretion, even a level of deceit when it came to treating patients. Aliases were common; that was legal in California. But Weber had never been asked to treat a patient outside his office. "It's a bit of a stretch," he had told Brad. "This is the wrong lighting and we're talking about doing things like a rectal exam on your couch."

But Brad was clear about his terms, reiterating them the way he had spelled them out to Rodger: no office visits, all blood work and lab tests were to be done under his legal name, Robert Davis, and bills were not to go through his insurance at SAG but directly to Zane. In other words, he would be treated anonymously on a cash-only basis. Even Weber's office staff was not to know who Robert Davis was.

Weber knew this put him out on a limb, medically and legally. It was why after Rodger had first phoned him, he'd insisted on meeting Brad. He knew and admired his work, but Brad's status as a celebrity wasn't sufficient. He wanted to make sure they "clicked," as he put it. Some metaphysical or psychological click.

Fortunately, they did click. Brad liked Weber and his dry, reticent manner; he also liked the fact that he had once been married but was now living with an HIV-positive lover. All that bespoke an honesty but also a respect for privacy, even secretiveness. And Weber responded to Brad. He liked his lack of bitterness and anger toward his illness, his wry sense of humor. "All this for that one good time," Weber said with a smile, quoting one of his other patients.

But Weber was also looking for a certain strength in Brad, some sign he wouldn't crack, wouldn't become "hysterical," as Weber put it, as the disease progressed. "I don't mean demanding, because I do think patients by their nature become demanding when they're ill," he explained to Brad. "But it's important that your own coping mechanisms stay strong."

Weber wanted that reassurance because he also saw in that first meeting that Brad was already very sick. Technically, he did not have AIDS. The CDC definition at that time required the onset of an opportunistic infection. "You're HIV-positive and symptomatic," Weber told Brad. But Weber knew full-blown AIDS was only a matter of time. Brad's weakness, his weight loss, the night sweats, the eczema on his face, the thrush in his mouth, and the fungus that was eating away his nails, all were telltale signs that Brad had advanced stages of HIV. Weber didn't have to wait for the results of the T-cell test. Brad was, in medical parlance, already on a clock.

Brad took the diagnosis calmly. Weber's attitude was that treating HIV was not about preparing for death or hoping for recovery but maintaining and, if possible, improving a patient's quality of life. That morning they talked about Brad's diet, his ability to travel, to work, even to go back to the gym. Weber reassured him that once they began drug therapy, Brad would feel better. "Philosophically, my idea is that life isn't over until it's over," Weber said. "This isn't 'the boy in the bubble.' You need to live your life to the fullest."

But all Weber's reassurances couldn't keep Brad from asking the one question he needed answered. "I'm going to die, aren't I?" Brad said lightly, getting up to open the office door, his back to Weber. "How long do you think I have?"

Weber didn't give him an answer. He didn't have to. Two days later, he called with Brad's test results. "There's good news and there's bad news," Brad said when I walked in the door that night. "The good news is, it's not AIDS yet. The bad news is I only have one hundred and forty T-cells."

I felt as if someone had reached out and slashed me with a razor. There was blood but no pain. Not yet. I knew what 140 T cells meant. I knew that 200 T cells meant AIDS, CDC or no CDC. I knew that many preliminary drug-trial groups wouldn't take people with under 200 T cells.

"What does Steve want to do?" I managed to get out.

"AZT, when we get back from Cannes," Brad said. "Other than that, he wants me to go back to the gym."

I didn't cry that night. Not then in front of him, and not later. Not once during Brad's illness did I ever break down in front of him or anyone. Not Alexandra, not my friends, not colleagues at work. As I had done for so much of my life, I would do my grieving in secret. The next morning, the day before we were to leave for Cannes, I got into the car like any other morning, but instead of heading to work, I drove around the corner and pulled over. I sat there for a long time, sobbing, just sobbing, until I no longer remembered where I had come from or where I thought I was going.

Cannes was exactly what Weber would have prescribed: not an escape, but a getting on with our lives. One thing Brad's T-cell count didn't change was our daily chaos. We had the usual last-minute rush to the airport, which became moot when the gate agent refused to let us board. We needed a special visa no one had bothered to tell us about. That was a hellish twenty-four hours, a day at the French consulate waiting in line for that blasted visa and then the ten-hour flight. By the time we got to Cannes, we were both wrung out. Brad had to go directly to a press conference, while someone shuttled me to our hotel. It was someplace off the Croisette, definitely not the Carlton. If I had been any less exhausted, I would have been upset by the damp, dismal room, but I simply lay down and passed out.

We spent five days at the festival. What a difference from that first trip more than ten years ago. For one thing, *Rosalie* was no *Midnight Express*. Not when Spike Lee's *Do the Right Thing* and Steve Soderbergh's *sex, lies and videotape* became the talk of the festival. *Rosalie* barely registered, especially when the critical consensus came in: a definite comedown for Percy from *Bagdad Cafe*.

Brad was disappointed the film didn't do better. He had been hoping, perhaps naively, for another career buzz out of Cannes. Percy was clearly less than thrilled, but that didn't stop him from playing the German paterfamilias. That was the other difference on this trip. There was no drama, no scenes at press conferences, no drunken fights with Alan Parker, who was so hell-bent on distancing himself from Brad. *Rosalie* hadn't done well, but at least Percy wasn't blaming Brad.

The night of the screening, we all trooped across the street to the party. It was on the beach, little tables with lanterns and strands of white lights strung everywhere. Although we knew the film wasn't a hit, we sat there that night—Brad, Percy, Eleanor, Marianne, and the rest of them—laughing and talking in the mild sea air. I have a picture someone took of Brad that night, sitting there in his silk scarf; how handsome he looked, happy even, and no longer a kid.

Time had definitely passed. That whole week, Brad didn't meet a single interviewer who didn't ask him what he'd been doing since *Midnight Express*. "Where did you go?" they'd say. "What have you been doing?" Even people on the street would stop him. "Brad

Davis! Brad Davis! We love you," they would say, crowding around him, and Brad's face would brighten, but only for a minute. "Where have you been?" came the inevitable chorus. They thought he hadn't worked in eleven years.

I wouldn't realize how deeply this cut Brad until several days after we were back in L.A. I was coming home late after a screening, picking my way in the dark from the garage to the back door, when I smelled smoke. Then I saw it, this huge pot, my big cooking pot, sitting on the lawn, blackened as if it had been in a fire. Brad had burned all his *Midnight Express* stuff—the reviews, photographs from the shoot, even the suspenders he had worn. Like some witch in *Macbeth* trying to alter the fates, he'd gone out in his black cashmere coat and burnt his past in a cauldron, sent it up in a cloud of ashes. It didn't matter that I'd been saving it all for Alexandra one day. He'd decided. He was cutting that movie out of his life.

Whatever Brad hoped to accomplish by his exorcism, it had little effect. By June 14, Brad had had his T cells rechecked. They numbered 93. Within two days, he was on AZT.

That summer of 1989 was hard, the worst since Brad was diagnosed HIV-positive. It wasn't just the AZT, although that would have been difficult enough given how sick Brad was now with blinding headaches and chronic fatigue. But Brad was hardly working. Most days he stayed in bed, the shades drawn, the bedroom fan droning, a pathetic antidote to the Valley heat. Despite his vaunted return to STE, he had only two jobs that summer, *The Edge,* a half-hour pilot for HBO that I had cast, and *The Rope,* a film version of O'Neill's drama for A&E. Each required no more than five days of shooting and neither payed more than $15,000.

Meanwhile, I was slowly losing my mind working on *Rock,* the ABC biopic about Rock Hudson's death. It was just a mess from the start. At one point there was a competing movie at NBC, which was at least based on Sara Davidson's book. This was a hodge-podge; some of it was the story of Mark Christian—Rock's lover who sued him right before he died—and some of it was based on Rock's wife's story.

But the rights problems were the least of it. I thought the script was really weak. At least I was on good terms with the producers, Frank Konigsberg and Larry Sanitsky, who were old colleagues.

The real problem, however, was that nobody wanted to play Rock. Given all the breast-beating that had gone on in Hollywood after Rock died, you'd think I could have found someone willing to play him on-screen. But that whole summer, from my first interviews in July up until I had my final list on September 15, I got pass after pass after pass. And not just from stars, but total unknowns, because after Frank and Larry got over thinking they could actually get people like Tom Berenger, they decided to go with a newcomer who resembled Rock. One weird day, they had Mark Christian audition to play himself. In the end, we wound up going with Billy Moses as Mark and Thomas Ian Griffith, another STE client, for Rock.

Working on *Rock* was bad enough as a job, but it also started to merge with my personal life. I was living at home with an actor sick with HIV while working on a film about an actor who died of AIDS. It really made me angry, looking again at what Rock had gone through, seeing how homophobic this town really is, seeing how his career was nearly ruined several times when people found out he might be gay, let alone that he had AIDS. It was a life defined by secrecy and denial and made me question our life. Did Brad live with that much denial? Did I?

I started to think I did the day Thomas Ian Griffith came on the set in full AIDS makeup. It was part of the makeup test to see how well he would age from young Rock to old Rock to dying Rock. I hadn't given this a thought until I spotted him, this handsome kid with shadows and hollows painted on his face, looking gaunt as if he were sixty and dying. I had to leave the room. I felt as if I had seen my future.

Brad was in no mood for my fears. Most of the summer, I kept up a running commentary on the movie, on Rock and on various AIDS treatments. I was bugging Brad to call Larry Kramer. It didn't seem that Brad was doing that great on AZT, and I wanted to make sure there wasn't some treatment in Paris, like the ones Rock had had, that we were missing. Finally, Brad called, but Larry set him straight.

"Look, there is no cure," he told Brad. "And if you go to a clinic in Paris, it will be a sure tip-off if anybody finds out."

That was enough for Brad. "Look, I don't want to hear about fucking Rock Hudson anymore," he exploded at me one night. "I don't want to hear about Paris, about how terrible it was for him at the end. I don't want to hear about it, not when I feel this bad."

Despite Brad's and my concern that summer, Weber had a more clinical attitude toward his new patient. As far as he was concerned, Brad was responding as he should. The headaches, the fatigue, even the anemia that kicked in, all were typical symptoms of someone starting on AZT. In fact, Weber was only seeing Brad every six weeks or so. Either Weber or Robert (name and details altered), his physician's assistant, would come by the house, examine Brad, draw blood, and leave, in all of fifteen minutes.

Weber's notes for July 21, 1989, read:

"Robert and I see Brad together and I introduced Robert to Brad. Brad had complained of headache in the past week, daily better now. Fatigue and a 3–5-pound weight loss. Tolerating 600 mg of AZT a day. Fairly well now. No shortness of breath. No new complaints. Minimal thrush or oral candida in his mouth. Ear, nose, and throat normal. Similar blood work is done. He shows some anemia. We decreased his AZT to 400 milligrams a day."

Financially this wasn't a strain either. Weber wasn't charging for his visits, although this is usually the least expensive part of AIDS treatment. "An office visit can run seventy-five dollars but you'll leave with six hundred dollars' worth of lab fees and another six hundred dollars in drugs," Weber told Brad. But even the drugs weren't killing us. Brad was only taking Bactrim, a prophylaxis that he got himself over at the Sav-on, and AZT.

When AZT was first prescribed as an AIDS treatment, it meant going to a hospital for almost three weeks and getting it by IV. Now, it was an oral medication, 100-mg tablets. Still at 600 mg a day, the prescribed dosage in 1989, that could run to $10,000 a year. But Weber was funneling Brad his medication for free.

Leftovers from other patients. I could always tell when someone had died because suddenly there would be these prescription bottles with someone else's name on them in our bathroom.

The one big change in our lives was the T-cell test, the blood test that determines a patient's level of immune deficiency. Healthy people have anywhere from 1,000 to 2,000 T cells. Anything below 200 is regarded as de facto AIDS. Below that it's virtually meaningless. But like every HIV-positive person, T cells began to rule Brad's days. From 140 he went to 93. On July 21, five weeks after he started on AZT, his T-cell count hit 179. Brad was elated. But by September, it had plummeted back to 78. That's when Brad decided to ignore his T-cell test. At least until the last year of his life. "I feel okay but this T-cell count is really getting to me," he said. "I'm not going to bother with them anymore."

That fall, it was as if a miracle had descended on us. Or perhaps it was only what Weber had said would happen, that Brad would adjust to the medication. In any event, Brad began feeling better almost overnight. The headaches stopped, his energy level went up, he even started going back to the gym. Light weights, high reps, as Weber advised, nothing too strenuous. When the September 8 T-cell test came back registering 78, Brad was beyond caring. He felt good and he had his first real job in more than six months.

He was leaving for Yugoslavia in four days, a month-long shoot for CBS's *The Plot to Kill Hitler*. It was a docudrama, a two-hour movie about Hitler's last days produced by Warner Bros. television. It wasn't a bad project, just a bad role for Brad. He was playing General Von Stauffenberg, a high-placed general in Hitler's command, one of the masterminds in the foiled plot to assassinate Hitler. Brad was no genius with accents, and understandably he had been way down the list. But as in *Rock,* they had a hard time finding actors. I knew Marcia Ross, the casting VP at Warner's, and she finally called in Brad. She thought he could pull it off, given his work in *Querelle,* and she knew we needed the money, his $225,000 fee. I felt bad when this came back to haunt her. Brad was so terrible in the film that CBS put out the word, no more roles to Brad Davis.

If Brad had any fears about playing a Nazi general, they paled in comparison to his worries about living in a Communist country for a month. He wasn't worried about getting a visa—only the United States and certain Arab countries had HIV immigration restrictions—or getting his drugs in; he kept the AZT in generic pillboxes. But he was worried about the food, getting enough to eat, and finding a doctor in Zagreb if he needed one. Weber told him, if something happens, just get on a plane to Rome. "You know you're in trouble when they're telling you to go to the Italians," Brad joked.

The rest of that fall while Brad was away was really okay. Hope seemed to be in the air, what with the fall of the Berlin Wall in November. We had Brad's *Hitler* money, and he was still feeling good. We had a new dog, Faith, a Doberman that Brad had got before he left for Yugoslavia. I had balked at the idea of a Doberman. We had the cats and Doc, our little terrier, who followed Brad around, and I didn't think we needed a guard dog even if Brad did. I'd take a German shepherd over a Doberman any day. But typically Brad found a breeder and came home with a puppy. She was already named Faith, but I had to admit it fit—after all we'd been through—and she really turned out to be a sweetheart. Nothing like I expected.

The rest of the year was a whirl and we were scheduled to go to New York in December with Alexandra for Christmas. It was a magical trip for some reason. All of it, the lights, the snow, the cozy dinners with friends, the Hanukkah party Erica, my old New York roommate, had, seeing Clifford Stevens again—it all seemed like a real life to us. I bought Alexandra her annual Christmas dress, a little French, long-waisted dress, and a red Laura Ashley coat with a black velvet collar. She looked like a little doll walking out with Brad the night he took her to see *The Fantasticks* down in the Village. Afterward we all met up with Clifford for dinner. It was a shame it all had to come to an end when we left on the twenty-fourth for a week in Tallahassee with Brad's parents.

But nothing that fall seemed to capture our mood that year so much as Brad's birthday that November 1989. It was his fortieth, and either Rick or I decided that it had to be a surprise party. I don't know how we pulled it off. Especially since everyone seemed to be trooping to Clacton & Frinton, Brad's favorite clothing store down on La Cienega, to get his gifts. He must have guessed since every time one of us went in, the sales staff rattled off Brad's list: "He wants this and he wants this and he wants this." John Erman thought it was hilarious the day he went in.

And then the night of the party. We had it at Tony Bill's restaurant on Maple Drive down in Beverly Hills. It's birthday central, but I still loved the room with its cool blond wood and the slate and their oyster bar. Brad loved it and it was a great time with Alexandra running around the table and everyone playing games with her and the pack of people there for Brad making toasts to him and to friendship and for forty more years together. Let it be, just like this, I thought, don't change a thing.

15

Starting the New Year off with a bang—Ian Charleson died of AIDS on January 6, 1990. Brad hadn't been in touch with him in years, not since they'd made *Chariots of Fire,* but he'd always liked him. Unlike Ben Cross, Ian had actually been pleasant to the Americans on the shoot. We had a photograph of him and Brad hanging in our living room. Now he was dead. We hadn't even known he was ill when John Hurt called, his voice faint and cracked, from his country house outside London. Ian's death hardly made a dent in Hollywood—just a notice in the trades—but it was big news in England. He'd been sick for some time; it was common knowledge at the National, where in his last months he was playing *Hamlet.* Three hours onstage every night and all those soliloquies about the meaning of life. And I was worried about Brad going on location. It was all so up-front over there, so different from L.A. Even before Ian died, Daniel Day-Lewis had been lined up to replace him.

I tried not to take Ian's death as an omen for our year to come. Brad's T cells rebounded to 114 on January 17, two days after *Unspeakable Acts* aired; a toss-up as to which portended worse news for Brad's future. Well, it was a toss-up until *Hitler* aired at the end of the month and CBS made Brad an actor *non grata.*

Brad never knew it, but it didn't take a rocket scientist to figure out his career was expiring almost as quickly as his body. He'd had such hopes after *Rosalie;* now, given its reception at Cannes, he was just praying the movie would open well when it was released in March.

But that January, Brad had nothing on his plate, one reason why he would bolt STE before the end of the year to go to the Gersh Agency. Not that it would do much good. We didn't know it then, but Brad would make only two more movies, both of them for TV, before he died.

If Brad was chronically underemployed, I was swamped, eyeball deep that month in the TV pilot version of *Look Who's Talking,* the hit movie that starred Kirstie Alley and John Travolta. Columbia was doing it, and Ed. Weinberger, one of the brains behind *Taxi* and *Mary Tyler Moore,* was the executive producer and doing his best to make my days a living hell. There wasn't a casting director in town who didn't have an Ed. Weinberger horror story. Everyone had warned me I was crazy to take the job, but I was beyond caring. My mantra was "We need the money," but I took it because work was my only antidote, my only guarantee of normalcy. Getting screamed at by Ed. was a small price to pay for the chance to forget about the rest of my life for a few minutes each day. Besides, my plan was working, or at least it was until Alexandra, of all people, put a stop to it. Kids' bullshit detectors, they'll get you every time.

There's nothing that will rile your friends faster than telling them you're taking your child to a therapist, but that's what we were doing that winter. It had been a long time in coming, although I hated to admit that, but when Brad had gone to Yugoslavia to do *Hitler* the previous September, the same month Alexandra started kindergarten, it was the last straw. Within three weeks of her starting at Children's Community, the principal called; Alexandra needed help and they could supply us with a list of recommended psychotherapists.

Now, six months later, we were facing our first appointment with Paul Liebowitz, a child psychologist out in Encino. Brad was dead set against this. He hated the idea of family therapy—weird given how he'd harangued me into going to his therapist with him—but I was convinced this was the only answer. Or maybe I was just projecting onto Alexandra what I would have liked for myself as a child, someone to listen to my problems.

I knew I did that a lot, but then I assumed most parents tried to get for their kids what they had never had. It's why I never wanted Alexandra to live in a repressed household. It's why I encouraged her to be so "out there," to follow her nose, to get into music, into painting, whatever she wanted. It's why I didn't worry when she turned into a little daredevil, the kind of kid who went off the diving board into the deep end before she was even two, the kind of kid who thought nothing of going to the gym with Brad and coming home covered with grease, the kind of kid who climbed up on the roof with her daddy to look at the stars. I didn't even mind it when Alexandra turned into a little bit of a smart mouth, holding her own at parties with our friends and other Hollywood types. I liked it because she wasn't turning out like me.

I guess that's also why I never questioned our decision to yell and scream at home, even in front of her. At least we were airing our differences instead of suppressing them the way my parents had. But what I hadn't seen was how all that primal screaming can affect a child, particularly an only child like Alexandra, and make them feel they're responsible for solving their parents' problems. That's why we were in Paul's office that February. Alexandra didn't know the half of it—that her father was dying—but she knew enough to know that something was wrong.

Starting that month, we had a standing appointment with Paul. Every week, I left work early to meet Brad and Alexandra at his office out in Encino. It was a long haul to get there, and once we were there, it was nothing but pain. As I said, kids' bullshit detectors. I suppose I wasn't totally shocked to hear that Alexandra wasn't "bonding" with me, as Paul put it; I was never home and my daughter wanted to murder me for it. I knew that because she told me in so many words. That was the rule: Alexandra had the floor for the first twenty minutes; she could say whatever she wanted and we couldn't interrupt or even respond. Then, for the next twenty minutes we would all talk together, and at the end, Paul would talk to me and Brad alone.

I actually grew to like Paul, he had a real way with Alexandra, but he thought Brad and I had horrible marital problems, that we were really screwing up our daughter. I didn't disagree, but I was desperate after a few weeks to tell him we weren't your garden-variety fucked-up marriage, that Brad was HIV-positive. I wanted to tell him because I wanted him to know why I couldn't bear to be at home, why I spent so many evenings at the office and at screenings, and why I spent Sundays alone holed up in a theater with my diet Coke and my notepad, sitting through a double feature, a triple feature if I could manage it. It was my way of coping. But I didn't tell him, because Brad wouldn't let me.

"It's none of his business and it's not your place to tell him," Brad said.

"This is Alexandra's life we're dealing with here," I shouted back. "I think he should know what's going on."

But Brad was adamant. "Forget it, it's not going to happen."

So I sat there in Paul's office, week after week, listening to Alexandra tell me what a horrible mother I was, listening to her nail me. At our first session, Paul turned to me: "If you want to have a relationship with your daughter, you're going to have to change your life. You're going to have decide what is more important, your work or your child." The good news, he added, was that we had caught it in time. "You've made mistakes," Paul said, "but you have time to correct them."

Time? Didn't he know I had everything but time? I had fear, paranoia, anger, but no time. Every day I lived with the fear of cancer, of AIDS, of dying, of Brad's dying, the fear of time cut short. If my sin was sitting through too many movies as a way of stealing back some of that time, then that was too damn bad. "Great," I said, smiling at them all. "Then we'll make changes."

I'm ashamed to say how hard I found it, in the beginning, to spend time with my own child. It meant big and little changes, cutting work short to help out on school field trips, turning off the radio so we could talk when I drove her to school. Mostly it meant an end to my Sundays. Now I spent them with Alexandra, Shana's day as we called it at home using the nickname she had given herself years ago when she couldn't pronounce her own name. Sundays were now my day to be with Alexandra, without Brad, without work. We would go out, just the two of us, and do what she wanted, lunch or shopping at the mall or just going and playing somewhere, bowling or a park or a movie. "But only if she wants it," Paul said sternly. "You cannot drag her along on your routine."

It was tough those first few weeks, giving up my one free day. But I did it. That first Sunday we headed out, I nearly lost it, not out of anger, but shame, as when I got Stark's letter before he died; no bitterness or recrimination, just cheerfulness in the face of great pain. It was like that with Alexandra. After all that anger, she was right there, welcoming me back. "You want to go, Mom?" she said, standing by the door, her jacket zipped up, her life back on its axis. "Because I'm ready."

Not that Brad didn't come in for his share of criticism during the therapy sessions. He played his own games with Alexandra. The more absent I was, the more present he got. "I'll take her, I always do," he would say when I was crashing around already late for something somewhere, leaving the two of them alone again. "She loves me more anyway." That was bad enough, but then he'd do it to her face. "Who do you love best, me or Mommy?" Brad would tease Alexandra, laughing. "That isn't even funny," I'd said, not that it made any difference. It's what happens with an only child: you use him or her to get at your spouse.

Fortunately, Paul didn't miss a trick. Neither did Alexandra. After she was done nailing me, Brad got his—all his compulsive behavior, his control issues such as refusing to let her eat meat and cut her hair. Brad had never let Alexandra cut her hair; since the day she was born, he had refused to let it be cut. But what started as a cute affectation when she was a baby was nonsense now that she was almost seven and her hair hung halfway down her back. Kids that age want to start dressing themselves, doing their own hair, but she couldn't because Brad wouldn't let her cut it.

And then there was the whole meat issue; Alexandra couldn't go to anyone's house for dinner without worrying about what they were serving. "Did you eat meat?" Brad would grill her when she got back. "Tell me what you ate." That one really got me, given my own food problems and how Brad would ride me. "Leave her alone," I would tell him. "You'll only make it worse." "You're one to give advice about eating," he would shoot back, and so it went. I was thrilled when Alexandra finally got Brad on that. "Daddy, I have to tell you it feels really bad not to eat meat," she said during one session. "I want to feel like other kids who get to eat meat." That night, the three of us went out, and she had her first hamburger in front of Brad. It was a huge breakthrough, this ordinary family dinner, but then that's the kind of family we were.

By the time Alexandra's birthday rolled around on April 23, 1990, we were doing well enough, Paul said, that we could meet every other week. It was good news for what was turning out to be a big birthday, Alexandra's seventh. Like any kid, she was over the moon about her birthday, even though I felt bad that we sort of had to do it on the fly. I had to be in Chicago that week, so the Saturday before, we gave her a sleep-over party with five other kids and all the trimmings, a cake, games, and a Teenage Mutant Ninja Turtle theme.

Alexandra wasn't the only one thrilled she was turning seven. Brad had really wanted to see this. In his mind, this was the magic number; if he lived until she was seven, she would always remember him. "She'll remember me, what I looked like, what I sounded like," Brad said. "She'll know her father from something besides his movies."

It was important to him, because right around that time Brad started to get sick again. It was his first relapse since starting the AZT the previous June. After that disastrous summer, he'd really rallied, the headaches had lessened, and he'd gotten some of his strength back. All fall he'd been better, he was back working out at Vince's, his color was good, and he didn't look as thin. But now, he was sick again, weak, pale, suffering some of the worst fatigue since he started the AZT.

"It's the anemia," Weber told him during one of his visits, "just a side effect of the drug treatment." Brad was encouraged, but what Weber didn't say was that it was only a matter of time before he would have to take erythropoietin, daily EPO injections, to combat the anemia. But Weber wanted to wait, give Brad a break from AZT, to see if his red blood cell count rebounded on its own. "Let's put you on a drug vacation," he told Brad, aware that his T-cell count was now 60. "Let's see what that does." So from April 10 until May 9, Brad went off AZT and Bactrim.

It was the same month I had to be in Chicago for a ten-day casting trip followed by a long weekend in New York. My old old friend Ellen was throwing her daughter's bas mitzvah that Saturday out in Forest Hills, a trip I'd had planned for ages. Six months ago, it had looked as if we could all make it; now it was out of the question. Even with Doris in the house every day, it was hard for Brad when I wasn't there. He was so weak now he couldn't drive Alexandra to school in the mornings. Week-ends were the hardest with Alexandra home all day and Doris only in on Saturdays. I couldn't leave them. But I also couldn't bear to think I had an invalid for a husband, not yet. So that first weekend in May, I did a U-turn, flew from Chicago to L.A., picked up Alexandra, and flew back to New York. We landed on Friday, the bat mitzvah was on Saturday, and we were back in L.A. on Monday.

It was nuts, but that's how our life was going; Brad got weaker and I got more frantic. It seemed as if every other week we were having conversations with Zane about something to do with money, the insurance, cash flow, updating our wills. I loved Zane, but those calls were like Chinese water torture, a reminder that we were falling further and further behind. As Brad's income stalled and dwindled, we seemed destined to live on my earnings alone, a frightening scenario given what Brad and I both feared, an ava-lanche of medical bills.

Not that we were there yet. That was the one ray of hope. Thanks to Weber's pro bono house calls and the free AZT, Brad's medical expenses from 1987 through 1989, the first year he saw

Weber, didn't amount to more than $3,000. But Brad was convinced that would not remain the case. Even more than me, he was already guessing what lay ahead.

Both of us got a good look at that future when *Longtime Companion* opened in May. It was the first Hollywood movie to deal directly with AIDS. Written by playwright Craig Lucas, the script had been commissioned by Lindsay Law for PBS's *American Playhouse*. Given what was happening in the country, it was hardly controversial: a gay couple in New York, one of whom is dying of AIDS, spends a long weekend at their beach house with several of their friends. Yet every major studio passed on it. Lindsay finally wrangled Goldwyn into distributing it, a major triumph when the reviews came in and Bruce Davison earned a Golden Globe and an Oscar nomination for his performance.

Brad and I both saw it, although we went separately. I had gone because I thought it was an important film, but also because I knew all those guys, the casting director, Jason La Padura, and most of the actors, such as Bruce, Campbell Scott, Dermot Mulroney. I loved it, sobbed my way through the whole thing, but I didn't relate Brad's situation to it directly since he had none of the symptoms that Mark Lamos's character had, the pneumonia and the Kaposi's sarcoma.

Brad, however, totally related. He loved the movie, thought it was beautifully acted and directed, but it terrified him. It wasn't so much the dying that got him, but the possibility that he might lose his mind, lose touch with reality, as his disease progressed. "Dementia," he said that night after he got back from the film. "I know that's going to get me." It wasn't even the AIDS really, but the fear that in a physically weakened state he would become like his mother. That was what scared him, that he would become like his mother.

It's why Brad was so crazed to redo our wills. We'd redone the will after Alexandra was born, but now he wanted Zane to put all our assets, our few assets—our house, his residual payments, our insurance money—in trust. He wanted them protected in case he lost his mind, in case of a tidal wave of medical bills, in case of whatever. He didn't want me and Alexandra bankrupt because of what was to come.

The insurance policy was the killer. Zane had wanted to redo that for years. It had been tough enough getting us $300,000 in 1983. Brad had been sober for two years, but it wasn't enough to override the policy stipulation regarding "barbiturate use." By 1986, Zane had thought enough time had lapsed that we could apply for more. For only slightly larger premiums, he told Brad, he could get us million-dollar coverage. But Brad refused. "I'll do it only if I don't have to take a blood test."

Zane's immediate reaction was that Brad was taking drugs again. But he dismissed that idea and chalked it up to Brad's reticence to expose any more of his medical history. Besides, Zane thought he could find an additional $250,000 policy that didn't require a physical. But after a few calls, he learned that by 1986, no insurer would do a policy over $100,000 without a full medical exam.

"Listen, I don't want to do this," Brad said that afternoon after Zane had brought up the insurance topic again. "But you have to know that I've discovered I'm HIV-positive." That was the end of the insurance discussions, and the start of talk about our wills and Brad's medical bills.

All of that was always in the back of our minds that year. I was trying to be good and spend more time at home, but with Brad not working, I was feeling pressured to take on two and even three jobs at once just to maintain our cash flow. That spring, while I was finishing up *Look Who's Talking,* or *Baby Talk* as its TV title became, I was also working on another pilot for Ed Weinberger, *Honor Bound. Baby Talk* had bogged down—nobody at Columbia was making any decisions—and in Ed's mind, I was on the payroll with all this time on my hands, so of course I could finish up *Honor Bound.* "There's only three parts left to cast," he told me. "It's nothing."

Of course it turned out to be much more than that, and I realized Ed was screwing me, getting two projects cast for the price of one. So when April rolled around and I got offered a movie of the week,

Dillinger, a biopic about the legendary gangster, I jumped at it. It was for ABC, a period film about an era that I loved. Of course I was doing it. I had every right to take another job. I had never signed an exclusive with Ed. But that's not how he saw it. When Ed got wind that I was doing the film, he fired me. "Get out," he told me the day I had my first meeting at Warner's. "Get your files and get out."

For the first—and only—time in my career I just let loose on a producer. All the frustration I was feeling about my life I dumped on Ed. "You're never going to care about me or even remember my name," I told him. "But I don't give a shit because working for you has been the single worst experience of my life."

I felt triumphant driving off the Gower Street lot, but whether I knew it or not, I was getting pushed to the limit. Brad knew that I was working too much. But what was the alternative given his career? *Rosalie* opened in March with okay reviews but absolutely no box office. The screening had been fun, a bit of the old days at the Writers Guild in February. Brad had gone with Rick Rosenberg, and even Robert, Weber's assistant, had tagged along to catch his patient play the star. But once the movie opened, Brad didn't bother to conceal his disappointment. His own notices were good, but even Clifford recognized this was one more missed opportunity. "It would have been so different if this was a hit," he told Brad over the phone. "Because you and I know this isn't about quality, but about being in a hit, that's when they want you."

Even without knowing Brad was ill, Clifford seemed to sense that time was not on our side, that Brad was getting restless, even a little panicky. Even before *Rosalie* opened, Brad had decided to go to New York. Some of it was a desire to see Rodger McFarlane and Larry Kramer again, but mostly he was going to talk to Clifford, to get some reading on his career from someone besides David Eidenberg, whom Brad now considered more an adversary than an ally. Ever since Brad's problems on *Unspeakable Acts,* he had felt distanced from David, angry that he had refused to back Brad in his fight with Linda Otto, and confused by what he saw as David's generally chilly attitude toward him.

It was during that week in New York in March that Brad told Clifford he was seriously thinking of leaving the agency. "David just isn't doing it for me," he told Clifford. "And I can't figure out why."

But Clifford knew. He knew the agency was suffering, that despite his big Broadway-based clients—Jason Robards, Colleen Dewhurst, Lauren Bacall, and the like—the L.A. office was losing clients. This kind of talent drain affects all the smaller houses who take on young actors, turn them into stars, and watch them get sucked up by ICM or CAA. It had nothing to do with Brad, but he was getting lost in the shuffle. It's one reason why David had tried to put him together with a manager, Mary Goldberg, after *Unspeakable Acts*. We had known Mary back in New York when she worked as a casting director at the Public Theater. Now she had moved to L.A. and become a personal manager for several actors. Ostensibly, she would deal with Brad daily, formulate a game plan, and act as his liaison with the agency. Managers are common practice now, a real trend in Hollywood, but Brad and Mary never hit it off, and when the situation came to a head, Mary was the one to bail. Brad was livid—it was like being fired by your housekeeper—and he blamed David.

Now Brad told Clifford he was seriously thinking of quitting STE largely because of David. But Clifford also knew that David himself was planning on leaving the agency later that month. In December, David had told Clifford he wanted to get out of the business, that he would retire right after the Oscars. He had also asked Clifford to keep the decision confidential. "Listen, I'm coming out to L.A. in April," Clifford told Brad. "Don't do anything until I can talk to everyone in person."

But Clifford didn't make it in time. By March 14, news of David's resignation was out and quite the talk of the town. It wasn't the abruptness of his departure—that happens all the time—but that David appeared to be sabotaging the agency. There were stories about how David was telling his clients the agency wouldn't survive his departure, and even nastier stories about how he had personally escorted clients such as Geena Davis up the street to ICM.

The agency was in chaos and Brad felt as if the ground had fallen out from under him. He had been angry at David, but now he was hurt that David was quitting, and even more that he hadn't even called to tell him. That afternoon, Brad fired off one of his letters:

David–

I'm not calling to say good-bye for several reasons, the least of which I wouldn't know who I was saying good-bye to. You made it quite clear that you wanted no personal involvement with me. I came to accept that. What I wasn't prepared for was how little support I would get from you on a professional level. . . . I made all the right excuses for your behavior during the Linda Otto incident [on *Unspeakable Acts*], but there was no way for me to disguise your behavior around the situation with Mary [Goldberg]. David, any other agent would have been livid that his client was treated in such a shabby and ultimately abusive manner . . . [then] feeling my most vulnerable, demoralized, insignificant, and out-of-work, I also get to be dismissed by you. Congratulations and touché, David. If you wanted to get back at me, you did.
—Brad

On April 1, David typed his response, a detailed point-by-point rebuttal and one tiny concession. "I had failed," David wrote, "to somehow force your career to work as I felt it should, and more importantly I had failed to make both you and me 'ok.'" He also admitted that in not calling Brad about his departure, "I acted like an asshole and chickened out. . . . I know I was wrong and am sincerely apologetic for that. . . . I was not even able or willing to do the one thing I knew you would have liked."

For Brad it was like Eddie Bondy's death. Another agent had left him. Clifford was moving quickly to staunch the blood, moving to Los Angeles to personally handle that half of the agency. But Brad sensed it would be months, maybe even years, before the agency would right itself. It was time Brad didn't have. It's why Brad decided to tell Clifford he was HIV-positive.

The night of May 9, Brad met him at his Burton Way apartment in Beverly Hills before heading over to Muse, one of Brad's favorite restaurants. Brad had gotten his latest T-cell test results that day, the first since he'd gone off AZT in April. In a single month, they had fallen by half, from 60 to 30.

"I've got something to tell you," Brad said. Clifford remembered looking at Brad's hands, his bitten nails, how nervous he seemed. "Oh, God," Clifford said to himself. "He's going to tell me he's leaving." His diary notes that night tell the story. "Midnight, another dear friend HIV-positive. SHIT!"

Clifford was already keeping one client's secret when he started keeping Brad's. Colleen Dewhurst, one of his oldest friends, was also dying of cancer. For Clifford, all the pieces came together with Brad's disclosure. It was no longer just the usual career panic, that realization that he "was someone who had been someone and who no longer was." Now there was a time clock, an urgency to Brad's need to work.

It's one reason why Clifford urged Brad to take *Hangfire* that June. It was a ghastly movie starring Kim Delaney and Jan-Michael Vincent, directed by B-movie director Peter Maris. It was a supporting role, only $75,000 for four weeks, after someone else had dropped out. I thought it was shit, but Brad took it. The days of the last-minute $250,000 movie of the week were apparently over. "Oh, let him do it," Zane had told me. "Their check will cash and at least he doesn't have to go on location."

It was an inauspicious start to what turned out to be a terrible summer. That month while Brad was shooting *Hangfire* out in Palmdale, another crisis erupted, this one involving Doris, our housekeeper. Her boyfriend had a drug problem and now he began to physically abuse her. We tried to work this out—we took her to a shelter for battered women, we even took her to a therapist—but Doris was Guatemalan, a staunch Catholic. God, she told us, would heal her boyfriend. Finally, I had to give her notice. I had hired a new housekeeper, Daisy, who was to start on July 9.

Almost immediately, I realized I had made a terrible mistake. Not only could none of us understand Daisy's El Salvadoran dialect, but Brad and Alexandra instantly hated her. The two of them were home all day now sharing a hot, crowded house with a virtual stranger. Alexandra was distraught over Doris's leaving—it was a huge abandonment issue for her. But Brad flat-out despised Daisy and the feelings were mutual. She didn't know he was sick; she thought he was lazy, a grown man spending all day in bed while his wife went out and worked. Brad thought Daisy was cold and unnurturing, especially when she refused to cook for him.

Food was a big issue for Brad now. He still had an appetite, but keeping weight on was another story; he was already losing the first of the more than sixty pounds he would drop in two years. His thinness was starting to invite comment from friends, from casting directors, those offhand but concerned observations: "Gee, Brad, you really look thin."

Weber had him eating three meals a day, something Brad had never done in his life. He was even forcing down protein shakes. A hot evening meal was imperative, Weber had told him, and Doris had obliged. She would make Brad and Alexandra lunch and then dinner, which we could heat up. But Daisy refused. Even though I had made it clear that this was part of her job, she simply didn't cook. Opening a can of soup or a frozen dinner was her idea of a hot meal. So I had to cook. All weekend I would make these huge meals, lasagna, casseroles, soups, anything I could make a bunch of and freeze for Brad to heat up at night. It was ridiculous: we had a full-time housekeeper and I was spending my weekends in the kitchen.

A lot of Brad's mistrust of Daisy was because, three days before she started, he had begun giving himself EPO injections for his anemia. They were just subcutaneous injections, like insulin, but Brad was still paranoid about Alexandra, and especially Daisy, seeing him shooting up. The morning of July 6, 1990, Robert came by to show him the procedure. It should have been simple, just a pinch of flesh and a jab of the needle, a lot simpler than what Brad had done during his drug-taking days. But Brad had no fat anywhere on his body. "Try your thigh," Robert suggested, but that was too painful. Brad wound up shooting it in his stomach—Robert swore he saw Brad's face flush at the first injection, that old junkie rush—but even that left a black-and-blue mark. They hadn't let the vial warm up enough—EPO needs to be refrigerated—and Brad said it was like shooting ice water in your veins.

So now there were needles in the house, a big box of them on the top shelf in the closet, right next to the red plastic toxic-waste container that Robert emptied every few weeks. I don't think I would have paid that much attention, except Brad made me watch him inject himself those first few days. He knew I hated needles. Even before I had my biopsy, I'd hated them. Now Brad was making a joke of it as he made me stand there. "I'm not doing this," I said. "I'm not watching you."

Finally, he lost his temper with my squeamishness: "You better well watch this, because you're going to be watching a lot worse before this is over."

The rest of the summer was just a blur of depression and work. I was doing two movies for ABC, while Brad was in endless negotiations to do the sequel to *American Cousin*. I felt as if we were two dogs at the track, running endlessly after a dead, metal rabbit.

On the face of it, we were exactly where we should have been. Brad was responding to the EPO and was no longer anemic. He was even becoming involved in some local AIDS activities. In July, he did an interview with Charles Champlin, the legendary Hollywood writer, about AIDS awareness in the industry. That was a favor to Rodger McFarlane. Later in the month, he spoke at the annual APLA garden party in Griffith Park. That was a favor to Mark Senak, the APLA lawyer.

But the reality was, as in any long, terminal illness, we were becoming exhausted and increasingly isolated. We were so broke that neither of us was in therapy. I hadn't seen Gaylan in months, and Brad had stopped seeing his therapist last fall. Zane had made it clear that with the exception of Alexandra's work with Paul, therapy could no longer be a priority.

I felt completely isolated. Without Gaylan in my life, I spoke to not a single person about Brad's illness. My every day was a living lie. Even Brad, who was so used to an extended support group—the nonstop phone calls, the constant stream of lunch and dinner dates—was down to a few essential people. There were daily calls to Roger and Larry in New York, Rick Rosenberg, and Mark Senak. He also spoke frequently to Clifford and to his therapist;

even though he could no longer pay her, she still spoke to him on the phone. There was also a psychic healer, a guy named Hilton Silverman, out in the north Valley, that Brad's therapist had found, whom he started to see. But it was a shadow compared to Brad's usual life. With the exception of Mark, whom he would meet at Dupars for a late breakfast when he felt up to it, Brad lived on the phone.

By August, we had both reached a crisis point. That month, I had appointment to see Paul Crane, my gynecologist. I hadn't been in for almost two years; Pap smears were not my favorite thing. So it wasn't that unusual for him to ask, "What are you using for birth control these days?"

Maybe it was the white coat or his calm doctor manner, but I just lost it. "I'm not using anything because I'm not having sex," I blurted out. "Because Brad is HIV-positive." It was the first time I had told anyone, anyone other than Gaylan, and I sat there in that stupid paper robe, just sobbing with relief.

Brad hit his own moment of crisis three weeks later. August 24, he got the results of his T-cell test. A new low: 20. Brad tells Weber he wants to name them, there are so few now. His journal entry reads:

D'day—August 24th, 1990
   I am sitting at a desk with pen in hand and writing this. Now what? Is anybody out there? Anybody want to give me a hand? I'm accepting all offers of a friendly and helpful nature, any guide or two hanging around? How about a little divine intervention. So! What to write about—my childhood? Ok.

Three days later, Brad completed his entry with a description of his own birth:

   I found it quite comfortable inside my mother's stomach, although she chain-smoked and was not above having a cocktail now and again, so I was in no hurry to be pushed out into God knows what. But it seemed clear that my time arrived. . . . There we all were gathered to welcome me into the world. My mother shrieking and the nurses sounding more and more like Prissy as the Yankees approached Atlanta and the doctor yelling at my mother to "Push" and "Come on, ya little bastard," to me. I was overwhelmed with everything working against me and I gave up, shooting out with such force that I nearly shot past the doctor's hands right onto the floor. "Look, the little bastard's trying to commit suicide," he said. And I remember thinking, we can always hold that as an option.

CHAPTER

16

Another year and another death: Lawrence Lott, one of Brad's costars in *The Normal Heart,* died of AIDS on January 24, 1991; he was forty and living with his mother in Colorado. As hard as I try to fight it, this seems an omen for us.

This is our sixth year of living with HIV, and life is unalterably hard. My days consist of crying jags and lies; Brad is all nerves and frustration. He is back at Gersh after jumping ship from STE in October. It was inevitable after David's bloody departure from the agency last spring. Clifford was sorry but not surprised since he knows now Brad is on a clock. I didn't know if Gersh was the right place, but anything was better than William Morris, all those wasted years after Eddie's death. Even I admit Bob has a talent for resurrecting careers. "A good actor is a good actor is a good actor" was always his mantra. All you had to do was scour his client list at the time—Harrison Ford, Kathleen Turner, Annette Bening—to get the picture.

So Brad is at Gersh and living on hope and painkillers. There are daily phone calls to the agency about *Blood Ties II,* the sequel to *American Cousin,* Alessandro Focazzi's script, and Brad's fee. Brad is pushing for more than the $250,000 he got the first time around. A lot more. He's really swinging for the fences now. That is when he's not laid low by the headaches and omnipresent fatigue. Both are debilitating, especially the headaches, which returned with a vengence after Brad's brief AZT vacation last May. Besides the AZT, Bactrim, and daily EPO injections, Brad plows through over-the-counter medicines, Advil, then Tylenol, then Bufferin. He takes them by the bottle, six, eight, ten, twenty pills a day. Our days are now prescribed by his health: if he has a good day, we have a good day; if not, our lives are even more hellish than they feel.

Christmas was a new low, the first year we stayed home and avoided the obligatory trek to Tallahassee. Brad pleaded the flu with his parents, although it's a toss-up what really kept us from going, his health or our finances. It hardly matters; it is only the first of the excuses we now manufacture when we can't make a dinner invitation, can't make a meeting, can't make parents' night at Alexandra's school.

By February 15, Brad switches from AZT to DDC and life becomes worth living again. Weber arranges it, some more of his wizardry since DDC is still largely experimental. This is good news and bad news. Clearly, the AZT is not working; Brad lost a third of his remaining T cells in a single month. He is down to 20 now, all of them named. But once off the AZT, his headaches and anemia disappear. Weber takes him off the EPO shots and puts him on two oral medications: acyclovir, an antiherpes prophylaxis, and dif-leukin, an antifungal agent. Weber's notes read: "We are now trying to prophylaxe [sic] him against everything—we are like a year ahead in doing this kind of prophylaxis—to prevent an opportunistic infection, which is inevitable for someone with only 20 helper cells."

Weber tells Brad that DDC will have its own side effects, painful neuropathy in his hands and feet, but that it won't set in for months. Now, all is sunshine again, relatively speaking. As far as I can see, the Diflucan is a miracle drug, an oral rather than topical medication for fungus infections. Almost immediately Brad's skin problems clear up: the thrush in his mouth, the blotches on his face. Even his nails, all but eaten up by fungus, start to grow back.

It's enough of a boost to make Brad think he is ready for one more big job, maybe even a series. Bob Gersh is certainly sending him out while they dicker on *Blood Ties II,* and for once Brad is willing to go. He meets with John Herzfeld on his pilot *Fifth Corner.* He goes in for an HBO movie, *The Story of Bobby Seale,* that Dennis Hopper is starring in. But he is most interested in *I'll Fly Away,* a TV series based on Harper Lee's classic *To Kill a Mockingbird.* The script is definitely a cut above average, and Brad is desperate to play the Atticus Finch character, a liberal Southern lawyer and single father. If Brad gets the role and grosses even $15,000 an episode, a full season of twenty-six would get us almost $400,000, exactly the kind of last payday he is looking for.

But none of these goes anywhere. The reasons are many and varied, as they usually are. But Brad is disappointed, especially when Sam Waterston lands *I'll Fly Away.* He's not remotely Southern and his TV Q-rating isn't any better than Brad's. I chalk it up to Brad's looks. It's not as if he looks sick, but he doesn't look well. It's almost a regular chorus now: casting directors give him the once-over and tell him, "You ought to put on a little weight."

Putting on weight is his grand obsession now, but nothing tastes good to him anymore. Even when I come home at night and try to make dinner, he can't get through it. It's why he forces himself to drink those high-calorie shakes Weber tells him to get at the Sav-on. Cases of this chocolate stuff sit in the corner of the kitchen. Brad hates it, but at nine hundred calories a shot, it's easy insurance against any nasty surprises when he steps on the scale every morning. For the first time in his life, Brad weighs himself every day. As if he's playing the slot machine. He bought the biggest, ugliest scale he could find, which takes up half our bathroom. The magic number is 140. It's fifteen pounds below normal, but even this is a struggle; the attrition is slow but steady. By spring, he will be 135.

In February, he gets a brief bit of good news workwise. A quick USA cable movie, *Child of Darkness, Child of Light.* It's a horror film, based on the novel *Virgin,* but the cast is okay, Sela Ward and Viveca Lindfors. Brad isn't one of the leads—he plays a doctor—but they're paying him $75,000, an amazing amount for all of six days' work.

I guess work does breed work because it's that month that Larry Kramer also calls Brad. It's more of a favor than a job. Larry's new play, *The Tyranny of Blood*, is finally getting a reading at Lincoln Center at the end of the month. It's the sequel/prequel to *The Normal Heart*, and Larry wants Brad to reprise his role as Ned Weeks. Brad is torn. It's a good cast—Colleen Dewhurst and George Grizzard. Ironically, both are Clifford's clients, and Marshall Mason, the former artistic director of the Circle Repertory Theater, is directing. But Brad has no intention of doing a full run of anything now; he doesn't have either the stamina or the financial resources to support an off-Broadway run. But he also knows this is Larry's official olive branch after their big falling out over the publication of *The Normal Heart*. In the credits, Larry had double-listed Ned Weeks to include Brad and his replacement Joel Grey. Brad was more wounded than I had ever seen him and fired off one of his letters.

He had written:

Dear Larry,

I am finally allowing myself to feel how deeply hurt and outraged I am at the way I am treated in the published version of *Normal Heart*. . . . Replacements are NEVER listed in the original cast. . . . [But] no matter how much I am excluded or ignored in the present or future where this play is concerned, there is one thing that is mine, and that is that I did originate that role. I did want to do it when NO Actor with Any Name would get NEAR it. (You couldn't cast it, Larry, REMEMBER?)

But Brad decided to do the reading, largely because he wanted to spend some time talking to the Gersh people in New York. He flew out on the twenty-fourth of February and spent that night at Larry's. The day of the reading dawned a gray, end-of-winter day. A steady rain had fallen all afternoon and was still coming down when the lights went up at the Bruno Walter Library up at Lincoln Center. Even the mood of the room was bleak; Larry was HIV-positive, Brad was sick, and Colleen was dying. Joe Papp, the producer of *The Normal Heart*, was in the audience and known to dying of bone cancer. He wasn't publicly admitting anything, but everyone was braced for his death, as if lights on Broadway were about to be extinguished. It was all doubly tragic since Joe's son, Tony, was dying of AIDS.

As if all that weren't grim enough, Colleen had started to hemorrhage that afternoon. As a Christian Scientist, she was refusing all medical help and amazingly made it through the reading. "I heard we had some problems today," Clifford whispered to her at the end of the night. He had been across the plaza at the opera and had snuck out at the interval hoping to catch Colleen, George, and Brad. He hated the play, too long-winded and didactic, but he was astonished that two dying people had such force. Afterward, Clifford went up to Brad and gave him a big hug. Even though he was at Gersh, there were no hard feelings.

Whatever fears Brad had about the reading were moot; *The Destiny of Me,* as Larry wisely retitled it, would not open off-Broadway for two years.

After he got back from New York, Brad went into deep negotiations on *Blood Ties II.* The cast was already coming together, but Brad was starting to get cold feet. Not only were they not going to pay him anything like the $500,000 he wanted, but it looked as if there would be months of filming abroad, in Rome and Hong Kong. Six months ago, this wouldn't have been an issue. But Brad wasn't up to that kind of travel now. Not only was he exhausted, but he was petrified of being found out abroad. "There's countries where they lock you up if they find out you're HIV-positive," he told Weber, "where they literally put you in prison." This was the case in a handful of Muslim nations, but Brad was adamant about not leaving the country now. Even before they made him an offer, *Blood Ties II* was history. How could he explain that to Bob Gersh? There was no way Brad was going to tell him he was HIV-positive, they weren't that close. In less than seven months at Gersh, Brad decided to quit the agency. "I've got to get out of there," he said one night. "I've got to get Clifford to protect me."

Even before he officially re-signed with STE on May 15, Brad landed his next job, a film version of Horton Foote's drama *Habitation of Dragons,* for TNT. Michael Lindsay-Hogg would be directing, which is why Brad got the call. It would be the first time they've worked together since Michael directed *The Normal Heart*. Brad is to play Brother, the younger of two brothers in a small Southern town; Frederic Forrest is set to costar. The money is shit—$5,000 a week for five weeks—something like a tenth of what Brad had hoped to get for *Blood Ties II*. But the role fits him like a glove; Brad calls the offer, which came without an audition, "a gift from God." It is, in the sense that it will be his last job, but none of us knows that. Certainly not Michael, who first meets with Brad in April at the producer's offices on Vine Street in Hollywood. Brad has fewer than twenty T cells and is convinced that he will never get the job because of his appearance, but he drives up in his Jaguar and Michael thinks he is doing okay.

He lands the role partly because Michael is right, Brad is perfect to play the jealous brother, "a guy who had suffered a lot and had bitterness because of it, but who also still had a wish to be good," as Michael explained it to Brad. But he also gets it because Michael Brandman, the producer, thinks Brad is still something of a star. Since he is producing a series of six movies—adapted dramas by playwrights such as Arthur Miller and David Mamet—for Amblin and TNT, his standards are vastly different from those of the rest of Hollywood. Star or no star, by the time Brad leaves for the shoot, five weeks in Texas starting May 13, he has ten T cells and has collected unemployment—two new lows.

One of the first conversations Brad and Michael Lindsay-Hogg have in Brookshire, a "bumfuck town" somewhere outside Houston, as Brad tells me over the phone, is about Billy DeAcutis's death from AIDS, nine days earlier. Another *Normal Heart* alumnus. "Let's keep it to one," Michael tells Brad, until he is reminded that Larry Lott died in January. "Oh, God, I forgot," Michael says, embarrassed. But Brad shrugs. This kind of deception doesn't get any easier, but it is automatic. Like weight lifting. "You just wonder how long it's going to take them to find a cure," he says easily.

For the next five weeks, Brad leads this kind of double life amid twelve-hour days on the set. He loves working with Michael again and the role is the kind that reminds him why he became an actor. Especially the fact that it's a twist on his own relationship with his brother. "This doesn't excuse the way Gene has behaved," he tells me over the phone, "but I understand it now, what it must have been like to have been Brad Davis's brother."

The rest of it is a nightmare, however, a Budget Host Inn and chicken-fried everything. There is nothing he can eat in the entire state of Texas; everything is meat and/or fried. The only good restaurant, Leandry's, is thirty miles away, and even there fresh vegetables are a rarity. At least no one thinks twice about Brad's complaints since everyone is ragging on the catering and the whole low-budget bit, such as there's only one car to ferry all the actors back and forth to the set. Even when Brad sets up a hot plate in his room and spends his evenings eating peanut butter sandwiches and writing letters, Michael chalks it up to the usual actor quirks.

If I was worried about Brad's being on location, I wasn't allowing myself to feel it. I had needed a breather, we both did. I was juggling two jobs, *Raven,* a CBS series starring Lee Majors that I'd been working on since March, and a feature at Disney, *The Incredible Journey,* the remake of the 1963 Disney classic. Besides, when compared to months in Hong Kong and Rome, Texas seemed like nothing, even those nights when Brad calls and is simply too tired to talk. "Hi," he says, sounding very very faint. "I can't talk because I'm really, really tired, but I wanted to say hi."

By the time they move to Houston for the last week of filming, Brad is eating only bread and cheese and complaining of stomach pains. Michael thinks it's a bout with some Mexican food, but Brad thinks it's an ulcer, or he would except for all the diarrhea. "I'm living on Maalox," he tells me. "I don't really know what's wrong." The night of the wrap party, a big to-do with the mayor in attendance, Brad was so weak he couldn't leave his room. Four days after he gets home from Houston, Weber calls with his latest T-cell results: Brad has zero T cells.

It happened the same way with my aunt Ida, when she was dying of cancer. There comes a day when you suddenly see they're dying in front of your eyes. It might be the pallor of their skin, a waxiness that wasn't there even two days ago. Or it may be the dullness of their eyes. Or the terrible thinness in the back. Or it may be the defeated way they turn their head in the light when they think no one is looking. In that moment, a chasm opens between you, and they are already beyond your grasp.

That's how it was when I first saw Brad after Texas. That Saturday night after the limo dropped him off and I was standing there in the kitchen making him something to eat, I first thought he looked fine. "Honey, you really don't look bad," I said, my back to him as I chopped whatever I was chopping. "I don't look thin?" he asked, his voice raspy in a way that I hadn't heard before. "No, really, I think you look pretty good." And I meant it, or I meant to mean it until I walked in on him in the bedroom a few minutes later and saw him, so pinched and naked as he struggled with his robe, this stupid pink terry-cloth robe he wore, and I knew then that he was dying.

But I put up a good front. The weaker Brad gets, the more obstinate I become. "Well, it isn't AIDS yet," I say resolutely. Brad may have no T cells, but there are still no definite signs of any opportunistic infection. At least that's what I tell myself.

But Brad is not assuaged. He feels sicker now than he's ever felt, and he is alarmed when Weber tells him he is leaving for a two-week trip to Europe; his lover is dying of AIDS and this is to be their last trip together. Robert will come by in his absence; another doctor, Peter Miao, will be on call.

But Brad is nervous, and when Robert Altman calls later that week, asking him to do a cameo in his new film, *The Player,* he is too exhausted to be anything but irritated. He loves Bob and he knows the film, based on Michael Tolkin's novel, is Altman's long-threatened comeback after years of living in virtual exile in Paris. Brad also knows that *The Player* has become something of a hot ticket in town since Bob is having his fun stocking the nasty black comedy with stars—Julia Roberts, Burt Reynolds, Cher, Jack Lemmon—playing themselves.

Under ordinary circumstances Brad would have jumped at the chance to do it, but now he just feels pressured. He tries to get Rick Rosenberg to go with him to be in the scene, moral support more than anything, but Rick refuses to horn in on Altman's parade. So Brad has to go alone. "What the fuck am I going to wear?" is his all-consuming thought on June 22, the Saturday he is to shoot his scene. Brad is to spend the afternoon at Le Restaurant down on La Cienega. It is supposed to double for the Ivy or Morton's, he doesn't remember which. But Brad spends the morning trying on a dozen different outfits, anything to disguise the thinness that he is certain will get him chucked from the film. He settles on a baggy black jacket and pants and an oversize gold shirt. The big look, he jokes, heading out to the car, but I can tell this will be a bad day.

And it is. He comes home, six hours later, wiped out. His scene was literally two lines, but it is the strain of putting up a front, the tension of being out, of seeing people he hasn't seen in four years. To top it off, Joel Grey is also there that day, Brad's nemesis ever since their double billing in the published version of *The Normal Heart*. Brad is so exhausted by the shoot that when Bob Altman calls again asking him—us actually—to be in the big gala scene to be held at the L.A. County Art Museum, Brad passes. I have nothing to wear and Brad refuses to trot himself in front of *le tout* Hollywood.

In the end, he is only window dressing anyway. His big scene never makes the final cut. Too bad, because I thought it was hilarious. Brad comes into the restaurant and tells the maître d' he is meeting Lisa Shapiro. "Shapiro? I don't have any Shapiro."

"Oh, wait a minute," Brad says. "Maybe it's 'Sha-pie-ro.'"

"Oh, yes, right this way, Mr. Davis."

If you had told Brad that his last lines on-camera would be cut, he would have laughed at the irony of it. There are too many lasts now, and like the final snowfall of the season, you never know it. The last dinner with Clifford Stevens is at Spumante on July 19. The last time we spend a weekend with Rick Rosenberg and Tim Thompson is over the Fourth of July at their house in Del Mar. And so it goes.

The Del Mar weekend was telling. It was absurd, given how close they were and how sick Brad was, that he had still not told Rick he was ill. I had bugged him about this for months; I for one was sick of lying to supposedly one of our closest friends. But this was typical of Brad's compartmentalized life. Brad's confidants included Clifford and Zane Lubin, Rodger and Larry, Weber and Robert and

Mark Senak, and that was it. Clifford and Zane essentially worked for Brad, Rodger and Larry he had known forever, when he was fucked-up on drugs, Weber and Robert and Mark were the HIV-specialists. Rick was none of these. He had met Brad only after he'd gotten sober, when his career looked to be coming back. Telling Rick he was HIV-positive meant shattering that image—he was a microcosm for the world as a whole—and that was something Brad was not prepared to do until the absolute last minute.

As far as I was concerned, that minute was now. A weekend in Del Mar, even in their big house? Surely they will know something is wrong given Brad's chronic stomach pain and the night sweats that have returned with a vengeance. But Brad won't budge. "Rick's so burdened with his own career now," he says, waving me off. And in truth, Rick is going through a bad patch over at Warner's, the kind of dry spell that can hit all producers.

So the weekend became a farce, a mismatch between Rick's expectations and Brad's abilities, a running battle that started that first morning when Brad slept in until noon and then spent an hour pawing through the refrigerator trying to find something, anything, he could eat while Rick just fumed about the day's evaporating. Ever since they'd moved to the beach, Rick and Tim had gotten into this whole health thing, running and mountain biking and heading off to San Diego to go to the Padres games. Our visit was like army maneuvers: field trips from the house to the beach, from the house to the restaurants, from the house to the movie, *Naked Gun 2½,* and from the house to the fair—and all of it on foot. "Parking's too nuts to drive," Rick said as he pushed us out the door for yet another outing. To get to the beach we had to scale this fucking dune—I just flat-out refused and went the long way around on the road—while Rick even had Brad carrying the beach chairs. At one point, Brad was on his knees in the sand, howling with laughter at the irony of this. "Maybe now would be the time to tell him?" I hissed. I'd been keeping up a steady stream of "Doesn't Brad look thin to you guys?" hints, hoping they would pick up on it.

But Brad ignored me. This was a contest of wills. The whole

weekend, he kept up a front, claiming that he was simply getting an ulcer. Even as he complained about being hot one minute and cold the next and could only really eat cottage cheese and the baby food we eventually had to get him, it was still only an ulcer.

And there were flashes of his old self, the way he ragged on Tim on the way back from the beach telling him that he should do something useful, "get into recycling," instead of this endless fun-in-the-sun life. And at the restaurant on Saturday, Pirettes over in Encinitas, Rick's hangout, "my Morton's south," he called it, Brad just ate it up when the waitress fussed over him, going on and on about *Midnight Express* and what a great actor he was. But by Sunday afternoon, after a two-mile walk to the fair and hours of Alexandra dragging us from one ride to the next, Brad was ready to drop. "God," he said, collapsing onto a bench, "if we could just drive to dinner, I'd be so grateful."

It was shortly after that—and his latest and last T-cell test on July 10 confirming his zero status—that Brad decided to tell Rick. He called his office at Warner's around eleven.

"What are you doing for lunch?" Brad asked. "I want to talk to you about something."

Rick said, "Look, what are you doing right now? I'll just come over."

When Rick got to the house, Brad opened the door. He'd made an effort to get cleaned up for Rick; his hair was damp from the shower and he'd cut himself trying to shave. "I have something to tell you," he said, patting at the blood with a Kleenex.

"Look, you don't have to tell me," Rick said. "It's AIDS."

"How did you know?"

Rick had started to put two and two together after the weekend. He'd told Tim he thought Brad was really sick and not dealing with just an ulcer. Rick had even brought a brochure from a group, Search Alliance, that was working with people with AIDS. "Listen," he told Brad. "I want you to fight this."

At least Rick knows now, at least it is one less person I have to lie to on the phone, a relief because things are getting worse. For the first time, Robert notes something other than "no complaints" in Brad's log. "July 9: substernal pain [diaphragm/stomach area], burning, fatigue, mild cough. T cells 0." But there are another twenty days, another three weeks of watching Brad get weaker and weaker and the nights when he shakes and sweats uncontrollably and days when he struggles to act as if he were fine, fine enough to take Alexandra to a friend's daughter's birthday party. There are three weeks of this before Brad finally goes to the hospital.

Robert has scheduled his outpatient test for July 29 at Sherman Oaks Hospital. Brad assumes I will drive him, but I suggest he get Rick. Brad is seeing virtually no one now—he hasn't even called Mark Senak in weeks—because of the way he looks and feels. "Call him," I tell him, "he'll want to do it."

Rick hates hospitals as much as Brad does, and Brad is nervous as shit about the test. It is essentially a rectal exam to check for bacteria in the stomach and bowels, but Brad is scared of the pain, of the hospital again, he's even dicey about the two Fleet enemas he has to take the day before. That weekend, he wants me and Alexandra out of the house. I make arrangements for her to spend the days with Doris, who has reappeared in our lives as an occasional baby-sitter, while I agree to go to Marcia Ross's birthday party she is throwing for herself at Trumps. This is the last place I want to be, but I'm amazed at how I drink tea and chatter with the best of them. On Monday, Rick picks Brad up before I'm even out of the shower; when I get home that night, he is already in bed asleep. He slept, it seemed, for two or three days.

The test has revealed nothing conclusive. Although Brad has symptoms of CMV, a gastrointestinal opportunistic infection, they can find no evidence of the microbacteria. But Rodger knows this is only a matter of time. He is pressuring Brad to keep his end of the bargain, to think seriously about going public. There is no question of Brad's working again, not in front of a camera anyway. His career no longer needs protecting. The question is how: a press conference, an interview, or just a day of phoning all our friends? At night in bed this is what we talk about now, not should we tell, but how. "I want to come out of hiding," he says. "And I don't want you ever to say I died of anything but AIDS."

Whatever fireworks Rodger McFarlane may have wanted, Brad decides that a book is the answer, a way to set the record straight in

271

his own words as well as one last chance to set aside a chunk of cash for me and Alexandra. "I'm not going to work again as an actor, I guess I'll become a writer," he tells me. "But you have to be the one to finish it."

I don't even hesitate. "It needs to come out," I tell him, "because I can't live like this anymore."

So the book, *this* book, was conceived in our bed, literally, the eight hours Brad spent propped up writing out the proposal in longhand, the pages piling up beside him.

"I'm an actor and I died of AIDS. But I also worked for six years [with HIV] and whether or not you liked me or whether or not you agreed with my decision to keep on working, you hired me. Just remember, I did some of my best work when I was HIV-positive. I didn't hold you up. You never had to worry about me showing up. I was there for you. I'm writing this because there are so many others like me, so many HIV-positive actors who are healthy and working, but who live lives of paranoia and fear because they can't tell the truth. Now, I'm telling it."

He is the most energized I've seen him in weeks. "I'm going to get a desk," he says. "Set it up in the corner and look out the window and write the story of my life."

Weber has decided they need to do a bone-marrow biopsy, the ultimate test for microbacteria. This is a nasty piece of work that requires several days' hospitalization. Also, he wants to stabilize Brad, who is hovering around 120 pounds and losing weight rapidly. He is at the point now where the sound of the dogs, or the smell of them or cat food, is enough to make him physically ill. In this heat, I can hardly bear our bedroom now, the damp sheets, the musty air, the ever-present tang of vomit.

That night when I got home, Brad gives me the news. "I have to go in," he says. "I'm too sick and the tests are going to take too long."

I knew what we were living with, but my response was still automatic. "Yeah, well, it still isn't AIDS yet."

"Susan, I have some sort of opportunistic infection, and it's knocking the shit out of me," Brad says, yelling. "This *is* AIDS! This

face," he says, pointing at his hollowed cheeks, "is the face of
AIDS."

This time I drive him.

August 13, 1991, a Tuesday morning, we head out on the route
that I will come to know in my sleep for the next six days—
Whitsett to Riverside to Van Nuys. It is a ten-minute commute to
the Sherman Oaks Hospital, Sherman AIDS Hospital as it is known.
The country's second-oldest ISU, immune-supressed unit, is here,
an entire wing, 3-West, with its own specially trained nursing staff, a
model for many other AIDS units. Weber has told Brad he will get
no better care anywhere else in the country.

I'm sure this is true, but my first impression is that it is all a little
shabby. The hospital is of modest size, only three stories, and inside
it looks worn, with the usual plastic chairs and laminated tables,
hardly the gleaming high-tech facility I was expecting. But Brad is
being admitted to the oncology ward, not the AIDS wing—Weber
and Robert have seen to this—so we are whisked directly to his
room on the second floor. The admitting clerk does all the
paperwork here rather than in the lobby, another Weber perk. Even
so, Brad has worn his red baseball cap, as if this will protect him
from the curious. He leans back on the bed, the red of his cap vivid
on the white pillow, while the clerk goes through her forms.
"Robert Davis," she writes in neat block letters. "Patient: Robert
Davis."

I look around. This is a private room, plush by hospital standards,
with a VCR, refrigerator, and even a little settee. But the furniture is
cheap and the fluorescent light is harsh; Brad looks gray in here. I
put my bag down and root around for the pictures I've brought,
photographs of Alexandra and me on the beach at Del Mar. I love
this one of Alexandra; she is screaming with laughter, almost
drowning in the waves. Brad tells me to put them on the table by
the bed. I do, and then I don't know what to do. While the clerk
finishes up with Brad, Robert tells me the bone-marrow test is
scheduled for that afternoon and that Brad will need to be
anesthetized soon. Brad will not want me to stay, so I tell him I'm
leaving, then swing by the office and then go home to wait for Alex-

andra to get home from camp. That was the smartest thing I did this summer, send her to day camp out in Calabasas.

The office is my antidote, my messy desk, the stack of messages demanding my attention. My assistant, Paul Goff, is there when I arrive. Does he suspect something is wrong? I've told him Brad is going into the hospital. "Tests," I've said, "for his stomach." It is the same excuse we've used on Alexandra, and so far it has worked. Everyone knows Brad has been under the weather.

But Paul must suspect something. Even before I knew Brad was to be hospitalized, I'd decided to close up my office temporarily. *Raven* had ended in July and my contract on *Incredible Journey* ran out on August 5, even though I still have the three animal voices to cast. The contracts make it easy to give my associate, Marsha Shoenman, an extended leave, but I asked Paul to stay on part-time, essentially to handle the mail and messages. He is there with coffee and messages when I come in. I make a stab at a few calls, but this is pointless. I am packing up to leave when Paul tells me Zane is on the line. I am instantly suspicious since Zane never calls me directly, but always talks to Brad. I am convinced he is calling to give me a hard time about Alexandra's camp expenses. But when I get on the phone, all he says is, "What the fuck is going on?"

"What are you talking about?"

"Brad's sick, isn't he?"

I am amazed—not at his timing, because I am the one to tell him Brad is in the hospital—but because this is the first time that anyone other than Weber has made the distinction between Brad's being HIV-positive and Brad's being sick.

"Yes, he is sick," I say. "Zane, he is very sick."

Brad's test reveals the worst: MAI, mycobacterium avium intra-cellular, also known as MAC, mycobacterium avium complex—one of the most common opportunistic infections in HIV-positive patients. In layman's terms, Brad has microbacteria raging in his very bones, and his body can do nothing to stop it. They found it by drilling into his pelvic girdle, the iliac crest, literally screwing a needle into his hip and sucking out the marrow. Brad doesn't remember any of this since he was knocked with an anesthetic, but officially, he has AIDS.

What this means, practically, is that Brad has a fever so high he needs to be given shots of morphine to control the violent shaking he gets every night, "the rigors," Robert says to me, squeezing my hand when I walk in that night when they are holding Brad down, hunched over him with a needle, searching for a vein. It is like watching someone being raped.

The morphine is only the beginning. Brad is now started on a slew of drugs, some oral, some intravenous, names I have never heard of. Robert tells me that MAI is a difficult infection to treat, that it is a form of tuberculosis, slow to grow, hard to kill, and with a high resistance to antibiotics. Like most mycobacteria, it lives dormant in almost everyone, kept in check by a healthy immune system. But in people with fewer than fifty T cells, MAI is a killer if untreated. Brad will not recover, he says, but they can get control of the infection and Brad will eventually go home. Response time, however, can vary enormously. Some infections come down fast, others can take five or six weeks. Brad is one of the tougher ones. His fever is difficult to break. It is high, 104, 105, with unrelenting night sweats and chills. Robert tells me this is one of the worst cases he has seen.

Although Brad is being fed on an IV now, he remains weak. When I visit him, twice each day, he tells me he wants water, bottled water, chocolate, and pajamas. He has never worn pajamas in his life, but now, with all the night sweats, he can't get enough of them. So my days become obsessed with pajamas.

At first I dig out all the old ones, Christmas presents from his parents years ago, but eventually I go to Bullock's and get an armful. He is going through them at night, three, four sets. I know because they are piled on the floor, soaking wet, when I come in the mornings. The nurses refuse to touch them, not even with their latex gloves. The clothes just lie there until I pick them up and take them home to wash them. Every afternoon, after my trip to the hospital, I head home to do the laundry and wait for Alexandra. Wash, fold, and iron. It is a soothing cycle, the hum of the washer and the dryer all afternoon, the crisp smell of the ironed cotton, so clean and comforting after the sour, antiseptic smell of the hospital. Even when Brad tells me to forget the ironing, I don't. I love the smooth, folded pile sitting on the kitchen table every morning, like a fresh stack of mail.

This is the rhythm of my days. I never think about the office, just hospital and home. In the evenings, I head back with Alexandra. Sometimes I bring Chinese food for us to eat together, a family dinner like the ones we haven't had at home since I can remember. But Brad isn't really eating and the smell makes him gag. Usually Alexandra just climbs into the bed with him and we all watch a movie, something stupid like *The Bride of Frankenstein,* until it's time for us to go. We do this every day, until I lose all track of what day of the week it is. By the time Brad leaves the hospital, I have begun to hate the place.

Brad comes home on Monday, August 19, limping out to the car because the neuropathy in his feet from the DDC is so bad now. It is the tenth anniversary of his sobriety, ten years since that day in Brittany with Helen when Brad finally stopped drinking. It's like looking at someone else's life to remember that trip, the three of us in France, its cool leafiness, the sound of Helen's rippling laughter.

But I can't think about that now, not with Brad sitting here so gingerly in the passenger seat of the Jaguar, holding himself as if he might break. He is wearing his red cap again, but his face is drawn and pale and he asks me to turn down the radio. The whole way home, he leans his head against the window, his eyes closed.

In the space of a week, our lives have changed again. His fever is gone, but Brad is taking seventeen medications, some of them oral, most of them intravenous. He left the hospital with a shopping bag full of bottles and vials and a PICC line in his arm. They installed it that morning before I got there, this big needle with a plastic sheath over it stitched into his arm; they were still taping it into place, wiping up the blood, when I got there.

I had no idea this was going to be part of the deal. I hate needles and even Brad seems a little freaked by this, this tube into his arm. I can't even imagine what we're supposed to put in it; the drug schedule they've given us is ridiculous. That whole phrase *home health care,* my God, if only I had known what that really meant.

They've given us another list for what we need at the pharmacy, Valley Pharmacy near the hospital, which specializes in AIDS-patient care and where Brad has been buying his high-calorie shakes. We make a stop there and I just hand the list to the pharmacist since I have no idea what half this stuff is. But when we get home and Brad crawls into bed, and I'm left to sort out the bottles and pills and vials, I realize the circus is only just starting. Some organization called Critical Care America, an outpatient care company, is going to send someone. Weber has arranged this and I can only guess at the cost. Someone is to come that night and then every day after that to train me, to show us what to do. I already know I am going to have to clean that damn PICC line every day, swab it and replace the bandage, tape right over Brad's arm where they've stitched the needle into his flesh with the black thread, like a sock that's been darned.

I'm sitting there trying to sort out what goes where when the doorbell rings. A deliveryman from the hospital with another huge box, all the apparatus—the syringes and vials and bandages and the pump to use in the PICC line for one of the drugs, the TPN, at night. He puts the box on the kitchen floor and starts to go through it with me because a lot of the medication needs to be refrigerated and I need to know which ones, and I also have to remember to take them out about an hour before Brad needs it or the temperature shock will be too painful when it hits his veins. So the Compazine needs to be cold—no, not the Compazine—the Anacasin needs to be cold and so does the TPN. And then all the boxes of swabs and boxes of dressing-changing kits, boxes of syringes, boxes of tubing. God, there's gobs and gobs of tubing because every time I give him a shot, I have to rinse the PICC line with heparin and saline, and there are three different shots between every different administration of anything new in the line.

The guy looks at me for a minute, as if he is worried that I will not be able to remember all this, and given the state of the kitchen—the piled-up newspapers and laundry and bowls of dog and cat food, just junk everywhere—I don't blame him. But then I just have to get him out of the house because I am suddenly so scared, scared finally of AIDS. Because I now know that this is AIDS, not a toilet seat, a rumor, a touch of a stranger's hand, even a kiss. This is AIDS, this stuff, this shit, all this stuff that I have to pump into Brad just to keep him alive for one more day. That's what fucking AIDS is.

The Care people help a lot. Helen, her name is, except she only comes once and then another woman comes once or twice and then a guy who tells us right out that he is HIV-positive. All of them are nice, although Brad immediately likes some of them and hates the others. They walk me through it, even the dressing-changing part, and so I'm just doing it now. They've rearranged our whole bedroom, moved everything away from the bed, so we can get the IV up by his side at night. We even have a bedpan—I ran out to the Sav-on for that—because when he has the TPN in his arm at night, he can't get up. At the end of the week, they tell me that I have learned to do everything an RN does in an intensive care ward. Except, I say to myself, that an RN doesn't lie down and sleep next to her patient at night, doesn't fall asleep listening to the pump and hiss of the machines that are keeping her husband alive.

Brad is trying to be good. He is willing his recovery, beating back the MAI into a workable submission. He talks about writing the book, of resuming what normal life he had even two weeks ago, where breakfast at Dupars is nothing out of the ordinary. But I have suspended all hope, all fear. I am in neutral, a drug delivery system. How many days will our lives be like this? I can't ask myself that question, not even when I know how much this costs, hundreds, thousands of dollars a day; each TPN is $800.

My only emotion is amazement at Alexandra, that she is living through this with us without trauma. She sees Brad's IV, the needles, and the syringes—she can't help it, it's part of our life now—but she never cries, never even talks about it, just sits next to Brad while I make dinner, pets his hands and tells him about her day at camp, about riding the horse and playing with the baby bunnies that have been born.

But in my own way, I am doing something similar. Friends call,

I'm fine. Yes, Brad is still not up to snuff, but I'm fine, busy. When Jeri Scott comes by to pick up Alexandra for a play date with Evan, I am chatty at the door; Brad even comes to the window to wave as they head down the walkway, long sleeves covering his PICC line. I even keep a lunch date with Howard, my old pal from Gersh, although I do some fast talking to keep him from coming in. That is Brad's one request, that no one come in the house but the Care people and Robert.

It's hard to tell if we're drifting away or if others are. Outside, we're having a heat wave, but L.A. seems cold and empty. Weber has disappeared, taken a leave because his lover is in his final days of battling brain lymphoma. Norbert Weisser has left the country, gone back to Germany to deal with his brother, Willy, the heroin addict, who is dying of AIDS. On August 21, three days after Brad gets home from the hospital, Clifford Stevens calls to say he is leaving L.A. to fly back East to be with Colleen Dewhurst at her home in upstate New York. He just makes it. The next day, Colleen dies. Jeri calls to tell us that Clifford has disappeared, he is so distraught. The next day, Robert calls. Weber's lover has died and he has left for Hawaii.

A cold wind is definitely blowing, but the coldest blast of all comes with the call I get from Mark Senak that week. "I think you should know that some of the things are getting out on the street," he tells me. His voice is rushed and low, as if he is either very very angry or very very calm. "There's this woman who is spreading a story about Brad—she's already managed to tell quite a few people that he has AIDS."

I ask Mark who it is: Karen Hendel, the head of casting at HBO, a woman Brad and I had socialized with. A friend of Mark's at HBO, Mike Lombardo, a senior VP, had heard her talking and called Mark. Karen had heard about Brad from Ken Foree, an actor Brad had worked with on *Hangfire*. Ken had gotten a call from someone who had seen Brad at the Gelsons recently, thought he looked thin, and put two and two together—Brad Davis has AIDS. Ken calls Karen because he assumes casting directors know all the dirt. But Karen hasn't heard this and so she starts calling people, people who know us, people who are our *friends*, people such as Kathleen and Jeri, and Marsha Kleinman and even Rick. She confronted Rick, one of Brad's closest friends. "Of course it's not true," Rick told her, because this was in July before Brad had told him. "I'm one of his closest friends and I would know."

"Well, if it's not true," said Karen, "then Brad better get out there and start being seen, because this is starting to go around."

There it was, what we had feared for six years, the Hollywood gossip mill. And it was impressive, one person had spread the rumor, put out the word that Brad had AIDS, to eighteen, twenty, maybe fifty people. In that one call, I saw what it could have been like, what it would have been like, how his career would have been dead in the water within days. "We hear he has AIDS. We're not interested."

Mark wasn't the only one to call and warn me. In the next two days, I heard about this from at least a dozen people.

I realized I was going to have to start telling people that Brad has AIDS. Or rather, I simply can't not tell them. The lying now seems pointless. I also realize that I might literally need some help, someone to take care of Alexandra if things get really bad. There was Rick of course, and Weber had miraculously reappeared, come to his senses in Hawaii and flown back to L.A., but I needed a friend I could call in the middle of the night if neccessary and say, get over here.

I met Judith for lunch at the Columbia Bar and Grill down in Hollywood. It was a favorite of ours because it's close to Paramount, where she often works. I hadn't seen her in weeks, so of course she began asking about Brad, questioning me the way a friend does: "What are they doing for this ulcer?" and "Why is his flu not going away?" Suddenly I just told her. Right there, in the middle of this industry lunch crowd, I just blurted it out. Brad has AIDS. After all those years of carrying this secret, I actually felt kind of calm talking about it. But Judith was distraught. "I can't believe this," she says, her eyes filling with tears as she scrambles to her feet.

And I sat there calmly, my salad half-eaten, as I watched her run, crying to the ladies' room.

Three days after Brad comes home from the hospital, Robert sends him back in. Another day of testing and some IV feeding. Brad is not responding. The infection is boiling back up and he is not eating. He can't. Almost all the weight Brad gained in the hospital is gone; he is back below 120. Robert thinks it's pneumonia. I can't bear to go back to the hospital, not this soon, so Rick drives him. It is the last time they will be together. That afternoon, when they get back home, Brad wants me to bring his papers, the copy of the will, the book proposal, and a legal pad. "Do you want me to write you a letter?" he asks me.

"A letter?"

"I'm writing one to Alexandra while I still have the strength. Whatever happens, I want this to be in order."

I am such a fool.

"No, no, no," I say, "I don't need a letter."

Three days later, Brad is readmitted to the hospital for the second and last time.

Two days after Brad has gone back in, Jeri calls. Michael Brandman needs to schedule Brad to loop *Dragons* sometime in September when Michael Lindsay-Hogg gets in from London. Oh, Christ, looping? Who can think about this now?

"Well, he's in the hospital again," I tell her, and suggest she make an excuse about Brad's still being sick. "Look, there's something I've got to tell you, but I can't do this now, so call me in a couple of days."

But Jeri, to her credit, doesn't let up: "Forget it. We're having this conversation today; I'm stopping by after work."

By the time Jeri made the drive over Coldwater Canyon, she'd convinced herself that Brad had AIDS. It wasn't that much of a stretch with the rumor going around and Brad in the hospital again. But still, it was a shock. I put on a positive face, telling her Brad was gaining weight on the IV, so we didn't really know what might happen. "I really wanted you to know in case I need some help with Alexandra." As with Judith, I'm calm, practical, even calling out to Alexandra to take Faith outside and play. But Jeri is unglued, tears streaming, fumbling for Kleenex in her purse. I watch her as I might watch someone cry in a movie.

Brad is in the hospital a total of seven days. They do a chest X ray because of the threat of pneumonia and put him back on IV feeding to put some weight on him. I am braced for my hospital and pajama ritual, but it is not necessary; Brad is spitting up blood. It is only a matter of time.

"I'm dying, aren't I?" he asks Weber.

Weber has just lived through this with his lover less than a week ago.

"Yes," he says quietly. "But I can't tell you exactly when."

They talk about Brad's options, the expense and the kind of care he can get at home and in the hospital. But Brad has his own ideas. He calls Michael Lindsay-Hogg at the Château Marmont and leaves a message. He won't be able to do looping in ten days because he will have the flu. He calls his therapist. "I'm coming home," he says, adding with a laugh, "they need the bed." Then he calls me. He is coming home, he says, to die on Sunday.

"Sunday? What are you talking about? How do you know you'll die on Sunday?"

He will die on Sunday because, like everything else in our lives, he wanted it like that. Brad is coming home to die because he's coming home to kill himself.

CHAPTER

17

It is the Friday after Labor Day, Rosh Hashanah begins at sundown on Sunday, and a stillness has settled over the city. Brad is to be released this afternoon. I can't bear this waiting at home, so I decide to take one of my crying drives. I wind up, after an hour or so, at the office. I am dimly aware that I need to get ready for this, for the onslaught of calls and whatever else is to come. When I get to the office, Paul is there. "Why don't you put on a pot of coffee and come in here for a second," I tell him.

I'm sure Paul has suspected something, given Brad's two hospital stays and that I've essentially quit working. But now, this is more than Brad's being sick. This is Brad's not going to make it.

I start out calm, as I'd been with Judith and Jeri. "Listen," I say. "I'm telling you because I'm going to need you to do some stuff, you're going to have to bounce some calls away, because nobody knows this is happening. Not his family, not his friends. Only a couple of people know, so you have to keep this quiet until it happens."

But then, suddenly I am not calm, I am crying because Brad is dying.

* * *

Telling Paul is nothing compared to telling Alexandra. Brad hadn't wanted to. He'd written his letter and now he was saying he was too weak to do this in person. But we were all on him. Weber, Rick, me. Especially after the rumor had started. That was what got him, that he didn't want Alexandra to hear about this on the street.

"Brad, she'll be able to live with this if you tell her," I said. "What she will not be able to live with is a lie, knowing that your last act towards her was a lie."

So, he agreed to tell her, but in his own way. Fine, I said, thinking this would happen when we got home that afternoon. But it was at the pharmacy across from the hospital where we stopped on the way home from the hospital that he told her. Alexandra was with us, she had insisted on coming to pick him up, and while I'm in the pharmacy, he tells her he is going to die.

Even before I get out of the store, I can see her through the glass door, see her in the backseat of the Jaguar, her face twisted in anger. I can't hear her, but I can see she is screaming, beating on the front seat where he is slumped, half-turned trying to grab her hands. But he is too weak to stop her, not her flailing arms, not when she yanks open the door and starts to scramble out. I don't know how I get to her that fast, but I have her now, bent over her, my arm across her chest, holding her tight, my head next to her head, and I hear her now, her endless screamed "Nooooo" 's so that you'd think all of our hearts would just break right there in the parking lot. And I hold her that way, hold her until she goes limp and I don't need to hold her anymore.

Saturday is a long day. Brad had already told me over the phone what he planned to do, but now he is going over the details point by point, what will happen when and how. It is clear that this is his idea, that he is ready for this, no question. I am sure I'm in shock, but this is not what I want to hear, not here in our bedroom, Brad lying in bed, going over the points in a low, rushed voice.

But I stand there, gazing out the window for several minutes, listening to the low rumble of his voice. Tomorrow Brad will be dead. He has never asked me, just told me, just called from the hospital and said this is how it would be. It is how he has done everything in our life together, how we'd gone out, how we'd gotten married. Now, it will be how he dies. Brad decides and I go along.

I tried to put up a fight: "You're not even asking me. You don't care about me, what I want, or about Alexandra. You don't care that I don't want this, that Alexandra doesn't want this, you don't even care that she's supposed to have a piano recital on Sunday."

And he didn't care. Not then. He was dying and he wanted to end it on his own terms. Before the pain, the expense, before the fear got overwhelming. "I'm doing this," he said, "and you and Rachel [name changed] are going to help."

Rachel? I couldn't believe he was dragging Rachel into this. It was bad enough to have to go through this, but to have another person there, another person share my last moments with Brad?

But this was a big point with him, something he was adamant about, the need for a third person, someone besides the spouse.

"Rachel is coming because someone has to be there with you," he tells me. "You can't do this alone, so it has to be Rachel."

So it was settled. It was to be the three of us. We had a date, 4 P.M. Sunday.

Like so many other times in our life, I know there is no point in fighting Brad. I also realize more than any other time in his life—more than the drinking and abusing, more than getting and staying sober—Brad is prepared for this. He is ready to die. What seems like an abrupt decision is, in fact, an answer to a prayer. For the first time in my life, I envy Brad his sureness about God, about his own spirituality, about his life beyond his body.

We sit and talk for a while longer. Without my even asking, he starts to tell me the story of Weber's lover, how two years ago, he had seemed to be dying and how he wanted to end it himself before it got too painful. But Weber had refused because he believed he really could rally, really could beat back the infection. And in fact, that's what happened. His lover did stabilize, his infection went down, and they had another two good years together before he finally died.

"This isn't like that," Brad says, looking me full in the face. I'm not going to rally, he tells me, because I'm bleeding to death. "But if I don't do it this way, it could be days, even a week or two, and I don't want to go through that. I don't want you to go through that."

I'm crying a little now, but Brad tells me now what is to happen, how he will take the drugs himself, but that first he will take the antinausea medication so he won't throw up the drugs. "You'll be frightened," he tells me. "And that's okay. But all I will do is go to sleep."

He tells me, too, that I should wait a good hour before I call the doctor—that he will come and issue a death certificate—and then I should call the funeral home. "No matter what happens," he tells me, "don't call 911, because they will try and revive me."

He also tells me that I should talk to whomever I need to talk to because there will be a lot of calls, a lot of requests from the media that I'm going to have to deal with. He also says that Alexandra and I will have to be retested immediately, "because her school is going to want to know if she is HIV-positive." He says that I am going to need to pay a lot of attention to Alexandra, that I should start to shift my focus to her. "Her father died of AIDS," Brad says, "but she has to know she is okay."

Brad had been sitting up in the chair in the bedroom, wearing that awful pink robe of his, but now he got into bed and stayed there. He is very weak, his breathing shallow. A huge part of me just wants him to die, to die in his sleep that afternoon, his breath mixing with that of Doc, our scruffy old terrier, who refuses to budge from the end of the bed.

It was around five when I woke him to tell him I'm driving Alexandra to Jeri's. I had made arrangements for her to stay there that night and the next day. She couldn't be here, not now. Brad couldn't bear it.

"Say good-bye to Daddy," I say as brightly as I can.

"But what if he dies while I'm gone?" she asks me.

This has been her fear for weeks now, that Brad will die when she isn't there. Now, I know, this time her fear will be realized.

"You have to say good-bye as if it might be the last time," I tell her, tell her the way I have told her each time she has left the house in the past two weeks.

And so she does. She is only eight years old, her thin arms wrapped around Brad's neck. I don't even remember being eight, but I know my daughter will not have that luxury. And then it is time for us to go.

While I'm gone, Brad pulls the phone onto the bed to make his good-bye calls. Like most of his life, it is a weird compendium of people: Norbert and his wife, Tandy; John Erman; Rick and Tim; and of course his parents. I don't really want to know or hear these calls. This is his business.

His parents are first, but only his father comes to the phone; his mother is too sick or too angry or too whatever she's been for most of her life to talk to her son. So it is Doodle who takes it, the call that his oldest son is dying. I'd worried about this conversation. Brad's father was almost stone-deaf, has been for years now. Communicating with him was a nightmare, shouting out the simplest of sentences, repeating them endlessly and never being sure what had sunk in. I had given up and let Brad deal with it. Now I was uncertain where he might find the strength to make this one final call. It was some sort of miracle, or maybe his father had expected it, but somehow Doodle heard him, heard without his having to shout, his son's hoarse and whispered good-bye.

Brad then moved on to his friends. He reached John first at his home in Bel-Air in the midst of a dinner party. "Let me call you back," John pleaded with him.

"You can't," Brad said. "I have AIDS and this is good-bye."

He reached Norbert at home in Venice. He had just come back from Germany that week after his brother had died. He was on the first of several bottles of wine to drown his sorrows when Tandy walked in. "Brad's on the phone," she said, tears in her eyes. "He's dying."

"What!" said Norbert, stumbling to his feet, regretting instantly that he was drunk.

"He's on the phone saying good-bye."

That was a long call, Norbert arguing drunkenly that Brad couldn't be saying good-bye, that Norbert needed to come see him, that he needed to read some Rilke poems to him, that he needed–

"Listen, I can't do this very much longer. I'm too tired," Brad interrupted him.

Norbert made one last stab. "Where do you think you're going?"

"I think I'm going where I came from."

He reached Rick last.

"Listen, try and hold on," Rick said. He was in the kitchen in the Del Mar house.

"Yeah," Brad said. "I don't think I can."

That night, Brad and I say our own good-byes. I get into bed and we just hold each other. He tells me that he loves me, that I'd really come through for him. He tells me there were so many times he hadn't felt he deserved a life that was so stable, with a wife and child who loved him unconditionally. He says over and over again, "God, you were really here for me, through all your fears, you really showed up." And I smile back at him because that's exactly what I thought of him, that he had really showed up for me.

As I lay there that night, it was clear to me that whatever we had lived through, all the horrors and the fears, Brad and I were closer then than we had ever been. But it was also clear to me that Brad and I were separating, separating the way the dying and the living do. Brad, I realized, had already faced the reality of his death. He knew that tomorrow was simply the final act of a play that had begun some time ago. He was ready to make that journey. He was ready to go, to leave me and Alexandra and our life here. He wasn't frightened and he wasn't even that sad. There was a peacefulness about him, a sense of certainty that I saw through my tears, and I realized Brad and I were, for the last time, moving into wholly different orbits.

* * *

Sunday, Brad wakes up agitated. He is nervous, fussing with the sheets and his robe, fretting about this and that. "I'm nervous," he tells me, and I think, Oh, God, you're nervous?

"Listen, you don't have to do this," I say, but he shoots back that he does. Thank God, he remembers to take a Xanax. He takes two and almost immediately calms down. "I can't believe how much better I feel," he says, sitting up. "Really, this is so much better."

Now he is calmer, more like his old self, just listening to me rattle on about this and that and should I sell the house and get rid of the cars and what did he want me to do with his mother's silver and her jewelry that he had stashed away in his dresser drawer. It is how I cope with the stress, but Brad is just nodding from the bed. "Start a new life," he says softly. "You have to go on and start a new life."

I see that all this, the details of our life, all the questions about money and lawyers and arrangements, were beyond him now, of no interest to him. He is only roused when I start to talk about the memorial service. His voice hoarse, he pipes up with a list of whom to invite and whom not to invite to the memorial service, grudges and loyalty to the end.

"And I want to be cremated in that shirt Alexandra got me," he says, and so I root around to find it, a red T-shirt they got from the Children's AIDS Foundation, these matching shirts with a kid's name on them, Zack, the name of a boy who died of AIDS. The whole day is this kind of nonsense until it is time for Brad to take the antinausea medication. I try to tell myself this is no different from all the other drugs he's swallowed or dropped into his veins, slipped down that PICC line. And then it's over, but it's still not four, so there's still some time, but then suddenly the doorbell rings and it is, it is the time.

"Don't get it for a second," Brad says, smiling at me from the bed.

"You don't have any regrets, you're not afraid?" I say.

And he shakes his head, still smiling, and I go out to let Rachel in.

After that, things happened very very fast, like images floating up in dream. I let Rachel in and Brad follows me, limping, his robe trailing. He gives Rachel a long hug and we all stand there a few minutes. And then, Brad tells us, he's going into the bedroom for a minute, "but wait for me to call you."

We stand there, immobile, like dogs waiting to be released, and in less than a minute it seemed, Brad called to us. And I looked at him already in bed, and I thought, he really looks bad. I hated myself for thinking that, that he looked so bad, so pale, with his face unshaved and the scabs of dried blood on his lips. I reached down to brush them off, but then I see he is bleeding from the mouth and I let my hand drop. I sit down next to him, and Rachel sort of stands off to the side and I hold his hand. Brad had said he should just go to sleep, that it would look as if it were happening fast but that it would really take at least an hour before he would stop breathing. And I sit there and look at him, he is getting so sleepy, and he smiles at me and mouths that he loves me and I am hanging on to his hand so tight. I didn't know what I would say to him, but then I just say, "Sleep with the angels, my darling." And then he did.

I was still sitting there, holding his hand, trying to brush away my tears with my free hand, when Brad suddenly jerked, hard, and sat bolt upright. "It hurts," he said, doubling over, his words all slurred. "Oh, God, it hurts."

You don't know what goes through your mind at a time like that—that you've made a horrible mistake, that he's going to die an agonizing death, that he isn't going to die, that you should try to save him.

I looked over at Rachel. She was white as a sheet, but somehow we both get Brad on his side, he was curled in the fetal position, and Rachel is rubbing his back and I am holding his hand—he is clenching it so hard—and in less than a minute, I feel all the life drain out of him. And I hold his hand like that, until I don't need to hold it anymore.

When it is all over, Rachel and I go into the living room for a minute. We don't say anything to each other, we don't hug. We just sit there, listening to our hearts race. Brad had said to wait an hour, but I know it is over, so I call Weber and then I call the funeral home.

When he arrives, Weber is quiet, quick. He goes in to Brad and then he comes out to me. He asks me if I'm okay and I tell him I'm fine, that I'm going to call Larry Kramer and ask him to call the *New York Times*, the *Los Angeles Times,* because I don't want the tabs to get the story first. He tells me to take care and that I should bring Alexandra to see him Tuesday morning at nine to get retested, and then he leaves.

And it was just after that that the funeral-home guys come, dragging in their gurney and the plastic body bag.

This is the worst part, hearing that zipper sound beyond the bedroom door. More than Brad's hand going limp, this was the real death, when Brad was no longer Brad but simply a body.

And then everyone is gone, the funeral-home guys, Rachel. I stand in the doorway of the bedroom. It is all still here, the IV stand, his pink bathrobe at the foot of the bed, his crystals and the stone Buddha I had given him on the bedside table. Even his wallet is on the dresser. It is as if Brad had just left, just for a second, and that if I waited, he would come back, he would come back the way he always had.

I went to Jeri's that night to tell them and to get Alexandra. But she is upset, we are all upset, crying in the kitchen, hugging. She doesn't want to come home that night and I understand, so I get in the car and come home alone.

That night, I try to think about what is coming, all the calls I have to make, the people I must tell. I feel tired just thinking about it. I can't sleep, not yet, not just yet in our bed, so I go into Brad's office, snap on the light over the desk, and sit down. I look around at all the pictures on the walls, so many photographs of Brad and our friends, Brad and Alexandra. I've been in here so many times when Brad was away on shoots it is hard not to think that he is in a hotel somewhere, fuming about something.

But he is not. On the desk he has left his list, the people to invite to the memorial service, his list of gifts for everyone, such as the script of *RFK* that he wanted Rick to have, the one with the coffee stains on it and that quote by Camus that he always liked. And the letter to Alexandra was there. That was hard, to open that and read that letter:

My dear, dear Alexandra,

If you are reading this, then you already know that I have left my body and gone to the other side where people don't need bodies. I hope you don't feel that I abandoned you. I have had the virus that causes this disease since before you were born. My very biggest fear was that I had infected your mother, which meant that you would've been infected as well. I was joyously relieved to find that both you and your mother were not infected. While I was waiting for the results of your mother's test for this virus, I prayed to God to spare you and your mother and promised that if you were spared that I would bear this virus bravely and not complain and accept my fate. . . .

I also prayed for God to let me stay on this earth long enough for you to have a father to help you in your early years, for you to remember that your father loved you more than anything . . . and for all these years you have been the love of my life. And that love will not stop. I will be loving you from the other side. And someday after a long and wonderful life and you leave your body (everybody does, honey), I will be waiting for you and we'll be together again. I promise you this.

My precious Alexandra, I know this will be very hard on you, but you are a beautiful, talented, strong little girl with a wonderful heart. I don't want you to lose that. . . . You'll have your Mommy to help you and lots of people there to help you get through. And don't forget I will be sending you lots of love from the other side, Always! You should know how very proud I am of you. I promise you, we will be together again.

I wish I could spare you this pain, honey, but I have no choice, when it's time to go, it's time to go. Alexandra there are a lot of people who think that people who get this disease are bad people. Not everybody thinks that way, but some people do. Don't let them make you feel bad. They are just prejudiced. It's a terrible disease, not terrible people, don't forget that. . . .

I couldn't get through that letter. I couldn't even imagine how I was going to give it to Alexandra. I just sat there, my tears dropping onto the pages until I couldn't cry anymore. I know I'd told Brad I didn't want a letter, but now I hoped that he had ignored me, that he had written me one anyway. I tore the office apart; it was something like 2 A.M. when I finally gave up. There was no letter, not to me.

Monday it began and it didn't stop, not for weeks. It was the first day of Rosh Hashanah, essentially a holiday in Hollywood. I got up early, made myself some tea—I even made the bed for the first time in months—and got right on the phone. I called Larry—he said he would call a reporter he knew at the *Times*—and then I started calling all my friends. And then the house started filling up: Rick and Tim had driven up to L.A. after Brad's call; Howard Askenase; Judith; my friend Phyllis Glick; and then Jeri and her husband, Mark, came and brought Alexandra. Everyone came and everyone brought food. And the phone rang all day, friends and then the media. Victor, Larry's friend at the *Times,* called and said the obituary would be in Tuesday's paper, and then I called the trades and they said the story would be in Wednesday, and it just went on and on. By the end of the day, there must have been sixty, eighty, a hundred calls.

I was completely overwhelmed with the press. I was taking calls, Rick was taking calls, Judith was. *USA Today* and then the TV programs started. *Good Morning America* and Peter Jennings and *Nightline.* Mark Senak called to say *Nightline* was hounding him to get me, telling him that they could get my number, "We can get any number," so he really had to get a move on.

It was all a shock. All those months when Weber had tried to let me know that Brad's death would be news, it hadn't sunk in, not when we were so consumed with hiding it. When I talked to Victor for the obit, he was quoting Brad's book proposal to me—Larry and Rodger had gotten it to him—and I said, "Why do you have that, why do you care about this?" I was so naive. Victor even told me later that he couldn't believe I was that naive. But I told him, "You have no idea how isolated we were."

But Brad's death was a little bit like a bomb going off. It was shocking in a way that Rock's death hadn't been. Brad wasn't the classic AIDS victim, not the way people thought of it, not then. And the fact that we'd kept it so secret was like a rebuke to Hollywood, as if we were saying, "Look what we went through, look what we had to go through even after Rock's death."

So it was news. I flew to New York the following Sunday to be on all three of the morning news shows as well as *ABC Nightly News*. And Brad's death continued to be news. Two weeks after he died, the *Los Angeles Times* ran a cover story in its Sunday Calendar section: "How Much Does Hollywood Really Care About AIDS?"

And that was the question. I hadn't realized that Brad's death was coinciding with the annual Commitment to Life benefit sponsored by the APLA. It was actually something of a flap because some board members wanted me to write a letter on behalf of Brad, but others thought I was going to slam the APLA. In the end, the board approved my letter and Richard Dreyfuss read it at the banquet.

And that was only the beginning of a whole self-examination in Hollywood. Even at Brad's memorial, which Rick organized for September 20 at the Doolittle Theater in Hollywood, the same place where Brad had attended Eddie Bondy's memorial service, people made speeches about it. Most of them were personal remembrances, but Percy Adlon came out and said that as much as he loved Brad, he wasn't sure, given industry practices, the insurance policies and whatever, that he could have hired Brad had he known he had AIDS.

It's one reason why Hollywood Supports was founded shortly after Brad's death. It had been on the drawing board for some time, the brainchild of Barry Diller, then CEO of Fox Inc., and Sid Sheinberg, then CEO of MCA/Universal, two APLA board members. It was to be the first industry-supported organization for people with HIV and AIDS in Hollywood. Now that Brad's death seemed to be galvanizing Hollywood, Barry asked Mark Senak to write up the proposal.

In the end, Hollywood Supports was unveiled and other things started to happen, such as MCA changing its insurance coverage to include domestic partners, something a handful of other studios would start to do. But getting to this point was such a typical Hollywood tale. Mark wrote up the outline for an outreach program designed to help and protect people like Brad, but at the first board meeting, Diller and Sheinberg started tinkering with it as if it were any movie script, adding this and taking out that so that Mark eventually spoke up. But Sheinberg glared at him. Six people were at the meeting, all board members, and Sheinberg said to Mark, "Who are you?" as if he'd brought in the coffee or something.

When I heard that, I thought, there is still a long way to go. It hit me, too, when Rick and I drove out to Forest Lawn to arrange the cremation and the woman who helped us had no idea who Brad was, not *Midnight Express,* not AIDS, not the *Times* article, the APLA, none of it, and I thought that really shows you what a huge gap exists between Hollywood and the real world. In the end, we tried to get a laugh out of the whole ordeal and picked out a coffin for the cremation that cost $250 because, as Rick pointed out, that was about the cost of a dinner at Morton's and Brad would have appreciated that.

There were a few nightmarish moments. Jill Clayburgh called the day after the obituary ran, wanting to know more about Brad's death and when did he get AIDS and on and on. And then all the problems with the coroner's barging into Forest Lawn and getting Brad's body because they decided they needed to do some drug tests. Brad had told me this might happen, but I told them I didn't know what drugs he was taking and how—I didn't know, not at the end, Brad had been very careful about that—so I couldn't tell them how all the Seconal had gotten into his blood. But there were bright spots. Going to Alexandra's school with her and addressing the older classes. I was so struck by their awareness of AIDS, the stories they told, a girl whose mother's best friend had AIDS, a boy whose father worked in a rehab center for people with AIDS, the other who had seen *The Normal Heart* and asked me if Brad hadn't been in that. In the end I was so amazed, touched really, because after all the hiding Brad and I had done, the world had really changed so that even these kids, these schoolchildren, knew better than I how much AIDS was a fact of all our lives.

The rest of that year and on into the next was really about going on, getting back to work and writing this book, Brad's book, in earnest. That January, John Erman offered me a job on a film he was doing, and so it began again. By that summer, I felt okay enough to redo Brad's office, clean out his files, take down a lot of those pictures, and turn it into an exercise room for me. I tried to think it is what Brad would have wanted, for me to get on with things, to get on with my life.

It was just about a year later, during a drive down Sunset Boulevard, that I saw it—the billboard for *The Habitation of Dragons*. I'd forgotten they were going to air it on September 8, the anniversary of Brad's death. Now, here it was, a giant poster of Brad, so much bigger than life, right here in West Hollywood. "Brad would have loved that," I thought as I drove by, and kept him in sight in my rearview mirror. "Oh, he would've loved that."

EPILOGUE

It has been more than five years as I write this that Brad died. In that time, our family, as well as Hollywood and the country as a whole, has experienced many changes. And yet certain facts remain obstinately in place. Although drug therapies have been refined, and it is now not uncommon for HIV-positive individuals to live ten, fourteen years without developing AIDS, the disease is still a killer. It is the leading cause of death among people aged twenty-five to forty-four, the exact years when Brad became sick and died. But even more depressingly, the fear and prejudice engendered by the disease have continued as well.

The past five years have also seen the rise of euthanasia, assisted suicide, to the top of the country's social agenda. Speaking from experience, I can say this is one of the most painful issues an individual can face. I don't pretend to have the answers. I only know the choices I made for myself and for my family.

I also know, from the past five years, how it is possible for someone to live through both of those experiences—AIDS and assisted suicide—and come out on the other side. I have had many ups and downs since Brad's death. Alexandra has had her share as well. But on the whole we are well and thriving. My hopes for change with the writing of this book have been tempered somewhat. But I remain optimistic, optimistic because against some of my first instincts, I have stayed in Hollywood and held my ground. We still live in our house in Studio City, we still have Faith our dog, and Doris is still with us. I still work as a freelance casting director, and in 1995 I won an Emmy Award for casting *N.Y.P.D. Blue*.

Perhaps that has been one of the biggest changes I have experienced—not the Emmy, but the validity of oneself and one's accomplishments. It is not something I'm sure Brad fully learned, a sense of his worth beyond celebrity. It is a hard lesson in a town that reminds you every day that image is all. Brad was never able to let that go; few actors can. But if there has been any silver lining, it is this: that I have a right to be here, not just as Mrs. Brad Davis, but as Susan Bluestein, and that is a legacy anyone would be proud to have.

But there are more personal, more painful lessons that I have learned in the past five years. My life with Brad was difficult, even dysfunctional. Since his death, I have seen more clearly than when he was alive how truly confused and hurt and even damaged we both were. The irony was, we thought the other held the answer, that we could solve each other's problems. Now, I know how wrong we were. Or were we? Whatever the turbulence of our marriage, we managed to stay together. Whatever anger I felt toward Brad, I also felt tremendous love.

I know many people will look at our life as an example of what *not* to do, of how *not* to live their lives. I expect many will point fingers. I have been candid in recounting our difficulties, perhaps more candid than I needed to be. Are there things I would do differently today? Of course. Are there things I hope to teach our daughter to do differently? Absolutely. But in writing this book, I hoped to honestly examine our past and in so doing possibly finally find the distance, the courage, to admit my mistakes, to take responsibility for my life.

And I see many errors. Those nights during our early days together in New York when I would wake to find Brad slicing his arms with a razor. Why did I refuse to see Brad for what he was, a deeply troubled young man? Why did I think time would improve him? Why didn't I insist he get professional help for his obvious emotional distress? These questions will stay with me the rest of my life.

And I wrestle with even more troubling questions about myself when we first learned that Brad was HIV-positive. How could I have blamed Brad, blamed the victim, for bringing this plague upon us, including our innocent child? And more than my anger, I regret my coldness, how I closed myself off when Brad was reaching out to me, how I turned away from the man who needed me more than he had ever needed me. I think now of my actions and I regret them more than I can say.

But I know now what lay at the root of my actions was fear, whether it was the fear of disease and death, the fear of losing our livelihood, or simply the fear of losing love. My life with Brad was a battleground, but not between two people, but between those two opposing emotions, fear and love. Brad was my partner, not my opponent, for he also knew great fear, perhaps even greater than my own. He was my confidant, my strength, my mate, as we faced our fears together. Reflecting the Camus quote that Brad loved and that begins this book, ours was a life filled with extremes, but it also had moments of greatness.

I miss Brad. There isn't a day that goes by that my thoughts don't turn to him for comfort, for guidance, and for humor. I know Alexandra feels his absence even more acutely. Her father was a difficult man, but as he wrote to her in that final letter, he was, he hoped, also a good man. If there is any meaning to this book, it is that—that as troubled as he was, Brad Davis was a good man, that he was capable of great love, and that he was loved greatly in return.